Decision-Making in Private Equity Firms

Mark Broere

Decision-Making in Private Equity Firms

An Empirical Study of Determinants and Rules

Springer Gabler

Mark Broere
Cottbus, Germany

Doctoral thesis, Brandenburgische Technische Universität Cottbus-Senftenberg, 2013

ISBN 978-3-658-03779-6 ISBN 978-3-658-03780-2 (eBook)
DOI 10.1007/978-3-658-03780-2

The Deutsche Nationalbibliothek lists this publication in the Deutsche Nationalbibliografie; detailed bibliographic data are available in the Internet at http://dnb.d-nb.de.

Library of Congress Control Number: 2013950218

Springer Gabler

Printed on acid-free paper

Springer Gabler is a brand of Springer DE.
Springer DE is part of Springer Science+Business Media.
www.springer-gabler.de

Acknowledgements

This doctoral dissertation would not have been possible without the support of many people. I would like to express my deep gratitude to my supervisor, Professor Dr Klaus Serfling, for accepting the project and for providing valued guidance and assistance in my thesis-writing. I would also particularly like to thank Professor Ulrich Hommel, Ph.D, for assuming the task as co-reviewer and giving much appreciated advice.

The quality of the results hinges on the quality of the empirical data; I am greatly indebted to all the private equity professionals who supported this project as interview partners and survey participants. I am especially grateful to our long-standing family friend Elaine Robson and my cousin Andy Adler for their encouragement, advice, and comments as well as for inspiring discussions on the essence of scientific writing.

My deepest gratitude goes to my wife and family for their never-ending patience and support.

Mark Broere

Brief Contents

Contents

List of Figures

List of Tables

List of Abbreviations

AAPOR	American Association for Public Opinion Research
AIMR	Association for Investment Management and Research
APV	Adjusted present value
BO	Buyout
BVK	Bundesverband Deutscher Kapitalbeteiligungsgesellschaften
CAPM	Capital asset pricing model
CEO	Chief executive officer
CFO	Chief financial officer
DCF	Discounted cash flow
EU	European Union
EVCA	European Private Equity and Venture Capital Association
GIPS	Global Investment Performance Standards
ILPA	Institutional Limited Partners Association
IPO	Initial public offering
IRR	Internal rate of return
MRR	Minimum return requirement
NPV	Net present value
NVCA	National Venture Capital Association
PC	Portfolio company
PE	Private equity firm
PEIGG	Private Equity Industry Guidelines Group
PI	Profitability index
PME	Public market equivalent
TWR	Time-weighted rate of return
UK	United Kingdom
U.S.	United States
US$	United States Dollar
USA	United States of America
USD	United States Dollar
VC	Venture capital
WACC	Weighted average cost of capital

Abstract

The decisions of private equity firms affect the development of industries and national economies, yet little is known about how these decisions are made. This doctoral thesis uses proprietary survey data from 136 private equity firms (mostly venture capital and buyout firms) located in the United States of America, Canada, and Europe to explore determinants and rules of decision-making in private equity firms. The results exhibit new facts about the objectives, minimum return requirements, success measures, decision metrics, exit decision power, and exit decision rules of private equity firms. Firstly, the data show that private equity firms incline towards simple decision heuristics and practitioner metrics; decision rules and metrics from established financial theory usually do not play an important role. In a private equity environment, market "imperfections" would appear to render the central models of established financial theory less useful for decision-making. The decision heuristics and metrics most popular among private equity practitioners can nevertheless (under certain conditions) deliver the same results as a policy to maximise net present value. Measured by this standard, the data suggest, however, that at least some private equity firms are forfeiting better performance due to inappropriate or inconsistent application of decision heuristics and decision criteria. Secondly, the data reveal numerous links between the responses of private equity firms and their individual characteristics, suggesting, for example, that external funding has a streamlining influence on a private equity firm's choice of success measures, that private equity firms are capable of choosing success measures that are better suited to their investment strategy, and that buyout firms tend to procrastinate the exits of poor quality investments more frequently than those of other investments. Some of these results reflect differences in the business models of buyout firms and venture capital firms. Others can be explained using theories and constructs which represent new institutional economics and include agency theory, asymmetric information, and Black and Gilson's (1998) implicit contract over control hypothesis. One such result is the important role that reputation and idiosyncratic risk play in the decisions of private equity firms. Thirdly, new hypotheses developed from existing literature are tested against the empirical data in this thesis. The results support the expectations that private equity firms generally consider money multiples and internal rates of return more important than other measures of success, that they tend towards an early exit of poor quality investments (early culling) more often than they tend towards an early exit of performing investments, and that price considerations usually govern the choice of exit channel. Fourthly, the views of European private equity firms on the determinants and rules of decision-making usually do not differ materially from those of private equity firms in the United States of America and Canada. Existing differences between these two geographical regions appear to relate mainly to external factors, such as legality and the liquidity of stock and buyout markets, rather than to factors within private equity firms. The results of this study should be useful to both scholars and practitioners in private equity. For scholars, this thesis provides novel data and insights into the determinants and rules of decision-making in private equity firms; its results should contribute to the development of new ideas and theories in this field of research. Practitioners are offered an understanding of potential pitfalls in decision-making. An increased awareness of these hazards should help improve the quality of their decisions.

1 Introduction

1.1 Research Topic

"Neither a borrower nor a lender be,
For loan oft loses both itself and friend,
And borrowing dulls the edge of husbandry." (Shakespeare, trans. 1997, 1. 3. 75–77)

This thesis explores determinants and rules of decision-making in private equity firms. Private equity has evolved within a few decades from a marginal phenomenon into a global industry with measurable impact on the economies of nations. Recent research has found, for example, that private equity stimulates the development of new products and services, improves the productivity of companies, and accelerates industry growth (Bernstein, Lerner, Sørensen, & Strömberg, 2009; Boucly, Sraer & Thesmar, 2011; Davis, Haltiwanger, Jarmin, Lerner, & Miranda, 2009; Lerner, Sørensen, & Strömberg, 2008; Romain & van Pottelsberghe, 2004). Despite the dramatic fall in private equity activity since the beginning of the recent financial crisis, the sector's control of financial and entrepreneurial resource is gigantic: Industry organisations currently estimate private equity assets under management (funds invested plus funds available for investment) at around $2.5 trillion, world-wide (Preqin, 2011, p. 15; TheCityUK, 2011, p. 3).[1]

This vast pool of capital and investments is managed by only a few thousand investment management firms (i.e. *private equity firms* — see below for a definition). Their investment and disinvestment decisions evidently influence the development of industries and even national economies — yet little is known about how these decisions are made. This deficit of knowledge could be ascribed to the often deplored reluctance of private equity firms to divulge information about their internal business practises, but there is possibly another, more elusive cause: Private equity markets are imperfect; asymmetric (or absent) information, illiquidity, and exposure to idiosyncratic risk render the central models of established financial theory — modern portfolio theory and the capital asset pricing model (CAPM) — less useful in a private equity environment, thus creating a challenge for academic research in this area.

This thesis endeavours to conduct an open-minded empirical investigation of decision-making in private equity firms; its aim is to improve our understanding in this field, whereas particular emphasis is placed on the following aspects: the objectives of private equity firms and the

---

1 Around 16% of this amount relates to real estate funds (Preqin, 2011, p. 15)

minimum rates of return they require from new investments (in the following, these rates of return will also be referred to as *minimum return requirements*), the metrics that private equity firms use to measure success (*success measures*) and the metrics they use as decision criteria (*decision metrics*), the exit decision power of private equity firms in relation to the portfolio company, the decision rules that private equity firms employ for deciding when to begin an exit process, and the principal determinants of the exit channel decision. It is hoped that this research will contribute to a better understanding of decision-making in private equity firms and stimulate the development of new theory. It is also hoped that the results of this research will help practitioners to improve the quality of their decisions.

Most of the existing literature on decision-making in private equity firms can be divided roughly into research on the investment decision and research on the exit decision. Research on the investment decision frequently concerns the criteria and cognitive processes for evaluating new investments (e.g. Borell, 2011; Dimov, Shepherd, & Sutcliffe, 2007; Elango, Fried, Hisrich, & Polonchek, 1995; Kollmann & Kuckertz, 2010; Lockett, Murray, & Wright, 2002; Murray & Lott, 1995; Muzyka, Birley, & Leleux, 1996; Petty & Gruber, 2011; Shepherd, Zacharakis, & Baron, 2003; Tyebjee T. T. & Bruno, 1981) and the rates of return that private equity firms require from new investments; research in this area has, for example, yielded information on the amounts of return that private equity firms require, identified associations between these amounts and the characteristics of private equity firms and investments (e.g. Lockett et al., 2002; Manigart et al., 2002; Murray & Lott, 1995; Ruhnka & Young, 1991; Vater, 2003), and identified factors that determine the risk premia of minimum return requirements (e.g. Dixon, 1991). But a number of seemingly elementary aspects of private equity decision-making are as yet unexplored. Existing research has devoted little attention to the objectives that private equity firms pursue, to how private equity firms specify their return requirements for new investments, or to the importance that private equity firms assign to factors that influence the levels of their minimum return requirements. Neither does existing literature provide satisfactory information on the metrics that private equity firms use for decision-making or for measuring investment success and investment risk.[2]

The present body of literature on the exit decision frequently focuses on factors that affect the exit time or channel of private equity investments (e.g. Black & Gilson, 1998; Cumming & Johan, 2010; Cumming & MacIntosh, 2003; Gompers, 1996; Lerner, 1994; Lin & Smith, 1998;

---

2 It should be noted that a related branch of research, which is concerned with the quantification of private equity performance, raises some fundamental issues of performance measurement in private equity (see, e.g. Chiampou & Kallett, 1989; Jones & Rhodes-Kropf, 2003; Ljungqvist & Richardson, 2003a; Peterson, Kasarda, & Grier, in press; Phalippou, 2009; Reyes, 2003)

Megginson & Weiss, 1991; Povaly, 2007; Schwienbacher, 2005; Wright, Robbie, Thompson, & Starkey, 1994). In the field of venture capital, various authors have also put forward theories or theoretical models for the timing decision (e.g. Cumming & MacIntosh, 2001; Tykvová, 2003) or the channel decision (e.g. Aghion, Bolton, & Tirole, 2004; Arcot, 2005; Bascha & Walz, 2001; Bayar & Chemmanur, 2011; Berglöf, 1994; Bienz & Leite, 2008; Black & Gilson, 1998; Hellmann, 2006; Schwienbacher, 2005). Empirical research in this field emphasizes the important role of price considerations (Relander, Syrjänen, & Miettinen, 1994; Wall & Smith, 1997) and has, for example, shown that venture capital firms tend to liquidate poor quality investments earlier than better quality investments (Cumming & MacIntosh, 2001; see also Tykvová, 2003, on the early liquidation of poor quality IPO candidates). Such research has not yet investigated the decision rules that private equity firms employ in practise for exiting portfolio investments, or the importance that they assign to certain decision criteria in their choice of exit channel.

In this thesis, *private equity* is understood as managed, dedicated pools of capital that are used for equity or equity-linked investments in companies, whereas its managers — referred to in the following as *private equity firms* or *fund managers* — seek to play an active role in growing the value of their investee companies and realise them at a profit within a limited period of time. This delineation builds on Gompers and Lerner's (2004) definition of venture capital[3] and is designed, on the one hand, to include venture, buyout, and growth capital, and on the other, to exclude mutual, evergreen, and hedge funds, fund of funds, most business angels, as well as non-profit organisations and debt investors. By this definition, private equity firms are therefore seemingly observing the judicious advice that Polonius gives his son Laertes in Shakespeare's Hamlet: "Neither a borrower nor a lender be" (trans. 1997, 1. 3. 75).[4]

The motivation for this study was prompted by a puzzle that occurred to me while working for an investment bank in the field of mergers and acquisitions. During this time, I frequently employed the capital asset pricing model to perform discounted cash flow valuations for corporate clients. I was surprised to find that private equity clients did not seem to care for these models; instead, they preferred to rely on simple multiples and internal rates of return (IRR).[5] It seemed odd to me that highly proficient and experienced investors should reject established

---

3 Gompers and Lerner (2004) define venture capital as "independently managed, dedicated pools of capital that focus on equity or equity-linked investments in privately held, high-growth companies" (p. 17)

4 Incidentally, some private equity firms (i.e. leveraged buyout firms) are often criticised for burdening their investee companies with too much debt

5 It should be noted, that these private equity firms typically calculate their multiples and IRRs on the basis of comprehensive cash flow models under varied market scenarios

financial theory in favour of crude metrics with well-known deficiencies. This conundrum has continued to occupy my thoughts and lies at the heart of the research in this thesis.

1.2 Method

1.2.1 Type of research

The appropriate methods for generating and justifying scientific knowledge have been the subject of longstanding philosophical debate (see, e.g. Chalmers, 1999, or Poser, 2001, for an overview of the main strands of thought). One popular classification of different viewpoints and methodologies in the social sciences is the dualism of quantitative research and qualitative research. Based on characterisations by Bortz and Döring (2006, pp. 296–302), Bryman (2008, pp. 21–24), and Mayer (2008, pp. 16–27) this dualism can be summarised as follows: Quantitative research typically employs measurement and statistical methods of analysis. It is associated with deductive reasoning and the testing of theory. Its philosophical foundation is attributed to Karl Popper's critical rationalism and the principle of falsification.[6] Qualitative research typically uses verbal data, which are analysed by interpretation and discourse. It is associated with inductive reasoning and theory building. Qualitative research is often employed for exploratory purposes, whereas quantitative research tends to be used for explanatory studies. Early contributions to the literature on scientific methodology frequently accentuated the contrast between the two types of research (often in conjunction with the "Methodenstreit" or "Positivismusstreit" of the social sciences; see, e.g. Bortz & Döring, 2006, pp. 302–307, or Paier, 2010, pp. 19–20, for summarising descriptions of the epistemological background). Today, many methodologists emphasize the complementarity of quantitative and qualitative research and propose that researchers combine the two strategies (e.g. Bryman, 2008, pp. 585–626; Mayer, 2008, pp. 26–27).

The research approach in this thesis accordingly uses elements from both categories of research. In view of the limited amount of existing literature on decision-making in private equity firms, the larger part of the study is exploratory and descriptive, and uses inductive reasoning to generate new ideas and hypotheses.[7] Yet most of the data are quantitative and are analysed using statistical methods. Where possible, I also develop falsifiable hypotheses from existing literature and confront these with the empirical data obtained in this thesis.[8] For the sake of clarity, such hypothesis-driven parts of research are always made apparent in the text.

---

6 See Lakatos (1989) for a concise presentation and discussion of Popper's ideas

7 Unlike the research understanding in the early period of inductivism, the conclusions of inductive reasoning are here regarded as starting point for future theory building and testing, not as 'scientific truths' (see Lakatos,1989, pp. 103–105 on inductivism)

8 An overview of the hypotheses tested in this thesis is presented in Appendix A

1.2.2 Research process and design

I began the research project with the screening of existing literature and the singling out of the aspects of decision-making in private equity firms that should form the main thrust of the investigation. Next, I considered two possible research designs for the project: These were a cross-sectional (survey) design and a case study design (see, e.g. Bryman, 2008, pp. 35–61, for an overview of possible research designs). Yin (2008, pp. 8–10) suggests that the survey design is more suitable for descriptive *what, who,* and *where* questions, and for assessing predictions and that the case study design is more suitable for explanatory type questions *how* and *why*. I chose a survey design for this thesis as the study aim, by implication, concerns primarily *what* questions, such as, "*What* objectives do private equity firms pursue?", "*What* metrics do private equity firms use for measuring investment success?", and so forth. This design also has the advantage of being more suitable for generalising results to units of the population not included in the sample (Bryman, 2008, p. 57). The ensuing steps of research depicted in Figure 1, excepting the data collection, were conducted separately for each aspect of decision-making. The review of available literature in the particular field was followed by an operationalization of the (implied) research question into functional survey questions and pre-formulated response items. Where possible, hypotheses were formed and adequate response items were integrated into the design of the survey instrument. The data collection was then carried out simultaneously for all aspects of decision-making. The subsequent exploratory data analysis and hypothesis testing lead to the central part of the thesis, containing the discussion of results and their theoretical and practical implications.

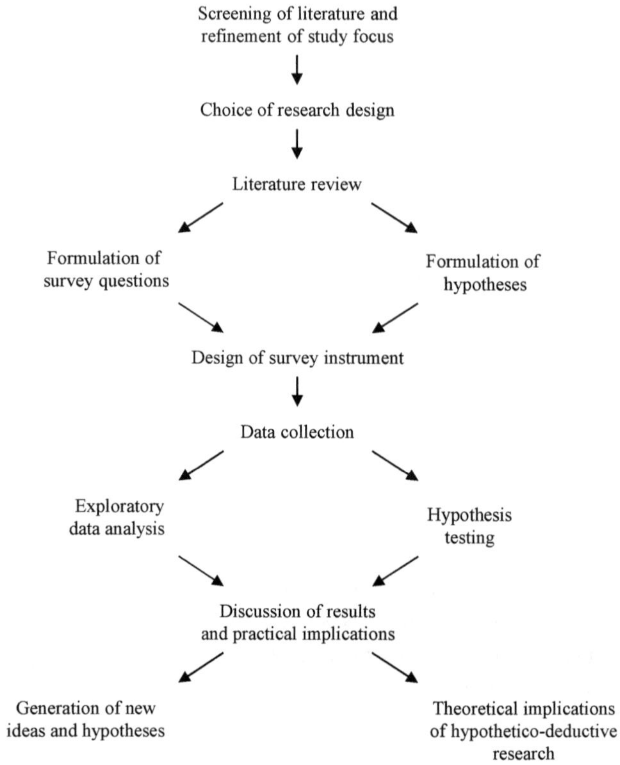

Figure 1. Overview of the research process.

1.2.3 Target population and sample frame

The target population for the study comprises all private equity firms located in the United States of America, Canada, and major private equity markets in Europe, whereas *major private equity markets* are defined as countries that count at least 20 fund managers (headquarter locations only). The exact number of private equity firms in these markets is unknown, but advertising by commercial information providers can give a rough idea of the respective world-wide population: In February 2009, *Pratt's Guide to Private Equity & Venture Capital Sources* (Thomson Reuters) claimed to list "over 4,000 actively investing private equity and venture capital firms operating around the world" (http://thomsonreuters.com/products_services /media/pratts_guide), the *2009 Galante's Venture Capital & Private Equity Directory* (Dow Jones) claimed to list "more than 2,900 active private capital firms in the United States and overseas" (http://fis.dowjones.com/products/galante.html), and the database *Fund Manager Profiles* (Preqin) advertised "profiles for over 4,400 fund managers [world-wide] specialising in buyout, venture, mezzanine, distressed debt and other direct private equity investments" (http://www.preqin.com/itemProduct.aspx?s=1&itemid=4).[9]

Prior surveys in private equity have typically sourced their samples from the membership directories of major private equity industry associations, sometimes also supplementing their data with information from commercial databases (e.g. Kraft, 2001; Manigart et al., 2002; Paffenholz, 2004; Povaly, 2007; Schwienbacher, 2005). But the use of membership directories for the sample frame can lead to systematic undercoverage of the target population because their entries are limited to registered members. Another disadvantage is that differences in membership criteria across private equity associations can lead to skewed samples. Because of this and additional practical considerations,[10] this study utilises the electronic Preqin database *Fund Manager Profiles* for sourcing the sample frame of private equity firms. Table 1 exhibits the steps in the selection of firms in the sample frame. The query was restricted to database entries flagged as *headquarter location* in order to avoid requesting data from both head office and subsidiaries of private equity firms. Muted response levels in an online pilot survey prompted the decision to address the entire sample frame of private equity firms in the main survey.[11]

---

9 Today, Preqin estimates the "total number of active fund managers in the [private equity] industry" at approximately 4,130, world-wide (Preqin, 2011, p. 18)

10 Practical considerations included the advertised regular maintenance and update of the database, and the ease with which multiple firm profiles containing respective contact persons' details could be searched for and extracted online

11 Adequate (random) sample sizes for statistical inference are dependent on a number of factors, such as the distribution of measured attributes in a population, the type of parameters under study, the methods of statistical inference, the type of research, and the desired levels of certainty and precision (Bortz & Döring, 2006, pp. 419–423, 604–605, and 627–635; Emory, 1985, pp. 283–301; Groves et al., 2004, pp. 99–102; Israel, 1992). In mail surveys, the actual sample size is also dependent on the response rate. Various back-of-the-envelope calculations suggested that a sample of at least 100 private equity firms would be adequate for most of the envisioned statistical analyses

Table 1
Selection of the sample frame

Selection step	Count
Total entries in the Preqin database *Fund Manager Profiles* in February 2009	over 4,400
└ fund managers - only headquarter locations - with investment type Venture or Buyout[a]	3,306
└ fund managers in the United States, Canada and Europe	2,651
└ fund managers in countries that are listed in the database with at least 20 fund managers[b]	2,527
└ fund managers with complete address details[c]	2,473
└ fund managers not addressed in the pre-test (= sample frame)	2,373

[a]Venture comprises categories Early Stage, Early Stage: Seed, Early Stage: Start-up, Expansion/Growth Capital, Late Stage, and Venture (General).
[b]The United States of America, the United Kingdom, France, Germany, Canada, Italy, Sweden, Switzerland, Spain, the Netherlands, Finland, Norway, and Denmark.
[c]Where possible, address details were manually updated or completed.

1.2.4 Data collection

Replicability, reliability, and validity are viewed as important criteria of (quantitative) social research (Bryman, 2008, pp. 31–33). The study results in this thesis are made replicable — to the extent that private equity firm behaviour is constant over time — by documenting the research steps and methods employed. The design and the execution of the data collection process were guided correspondingly by the aim of generating reliable and valid survey results. I used a self-administered, standardised questionnaire to collect data from private equity firms. This makes it possible to compile a large amount of data in a cost- and time-efficient manner, while reducing detrimental effects from interviewer involvement (see Bortz & Döring, 2006, pp. 252–253; Bryman, 2008, pp. 217–219; Groves et al., 2004, pp. 138–165, on the advantages and disadvantages of self-administered questionnaires). The formal design of the survey questionnaire employs various elements from tested designs of earlier studies (i.e. Kraft, 2001; Manchot, 2010;[12] Paffenholz, 2004; Povaly, 2007; Schwienbacher, 2005; Vater, 2003; Wegner, 2007) and makes use of literature recommendations on survey methodology (see Bortz & Döring, 2006, pp. 137–262; Emory, 1985, pp. 187,189 and 198–272; Groves et al., 2004, pp. 189–195 and 226–236; Mayer, 2008, pp. 58–100; University of Massachusetts Amherst, 2009). Particular emphasis was laid on the clarity, brevity, and relevance of all questions and response items. Frequent use was made of rating scales with five numbered steps and defined end points; where appropriate, an *other* category was included so as to identify issues and constructs not covered by the pre-formulated response items.

[12] An early version of the survey form by this author was kindly made available for the preparation of this research in January 2008

Draft versions of the questionnaire were discussed in expert interviews with senior representatives (partner level) of three buyout firms and with one investment manager of a generalist firm. Additional telephone interviews were held with representatives of the National Venture Capital Association (NVCA) in the United States of America and the Bundesverband Deutscher Kapitalbeteiligungsgesellschaften (BVK) in Germany.[13] The design of the survey was concluded in mid-February 2009 with a pre-test of the questionnaire in an online pilot survey of 100 private equity firms randomly selected from the frame population. A copy of the print version of the finalised survey form is shown in Appendix B.

The field phase of the survey began on 11 March 2009 with the dispatch of invitation letters and survey questionnaires by a postal service provider.[14] The database listed at least one personal contact for more than 90% of the private equity firms contained in the sample frame. Where multiple personal contacts were available for a single entry, one was picked at random (excluding non-executive board members and persons responsible for geographic areas outside the study focus). Most selected contact persons held senior positions (e.g. Partner, Managing Director, CEO, or CFO). The contact details and addresses of the selected private equity firms were then screened for completeness and obvious mistakes; erroneous entries were manually corrected, where possible, using information from the respective company websites. The survey instrument was made available to the addressees by post, as a printable download, and also as an internet survey, so that respondents could choose to complete the questionnaire, at their convenience, in writing or online (see Bryman, 2008, pp. 646–647, and Groves et al., 2004, pp. 163–165, on using multiple modes of data collection). An advance notice of the survey was sent by fax to those private equity firms for whom fax numbers were available in the database (more than 80% of all addressees) one day after the postal dispatch of invitations. Reminder letters were sent by email or fax after two to three weeks. In cases where these reminders

13 The European Private Equity and Venture Capital Association (EVCA) was unfortunately not available for an interview before the field phase of the survey began

14 All letters were classified as airmail, excepting those addressed to recipients in Germany

returned a failure notice, contact details were manually researched and corrected before making another delivery attempt. Altogether, the field phase of the survey lasted a little over two months. During this time, each addressee received up to two reminders (see examples of written communications in Appendix C).[15]

1.2.5 Data analysis

Altogether 149 completed questionnaires were received from survey respondents. To begin with, the questionnaires received were screened for incomplete, incomprehensible or obviously erroneous data. As a matter of course, the initial analyses also included a repeated verification of responding firms' eligibility.[16] Incomplete private equity firm specifications, such as firm type, capital under management, or investment focus, were subsequently edited or completed using information from the company websites (two instances).[17] All other missing items were labelled *missing value* and excluded from the analyses. In some instances, respondents had checked two neighbouring steps of a numbered rating scale, or inserted a cross between two such steps. These entries were coded as intermediate (.5) values. In the course of the assessment, 13 returned questionnaires had to be laid aside, either because they contained insufficient data, or because the corresponding private equity firms had been re-categorised as ineligible (see Chapter 2.2.1 and Appendix D for more detail on the categorisation of survey responses). As a result, the final sample contains 136 questionnaires.

In a next step, various methods were used to assess the survey quality. Survey outcome rates were calculated according to the guidelines and standard definitions of the American Association for Public Opinion Research (AAPOR, 2009) and compared with the response rates of earlier private equity surveys. The possible effects of survey non-response on data quality were assessed by examining the causes of non-response, by comparing characteristics of respondents and non-respondents, and also by comparing characteristics of "early respondents" and "late respondents". As a final quality check, the validity of the survey data was examined by comparing survey responses with available external data for the same construct. None of these analyses yielded material issues of data quality. An identified location bias (towards

---

15 A small number of follow-up telephone calls with private equity firms were also undertaken. This endeavour was abandoned after around 50 calling attempts due to disproportionate time requirements

16 The eligibility of the responding person was not separately verified. Although the survey was conducted as a personalised survey, not all forms returned were necessarily completed by the senior managers to whom the survey forms were addressed. This is not seen as a major concern for the quality of data in this study, as lower-level professionals can be expected to be sufficiently familiar with most of the information requested in the survey

17 All edits and data additions are documented and available from the author upon request

European private equity firms) is compensated by the use of country weights (see Chapter 2.2 for more detail on data quality and weights).

The central part of (quantitative) data analysis in this study concerns descriptions of single variables, the exploration of associations between variables, and the testing of relationships between variables. For these purposes, I employed mostly univariate or bivariate statistical methods, for example, Chi-Square tests, independent or paired samples *t*-tests, Mann-Whitney *U*-tests, Wilcoxon signed ranks tests, and tests of Spearman rank correlation. As a matter of caution, statistically significant bivariate results are always examined in light of possible influences from related variables (the respective correlation tables are included in the Appendices) and occasionally I supplement the investigation with an analysis of variance. Control variables are added if they are thought to improve the quality of the analysis. In preparatory and auxiliary analyses, I also made extensive use of histograms, scatterplots, and contingency tables.[18] Multivariate statistical methods are employed only when their assumptions are reasonably well met and where the results are sufficiently robust. One linear regression and one logistic regression are each employed for the analysis of non-response; additional (multiple) linear regressions are performed for the purposes of hypothesis testing in Chapter 3.4.2, and for the analysis of determinants of firm performance in Appendix E. In each case the analysis was preceded by a qualitative assessment of distributions, correlation tables, scatter plots, subsample counts, bivariate test results and expected explanatory power. Ordinal logistic regression analyses could not be employed (though generally suitable) because the respective crosstabulations of dependent and independent variables yielded too many cells with a count of less than five (see Garson, 2011, assumptions section, for an overview of the assumptions for ordinal logistic regression analysis).

Many quantitative data items are recorded on rating scales with five numbered steps and defined end points. For example, the degree of importance that respondents attribute to a particular objective is measured on a scale from 5 (*very important*) to 1 (*not important*). The corresponding variables are, under strict interpretation, ordinal scaled, and not interval scaled, as there is no warranty that distances between scale values are identical across the range of values (see Bryman, 2008, pp. 321–322, on possible types of variables). The use of parametric tests for such data is controversial (Bortz & Döring, 2006, p. 181), but a number of studies suggest that the results of parametric tests are rather robust to changes in the quality of the underlying scales (see, e.g. Bortz & Döring, 2006, p. 182, or Emory, 1985, pp. 358–359, for

---

18 Much of the statistical analysis was completed using current versions of IBM SPSS Statistics, MS Excel, and G*Power

more detail of these studies). For the purposes of this thesis, I generally assume that the rating scale variables generated in the survey meet the criteria for interval scale data well enough to allow meaningful interpretation of arithmetic operations, such as mean value or standard deviation, and to enable reasonably valid parametric testing. Nonetheless, non-parametric tests were always performed alongside the parametric tests and the results of these are reported where they differ materially from those of the corresponding parametric tests. Following general literature recommendations (e.g. American Psychological Association, 2010, pp. 32–34; Wilkinson & Task Force on Statistical Inference, 1999), the results of hypothesis tests are always evaluated in consideration of effect sizes and p values; non-significant test results are also discussed in light of statistical power, and, in exploratory parts of the thesis, statistical significance is used only to express levels of confidence in the (external) validity of sample results. As deemed necessary, parameter estimates are complemented by confidence intervals.

1.3 Limitations

The study is subject to various limitations. Firstly, the study results may not apply to populations outside the scope of the survey (limitation of external validity): Geographical coverage of the survey is restricted to the United States of America, Canada, and major private equity markets in Europe. The results may therefore not apply to other private equity markets, such as those in the Asia–Pacific region, which have grown rapidly within the last decade and today account for a sizeable proportion of the total private equity market. Similarly, the results may not apply to organisations outside the definition of private equity firms in this thesis, for example, funds of funds, evergreen funds, or non-profit organisations. Secondly, despite all precautions, the validity and reliability of results might be affected by survey error (see Groves et al., 2004, pp. 39–65, for a systematic classification of types of survey error). One possible source of survey error concerns the accuracy of the sample data: Responses might not correctly reflect the information that was sought from the private equity firm, for example, because of intentional or unintentional misreporting by the respondent, or because survey questionnaires were completed by persons other than the addressees. Another possible source of survey error concerns the validity of generalisations. Inferences from the sample of respondents to the target population could be impaired by coverage error, sampling error, or nonresponse error. In particular, the comparatively high level of survey non-response calls for a cautious treatment of inferences to the underlying population of private equity firms. Thirdly, the internal validity of the study is limited by the applied methodology. The available sample data only rarely permitted the use of multivariate methods. Some of the significant effects that are identified in bivariate analyses might be found in more complete multivariate analyses to be spurious, or in other ways affected by other variables; and due to the cross-sectional design of the study, directions of causal influence are frequently ambiguous (Bryman, 2008, p. 44). Finally, the study does not explore connections between reported performance and evaluations of individual decision methods and criteria as the quantity and quality of the collated performance data are viewed as insufficient for such analyses.

1.4 Organisation of the Thesis

Following this introduction, Chapter Two discusses the quality of the survey data and presents key descriptive statistics for the sample of private equity firms. The central body of empirical research is contained in chapters three to five, each of which is organised largely in the style of an independent research paper. Chapter Three concerns the objectives of private equity firms and the minimum rates of return that they require from new investments. Chapter Four explores the metrics that private equity firms use to measure and manage the performance of portfolio investments, and chapter Five investigates the exit decisions of private equity firms, with a particular focus on the exit decision power of private equity firms, the decision rules that private equity firms employ for deciding when to begin an exit process, and the principal determinants of the exit channel decision. Chapter Six concludes the research with a summary of the study results and additional conclusions. The final chapter provides a summary of the thesis in the German language (see Figure 2 for an overview of the thesis structure).

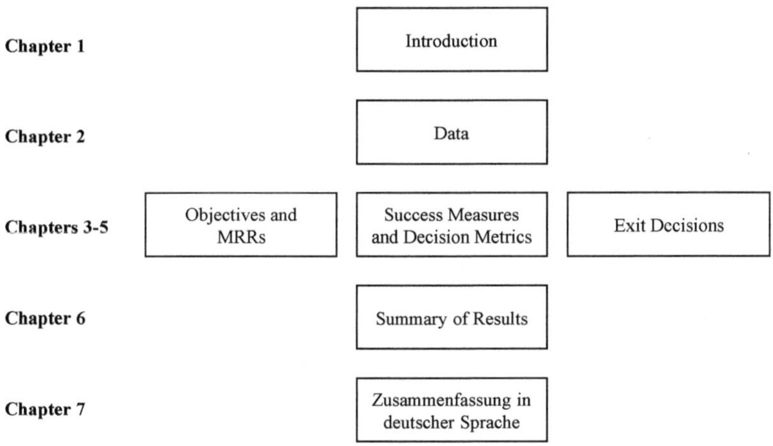

Figure 2. Structure of the thesis.

2 Data

2.1 Abstract

This part of the thesis examines the quality of the survey data and presents descriptive statistics for the sample of private equity firms. The study employed a cross-sectional survey design to collect data on key determinants and rules of decision-making in private equity firms. Following a preparatory phase, which included expert interviews as well as an online pilot test, a self-administered, standardised questionnaire was made available to more than 2,300 private equity firms located in the United States of America, Canada, and eleven countries in Europe. The field phase of the survey lasted a little over two months, during the course of which each addressee received up to two reminder notifications. After screening returned questionnaires for completeness and verifying the eligibility of responding private equity firms, the final sample consisted of 134 complete, and 2 partially complete survey questionnaires. The corresponding survey response rate of 5.8% is lower than response rates specified in other private equity mail surveys. A regression analysis of response rates and the numbers of units addressed in 16 private equity mail surveys suggests that this outcome is largely a result of the unusually large sample frame size of the survey in this thesis. I use multiple methods to examine whether the survey non-response has any detrimental effect on the quality of data; the results of these analyses yield no evidence that the group of non-respondent firms differ materially from the group of respondent firms in any way, other than perhaps employing a more stringent policy of confidentiality and being more likely to be located in the United States of America or Canada. Country weights are introduced to compensate any bias that might flow from a skewed geographic distribution of private equity firms in the sample. As a final quality check, the validity of the survey data was assessed by comparing response data to information from an external database; the results are reassuring in that most matching variables are highly correlated with each other. The sample of respondent firms is almost equally balanced between venture capital and buyout firms. In the year of the survey, responding private equity firms had been in existence for, on average, 9 to 11 years and had raised an average of 2 to 3 private equity funds. The mean (median) capital under management of the sample amounted to €426.0 million (€150.0 million). Respondent specifications regarding the "rough average return" of their private equity firm "across all funds" imply a mean IRR of 33.5% and a mean multiple of 2.6, whereas the respective average amounts of the subsample of buyout firms are higher than those of venture capital firms.

2.2 Data Quality

2.2.1 Calculation of survey outcome rates

The survey outcome rates shown in this thesis are calculated in accordance with the guidelines and standard definitions for final dispositions of case codes and outcome rates for surveys as set out by the American Association for Public Opinion Research (AAPOR, 2009).[19] As illustrated in the introduction to this thesis, the original (pre-survey) sample frame contained 2,373 private equity firms. During the course of the mail survey 73 of these firms were eliminated from the sample frame — irrespective of whether or not they had completed a survey form — because they had ceased to exist, were inactive, had been identified as duplicate listings, or because of serious doubts concerning their profit-seeking nature. Thus, the final (post-survey) sample frame consisted of 2,300 private equity firms located in the United States of America, Canada, and eleven countries in Europe. Following a review of the altogether 149 questionnaires that were received in the field phase of the survey, thirteen questionnaires were removed from the analysis because they contained insufficient data or because the corresponding private equity firms had been eliminated from the sample frame. The remaining sample of 136 returned questionnaires comprises 134 *completed* questionnaires, and 2 *partially completed* questionnaires.[20]

---

19 This excludes specific statistics relating to online participation, for which no guidelines were available

20 A table with more detail on the final disposition codes of the sample frame is available in Appendix D

Table 2
Survey outcome rates by location

Location	Frame	Sample[a]	Response Rate 1	Co-operation Rate 1	Refusal Rate 1	Contact Rate 1
	Count		%			
US	1,573	57	3.6	72.2	1.3	5.0
UK	218	18	8.3	66.7	4.1	12.4
France	92	6	6.5	75.0	2.2	8.7
Germany	88	14	15.9	70.0	6.8	22.7
Canada	82	5	6.1	71.4	2.4	8.5
Italy	43	5	11.6	71.4	2.3	16.3
Sweden	43	4	9.3	66.7	4.7	14.0
Switzerland	38	6	15.8	85.7	2.6	18.4
Spain	36	3	8.3	100.0	0.0	8.3
Finland	24	2	8.3	100.0	0.0	8.3
Netherlands	24	4	16.7	80.0	4.2	20.8
Norway	22	8	36.4	100.0	0.0	36.4
Denmark	17	2	11.8	66.7	5.9	17.6
Total	2,300	134	5.8	73.6	2.0	7.9

Note. All outcome rates are calculated in accordance with the 2009 Standard Definitions for final dispositions of case codes and outcome rates for surveys as set out by the American Association for Public Opinion Research (AAPOR).
[a]Questionnaires categorised as *complete* only.

Table 2 shows a breakdown of the survey outcome rates by location. Response rates in European countries varied widely between 6.5% (France) and 36.4% (Norway). The lowest response rate by country was generated in the United States of America (3.6%) — the country, which accounts for more than two thirds of private equity firms in the sample frame. Roughly two thirds of all completed questionnaires were submitted via the online survey tool. 94 of the 110 persons who logged on to the internet survey tool returned a complete form, representing a conversion rate of 85.5%. The mean average time that online participants were logged on to the internet survey tool was 13.7 minutes.[21]

2.2.2 Comparison with previous private equity mail surveys

The overall response rate of 5.8% is lower than response rates specified in other private equity mail surveys. One possible explanation for this outcome is the large size of the survey in this

21 The calculation of mean duration is based on the data of 85 online survey participants who completed the questionnaire in one session

thesis. All else being equal, more survey addressees imply less time and resource available for processing each individual unit (e.g. eligibility checks, verification of address, and communications with units). But perhaps more importantly, the addressees of large scale surveys might be less inclined to respond to the survey request than addressees of small scale surveys because their relative contribution to the survey is smaller.[22] Figure 3 shows a scatter plot of response rates and numbers of units addressed for previous private equity mail surveys and the survey in this thesis. Evidently, the graph supports the assumption of a link between the two variables; the coefficient of Spearman rank correlation is large and statistically significant ($r_s = -.90$, $p < .0005$, two-tailed, $n = 16$).[23] A linear regression of logarithmic transformations of the two variables yields the approximating curve depicted in the graph.[24] The regression model is statistically significant, $F(1, 14) = 44.9$, $p < .0005$, and explains 76.2% of the variation in response rates.[25]

22 This, of course, only applies to surveys in which the recipients are conscious of the sample frame size (as in the survey in this thesis)

23 The outcome of the test remains unchanged when using critical values of the Spearman rank order correlation coefficients for small sample sizes specified by Zar (1972): $r_{s\,crit}$ ($n = 16$, alpha = .01, two-tailed) = .635

24 A scatter-plot of regression residuals showed increased variance for sample frame sizes below 250 (heteroscedasticity). This suggests that the sample frame size is a less reliable predictor of response rates in small-scale surveys

25 A regression of the data excluding the present survey led to results of similar strength; the response rate of the present survey lies within the 95% confidence band of such a model

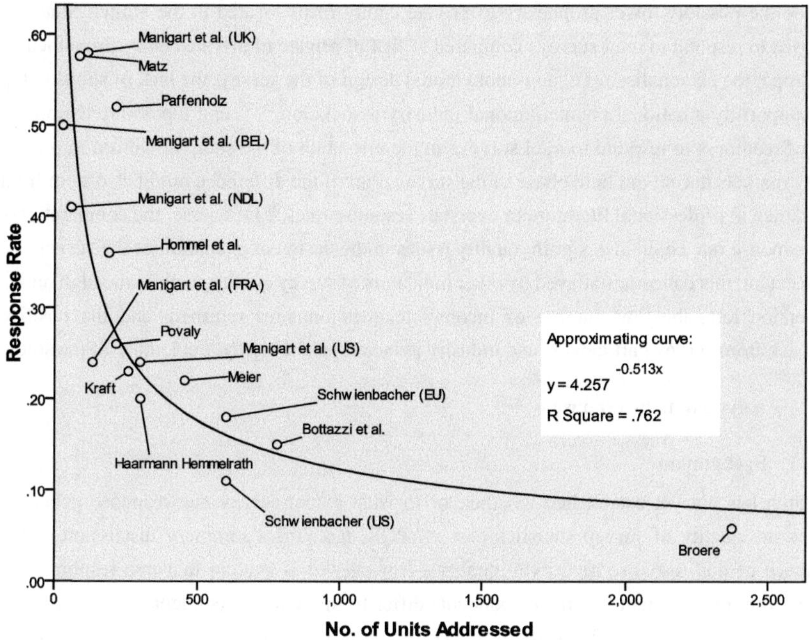

Figure 3. Scatter plot of response rates and sample frame sizes (No. of Units Addressed) for private equity mail surveys. All figures are reported values, except the response rate for Matz, which is derived from other figures reported in the study. The response rate for Haarmann Hemmelrath is a minimum value. The response rates are sourced from the following publications: Bottazzi, L., & Da Rin, M. (2002). Venture capital in Europe and the financing of innovative companies. *Economic Policy, 17*(34), 231–269; Haarmann Hemmelrath (Ed.) (2002). *Exit-Management in Beteiligungsgesellschaften: Ergebnisse einer Studie der Haarmann Hemmelrath Management Consultants GmbH in Zusammenarbeit mit der der Technischen Universität zu Braunschweig*. Düsseldorf, Germany: Author; Hommel, U., Ritter, M., & Wright, M. (2003). Verhalten der Beteiligungsfinanzierer nach dem "Downturn": Ergebnisse einer empirischen Untersuchung. *Finanz Betrieb, 5*(5), 323–333; Kraft, V. (2001). *Private Equity-Investitionen in Turnarounds und Restrukturierungen* (Doctoral dissertation, University of St.Gallen, Switzerland). Frankfurt am Main, Germany: Campus; Manigart, S., de Waele, K., Wright, M., Robbie, K., Desbrières, P., Sapienza, H. J., & Beekman, A. (2002). Determinants of required return in venture capital investments: a five-country study. *Journal of Business Venturing, 17*(4), 291–312; Matz, C. (2002). *Wettbewerbsentwicklung im deutschen Private-Equity-Markt: Strategieoptionen für Beteiligungskapital-Gesellschaften* (Doctoral dissertation, WHU – Otto Beisheim School of Management, Koblenz, Germany, 2001). Wiesbaden, Germany: Deutscher Universitäts-Verlag; Meier, D. (2006). *Post-investment value addition to buyouts: Analysis of European private equity firms* (Doctoral dissertation, RWTH Aachen, Germany, 2005). Wiesbaden, Germany: Deutscher Universitäts-Verlag; Paffenholz, G. (2004). *Exitmanagement: Desinvestitionen von Beteiligungsgesellschaften* (Doctoral dissertation, University of Cologne, Germany, 2004). Lohmar, Germany: Eul; Povaly, S. (2007). *Private equity exits: Divestment process management for leveraged buyouts*. Berlin, Germany: Springer; Schwienbacher, A. (2005). *An empirical analysis of venture capital exits in Europe and in the United States*. EFA 2002 Berlin Meetings Discussion Paper. Retrieved from http://ssrn.com/abstract=302001.

Although the large sample frame size goes a long way towards explaining the lower response rate of the survey in this thesis, a number of other factors may also have played a role. These include the possibly lower propensity of private equity firms located in the United States of America to respond to mail surveys compared to that of private of private equity firms located in Europe, the personalised (i.e. non-anonymous) design of the survey, the lack of sponsorship and support by a national or international industry association,[26] [27] and a possible temporary lack of readiness to respond to mail surveys in the aftermath of the sharp downturn in private equity markets during the field phase of the survey. Part of the difference might also stem from a tendency in professional literature to overstate response rates.[28] Of course, the comparatively low response rate could also signify quality issues in the design or execution of the survey. To some extent, this concern is allayed by other indicators of survey quality, such as the high online conversion rate, the low number of incomplete questionnaires returned, and the positive feedback from survey participants and industry associations during the field phase of the study.

2.2.3 Analysis of non-response

2.2.3.1 Background

Research has not yet established whether, or to what extent survey non-response generally affects the quality of survey statistics (see AAPOR, n.d., for a summary discussion of the influence of non-response on survey quality). However, it is evident that non-response can cause error "to the extent that the respondents differ from the nonrespondents on the statistics of interest" (Groves et al., 2004, p. 182). The first part of this analysis investigates the types and causes of non-response, with a view to establishing whether causes for refusals to participate could be connected to the data measured in the survey. The second part of the analysis compares the characteristics of respondents and non-respondents, using data from the sample frame database. The last part of the analysis compares the characteristics of "early respondents" and "late respondents", using data from the sample frame database, whereas the extent of a participant's resistance to respond to the survey request is proxied by the number of reminders that a participant had received before responding.

---

26 A small number of recipients declined to partake in the survey, stating that they participate only in surveys of particular industry associations

27 Conversely, local university patronage could explain the comparatively high survey response rate in Germany

28 Johnson and Owens (2003) identified large inconsistencies in reporting standards in professional literature. After studying 95 journal articles in social sciences and health sciences, they observe that response rates without definition "can mean anything, particularly in the absence of any additional information regarding sample disposition" (p. 130) and that they "have yet to encounter any case in which a response rate has been *underestimated* (vis-á-vis AAPOR standard formulas)" (p. 132). A cursory review of the private equity mail surveys referred to in Figure 3 shows that only Matz (2002) provides information on disposition status (though without reporting a response rate); none of the studies specify, for example, whether the reported rates include partial responses

2.2.3.2 Analysis of types and causes of non-response

According to Groves (2004, p. 178), "bias flows from nonresponse when the causes of the nonresponse are linked to the survey statistics measured". The breakdown of survey non-response in Appendix D shows that the vast majority of non-response (around 96%) is made up of addressees from whom "nothing ever returned"; other types of non-response mostly comprise documented failures to contact the addressee (returned error messages) and explicit refusals. The causes of non-response for the large group of silent private equity firms are unknown. Some non-respondents may not have received the survey request due to erroneous contact details and postal failures; others may have ceased to exist or may have considered their firms ineligible for the survey. However, it appears likely that a large number of addressees were simply not inclined to respond to the survey request. Their reasons might be similar to those provided in the 22 explicit refusals. 19 of these non-respondents stated one or more of the following reasons: (a) the firm policy does not permit their responding to survey requests (41%); (b) insufficient time or personnel to respond (36%); and (c) no disclosure of such information to outsiders (18%). In addition, two non-respondents declared that they were not interested in the survey, and one non-respondent from France claimed to not speak English.

The high percentages of responses under (a) and (c) suggest a bias in the survey sample towards private equity firms with less stringent confidentiality policies. However, it appears rather unlikely that such a bias should affect the statistics measured in the survey (i.e. private equity firm objectives and minimum return requirements, success measures and decision metrics, rules for exit decisions and general firm characteristics). This is largely consistent with the results of a comparison between respondents and non-respondents presented in the following (aside from a location bias). Other than that, the language issue specified in one refusal could indicate that private equity firms from non-English-speaking countries are underrepresented in the sample of respondents. This concern was rejected after observing that non-English-speaking countries in the survey generated a higher average response rate than English-speaking countries in the survey (see Table 2 in Chapter 2.2.1).

2.2.3.3 Comparison of respondents and non-respondents

2.2.3.3.1 Bivariate analyses

The characteristics of respondents and non-respondents were compared, using data from the sample frame database. Table 3 exhibits the results of the bivariate analysis. The Pearson Chi-Square tests reject the independence of the survey participation status from Type and Location; the strength of association is small in both instances, with each variable accounting for less than 3% of variance in participation status. The descriptive statistics for continuous variables show that responding private equity firms were on average younger, had raised less funds, and were smaller (by Staff Count, Funds, and Funds Raised) than non-responding private equity firms. Independent samples *t*-tests yielded statistically significant results for the parameters Age and Funds Raised, whereas the size of effect is small in both cases.

Table 3
Connections between survey participation status and firm characteristics

	Pearson Chi-Square test				
Variables	n	df	χ^2	p^a	Φ
Participation status and Type	2,300	2	9.6	.008 ***	.06
Participation status and Location	2,300	5	61.8	< .0005 ***	.16

	Status		Status		Status		Independent t-test		
Variable	R	NR	R	NR	R	NR	M_{diff}	p^a	d
	Subsample size		Mean		Standard deviation				
Age (yrs)	83	1,348	12.3	15.4	8.9	12.2	-3.1	.021 **	-0.26
Staff Count	78	1,110	13.3	16.5	11.1	43.0	-3.1	.521	-0.08
Funds	109	1,642	2.4	2.8	1.7	3.0	-0.4	.168 b	-0.14
Funds Raised ($m)	104	1,491	466.5	1,075.4	845.9	3,751.6	-608.8	< .0005 ***	-0.17

Note. The sample frame of 2,300 private equity firms is divided by participation status into 136 respondent firms (R) and 2,164 non-respondent firms (NR). The firm characteristics of the sample frame were obtained from the Preqin database *Fund Manager Profiles* in February 2009. Type specifies the type of private equity firm, whereas database entries denoted as Early Stage, Early Stage: Seed, Early Stage: Start-up, Expansion/Growth Capital, Late Stage, and Venture (General) are categorised as *venture capital*; database entries Buyout, Management Buy-out, Privatisation, Turnaround, Succession, Management Buy-in, Spin-offs, Divestiture, and Public to Private are categorised as *buyout*; all remaining entries are included in the category *other*. Location specifies private equity firm headquarter location, divided into six categories: United States of America and Canada, United Kingdom, France, Germany, Nordic (Denmark, Finland, Norway, and Sweden), and Other European (Italy, the Netherlands, Spain, and Switzerland). Funds denotes the number of funds a private equity firm has raised. Funds Raised denotes the value of funds raised over the last ten years in US$ millions.
[a]*ps* are two-tailed. $^*p < .10$. $^{**}p < .05$. $^{***}p < .01$.
[b]Equal variances not assumed.

2.2.3.3.2 Logistic regression

A binary logistic regression analysis was performed with the participation status as dependent variable. To increase the statistical power of the analysis, the predictor variables comprise only variables that were found to be significant in the bivariate analyses, that is, Age, Funds Raised, Location (coded in five dummy variables for the logistic regression), and Type (coded in two dummy variables).[29] The database contained sufficient information (listwise) for a regression

[29] The table of correlations between predictor variables (see Appendix F) shows no sign of excessive correlation (*multicollinearity*)

analysis with a sample of 1,111 private equity firms, comprising 64 respondent firms. The results of the regression analysis show that inclusion of predictor variables into the model with intercept only, significantly increases the model's ability to predict the participation status of private equity firms (see Table 4). A Hosmer and Lemeshow Goodness-of-Fit test suggests that the model estimates fit the observed data at an acceptable level. The strength of association is limited: Pseudo R Square ranges between 5.0% (Cox and Snell) and 14.0% (Nagelkerke). Only the dummy variable US & Canada has a significant partial effect ($p < .0005$). Inverting the odds ratio for this variable implies that (all else being equal) a private equity firm located in any of the countries Italy, the Netherlands, Spain, or Switzerland (together the reference dummy variable for Location) was 6.7 times (95% CI [3.0, 14.9]) more likely to respond to the survey than a private equity firm based in the United States of America or Canada.

Table 4

Binary logistic regression of variables predicting the survey participation status of private equity firms in the sample frame

Predictor	B	Wald χ^2	df	p	Odds ratio (e^B)	95% CI for e^B Lower	Upper
Constant***	-1.40	11.3	1	.001 ***	.25		
Age (yrs)	-0.02	0.9	1	.333	.98	0.95	1.02
Funds Raised ($m)	0.00	1.4	1	.245	1.00	1.00	1.00
Location***		42.8	5	< .0005 ***			
US & Canada***	-1.90	21.6	1	< .0005 ***	.15	0.07	0.33
UK	-0.70	2.2	1	.139	.50	0.20	1.26
France	-0.71	1.5	1	.219	.49	0.16	1.53
Germany	0.28	0.3	1	.590	1.32	0.48	3.66
Nordic	0.18	0.1	1	.699	1.20	0.47	3.04
Type		3.5	2	.175			
Venture capital	-0.23	0.5	1	.466	.79	0.42	1.48
Buyout	0.41	1.4	1	.235	1.51	0.76	2.98

Test	χ^2	df	p
Omnibus test	56.9	9	< .0005 ***
Hosmer and Lemeshow test	4.9	8	.772

Note. The sample of 1,111 private equity firms with valid data (listwise) is divided by Participation Status (the dependent variable) into 64 respondent firms and 1,047 non-respondent firms. The firm characteristics of the sample were obtained from the Preqin database *Fund Manager Profiles* in February 2009. CI = confidence interval. Funds Raised denotes the value of funds raised over the last ten years in US$ millions. Location specifies private equity firm headquarter location, coded in five dummy variables. *Nordic* includes Denmark, Finland, Norway, and Sweden. The reference dummy comprises Italy, the Netherlands, Spain, and Switzerland. Type specifies the type of private equity firm, whereas database entries denoted as Early Stage, Early Stage: Seed, Early Stage: Start-up, Expansion/Growth Capital, Late Stage, and Venture (General) are categorised as *venture capital*; database entries Buyout, Management Buy-out, Privatisation, Turnaround, Succession, Management Buy-in, Spin-offs, Divestiture, and Public to Private are categorised as *buyout*; all remaining entries are included in the reference category *other*. Cox and Snell R^2 = .050. Nagelkerke R^2 = .140.
*$p < .10$. **$p < .05$. ***$p < .01$.

2.2.3.4 Comparison of early respondents and late respondents

According to the continuum of resistance model (Lin & Schaeffer, 1995), participants who were difficult to contact can be used to estimate the impact of non-response on survey results. This study employs the number of reminder notifications that private equity firms received before responding to the survey request (*Reminders*) as the condition reflecting the level of effort that was required to elicit a response. Accordingly, the analysis compared average sample frame characteristics of respondents across different conditions. Table 5 shows that the Pearson Chi-Square test rejects independence between variables Location and Reminders (p = .001, two-tailed). The magnitude of association is medium and implies that the location of a respondent accounts for around 13.7% of variance in the number of reminders. The associations between continuous firm characteristic variables and the number of reminders were examined using one-way between-subjects analyses of variance. The descriptive statistics show that respondent firms are, on average, younger, less experienced (by Funds), and also smaller (by Staff Count and Funds Raised) with each additional reminder.[30] Table 5 shows that none of the corresponding test results are statistically significant. No multivariate analyses were performed, as the valid sample (listwise) for the four variables consisted of only 38 private equity firms.

Table 5

Connections between the numbers of reminder notifications received and firm characteristics of respondent firms

	Pearson Chi-Square test				
Variable	n	df	χ^2	p^a	Φ
Reminders and Type	136	4	1.6	.810	.11
Reminders and Location	136	4	18.6	.001 ***	.37

	Reminders			Reminders			Reminders			One-way ANOVA			
Variable	0	1	2	0	1	2	0	1	2	df	F	p	η
	Subsample size			Mean			Standard deviation			Betweeen subjects			
Age (yrs)	32	23	28	13.5	13.2	10.1	10.0	9.9	6.0	2	1.26	.289	.03
Staff Count	35	19	24	14.8	14.4	10.4	11.5	13.3	8.1	2	1.24	.295	.03
Funds	43	29	37	2.6	2.4	2.2	1.6	2.0	1.6	2	0.39	.676	.01
Funds Raised ($m)	41	26	37	537.9	568.7	315.7	823.2	1246.3	423.0	2	0.92	.401	.02

Note. The firm characteristics for the sample of respondent firms (n = 136) were obtained from the Preqin database *Fund Manager Profiles* in February 2009. Reminders specifies the number of reminder notifications a respondent firm received before submitting the questionnaire. Type specifies the type of private equity firm, whereas database entries denoted as Early Stage, Early Stage: Seed, Early Stage: Start-up, Expansion/Growth Capital, Late Stage, and Venture (General) are categorised as *venture capital*; database entries Buyout, Management Buy-out, Privatisation, Turnaround, Succession, Management Buy-in, Spin-offs, Divestiture, and Public to Private are categorised as *buyout*; all remaining entries are included in the category *other*. Location specifies private equity firm headquarter location, divided into three categories: United States of America and Canada, United Kingdom, and Other European (Denmark, Finland, France, Germany, Italy, the Netherlands, Norway, Spain, Sweden, and Switzerland). Funds denotes the number of funds a private equity firm has raised. Funds Raised denotes the value of funds raised over the last ten years in US$ millions.

[a]two-tailed. $^{*}p < .10$. $^{**}p < .05$. $^{***}p < .01$.

An analysis of response patterns by location reveals considerable differences across geographic regions (see Figure 4). In the United States of America and Canada the number of responses

[30] One exception is a minimal increase in the average value of funds raised from respondents without reminder to respondents with one reminder (this goes along with high standard deviation)

increased with each reminder notification, in the United Kingdom a constant number of responses was generated with each reminder, whereas in other European countries more than half of all responses (60%) were submitted before any reminder was issued. These observations support the speculation in Chapter 2.2.2 that private equity firms in the United States of America and Europe respond differently to survey requests.

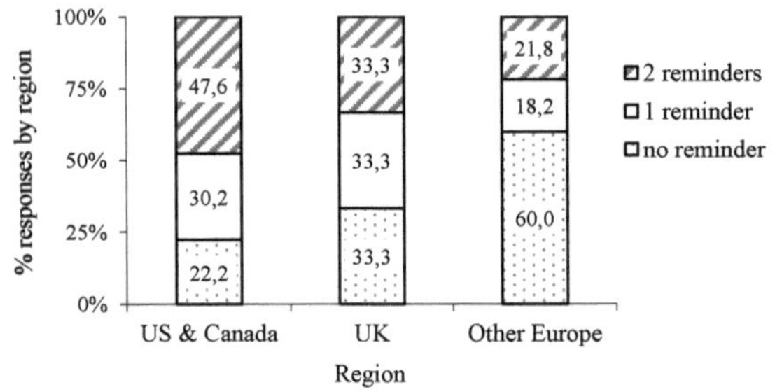

Figure 4. Numbers of reminders required to elicit a response from survey participants by geographic region (n = 136). Region denotes private equity firm headquarter location. Other Europe comprises Denmark, Finland, France, Germany, Italy, the Netherlands, Norway, Spain, Sweden, and Switzerland.

2.2.3.5 Implications for the study

Overall, the analyses yield no evidence that the large group of non-respondents differs materially from the group of respondents in any way, other than possibly employing a more stringent policy of confidentiality and being more likely to be located in the United States of America or Canada. As regards the policy of confidentiality, it does not appear very likely that the key statistics measured in the survey (i.e. the objectives, minimum return requirements, success measures, decision metrics of firms and their rules for exit decisions) should be materially affected by this characteristic. As regards the location, it is quite conceivable that the recorded survey statistics should vary between geographic regions, for example, due to a differing maturity of private equity markets (see, e.g. Black & Gilson, 1998). The non-response analysis shows in particular that private equity firms located in the United States of America and Canada were generally less responsive and required more reminders to elicit a response than their counterparts located in Europe. Consequentially, this underrepresentation of U.S. and Canadian private equity firms in the survey sample could give rise to error when using sample data for inferences to the underlying population of private equity firms.

In order to reduce the potential error from country bias, private equity firms in the survey sample are assigned country weights. These are calculated so as to make the percentage distribution by country of weighted respondents match the percentage distribution by country of private equity firms in the sample frame population (see Groves et al., 2004, p. 326, for information on methods of sample weighting). All ensuing data analyses in this thesis, excepting those relating to countries and regions use the weights presented in Table 6.

Table 6
Assignment of weights by country

Location	Frame	Sample	Frame	Sample	Weight
	Count		Percent		
US	1,573	58	68.4	42.6	1.60
UK	218	18	9.5	13.2	0.72
France	92	6	4.0	4.4	0.91
Germany	88	14	3.8	10.3	0.37
Canada	82	5	3.6	3.7	0.97
Italy	43	6	1.9	4.4	0.42
Sweden	43	4	1.9	2.9	0.64
Switzerland	38	6	1.7	4.4	0.37
Spain	36	3	1.6	2.2	0.71
Finland	24	2	1.0	1.5	0.71
Netherlands	24	4	1.0	2.9	0.35
Norway	22	8	1.0	5.9	0.16
Denmark	17	2	0.7	1.5	0.50
Total	2,300	136	100.0	100.0	

Note. Location specifies private equity firm headquarter location. Weights reflect the ratio of a country's share of private equity firms in the frame population to its share of firms in the survey sample.

2.2.4 Correlations between survey responses and comparable external data

One way of estimating the validity of survey data is to measure the correlation between survey responses and external data that evaluate the same construct (Groves et al., 2004, pp. 254–258). Incidentally, a small number of private equity firm characteristics that were collated in the survey are also supplied in the external database that was used for selecting the sample frame (the Preqin database *Fund Manager Profiles*). But using the Preqin database as the "gold standard" for assessing the quality of the survey data in this thesis has its own implications: The validity of its data is unknown; therefore, deviations between the two sets of data could stem from errors in either database. Moreover, such deviations could also arise from time differences between the two data sources, or from differences in the targeted construct. However, these complications do not render the test meaningless: Whereas an absence of collinearity does not yield conclusive evidence on the quality of data because the source of deviation is ambiguous, high degrees of positive correlation should serve as an acceptable sign of the validity of both datasets.

Table 7
Correlations of survey variables with external data

		Pearson		Spearman	
Survey variable	Matching data from external database	r	n	r_s	n
Age (yrs)	Age derived from year of establishment	.85 ***	71	.92 ***	80
Funds	Total number of funds raised	.22 **	96	.69 ***	108
Capital (€m)	Estimated available capital in US$ millions	.89 ***	91	.73 ***	103
Firm Type	Firm types derived from data on "Strategies"[a]	.	.	.63 ***	156
BO - VC	Firm types derived from data on "Strategies"[b]	.80 ***	92	.81 ***	108

Note. Correlations were tested pairwise, using country-weighted data. The weights reflect the ratio of a country's share of private equity firms in the frame population to its share of firms in the survey sample. The matching external data were sourced from the Preqin database *FundManager Profiles* in February 2009. Survey variables: Age is the number of years a respondent's firm has been in existence. Funds is the number of private equity funds a respondent's firm has raised. Capital is the rough total capital under management of a respondent's firm in € millions. Range specifications were replaced by their means, and amounts in other currencies were converted to € amounts using the averages of market exchange rates over the time of the survey. Firm Type contains all sample firms, categorised as either buyout (BO), venture capital (VC), or *other*. VC includes eight firms of related firm types, such as "growth equity" and "business angel"; BO includes two firms of related firm types ("industry specific buyout" and "restructuring buyout"). BO – VC contains only sample firms with firm types BO and VC.
[a]Early Stage, Early Stage: Seed, Early Stage: Start-up, Expansion/Growth Capital, Late Stage, and Venture (General) are categorised as VC; Buyout, Management Buy-out, Privatisation, Turnaround, Succession, Management Buy-in, Spin-offs, Divestiture, and Public to Private are categorised as BO, all remaining entries are allocated to the category *other*.
[b]Allocations as before, but excluding firms allocated to the category *other*.
$^{*}p < .10$. $^{**}p < .05$. $^{***}p < .01$. All *p*s are two-tailed.

Table 7 shows overall fairly high degrees of correlation between the survey responses and the corresponding data in the external database. The comparatively low coefficient of Spearman rank correlation for Firm Type is caused by a larger number of *other* type private equity firms in the Preqin database than in the study sample — this is most likely the result of an incomplete allocation of database entries to the firm types venture capital and buyout. If the analysis is limited to venture capital and buyout firms only, the coefficient of Spearman rank correlation increases to .81 ($p < .0005$, two-tailed, $n = 108$). Overall, the results are reassuring in that most matching variables are highly correlated with each other.

2.3 Descriptive Statistics

The sample contains 136 private equity firms located in the United States of America, Canada, and Europe. Table 8, Table 9, and Table 10 show key descriptive statistics for the sample firms in total and broken down by firm type (see Appendix G for variable definitions). In the year of the survey, responding private equity firms (not funds) had been in existence for, on average, 9 to 11 years and had raised an average of 2 to 3 private equity funds. The mean (median) capital under management of the sample amounts to €426.0 million (€150.0 million). The respective values for the subgroups of venture capital and buyout firms amount to €232.3 million (€130.0

million) and to €671.0 million (€200.0 million). The dispersion of capital under management is high, particularly for buyout firms. Median values are lower than mean values because the distributions are right-skewed. A comparison of statistics for venture capital and buyout firms in the sample shows that the average venture capital firm is smaller (by capital under management), undertakes smaller investments, and manages a larger number of investments than the average buyout firm. Independent samples *t*-tests and Mann-Whitney *U*-tests show that these differences are statistically significant (alpha = .05, two-tailed).[31]

The mean (median) IRR of private equity firms that had provided valid responses for this item (n = 88) amounts to 33.5% (26%). The mean (median) multiple of the subsample of private equity firms that had submitted valid details for this item (n = 66) amounts to 2.6 (2.7). As the survey questionnaire referred only to the "(rough) average return" that a firm had "achieved across all funds", the amounts specified by respondents may not always be fully comparable with each other. Notwithstanding this, the data show a noteworthy pattern: The average IRR and multiple for the sample of venture capital firms is lower than the average IRR and multiple for the sample of buyout firms. An independent samples *t*-test is statistically significant for the difference in multiples; the size of effect is large. A corresponding test with IRR data was conducted using a logarithmic transformation because the distribution of "simple" IRRs was found to be right-skewed (skewness of 4.1 and 2.3 for venture capital and buyout firms, respectively). The mean difference in ln IRR is statistically significant,[32] suggesting that the ratio of the geometric mean IRR of buyout firms to the geometric mean IRR of venture capital firms is 1.9 (95% CI [1.3, 2.7]);[33] the size of effect large. Additional exploratory analyses yielded connections between IRR performance and other firm attributes: The IRR of venture capital firms in the sample is positively related to firm experience (as measured by the number of funds raised); the IRR of buyout firms in the sample is negatively associated with geographical specialisation and, to a lesser extent, with the number of investments (see Appendix E for further detail).

31 In Table 8, the results of Mann-Whitney *U*-tests are only shown where they differ materially from the results of the independent samples *t*-tests

32 Table 8 shows that a non-parametric Mann-Whitney *U*-test using simple IRRs leads to the same outcome

33 The antilog of the arithmetic mean difference between the logarithm-transformed values yields the geometric mean. In this particular case, the ratio of geometric mean IRRs also roughly reflects the relation between the respective median IRRs, because the distributions of ln IRR are largely symmetric

Table 8

Key characteristics (ordinal scale and continuous variables) of private equity firms in the survey sample by type

Characteristic	Type			Type			VC - BO		
	VC	BO	All	VC	BO	All	M_{diff}	p^a	d
	Mean			Median					
Age (yrs)	10.0	12.2	10.7	9.0	10.0	9.0	-2.3	.146	-0.27
Funds	3.3	2.5	2.8	2.0	2.0	2.0	0.8	.182	0.25
Capital (€m)	232.3	671.0	426.0	130.0	200.0	150.0	-438.7	.026 ** b	-0.43
Investments	18.0	8.4	12.7	14.0	7.0	9.0	9.6	.004 ***	0.55
Investment Size (€m)	5.9	32.5	18.1	4.0	15.0	7.5	-26.6	< .0005 ***	-0.94
IRR (%)	32.9	35.2	33.5	15.0	30.0	26.0	-2.4	.828 c d	-0.06
Multiple	2.1	2.8	2.6	1.9	3.0	2.7	-0.7	.007 ***	-1.05
	Standard deviation			Subsample size					
Age (yrs)	7.0	9.8	8.4	62	60	133			
Funds	4.1	1.8	3.0	57	58	126			
Capital (€m)	357.2	1,386.3	984.5	56	55	123			
Investments	22.9	9.0	17.3	58	61	130			
Investment Size (€m)	5.6	40.4	30.0	64	59	134			
IRR (%)	61.8	17.7	41.2	34	45	88			
Multiple	0.9	0.5	0.7	18	42	66			

Note. All figures are based on country-weighted survey data. The weights reflect the ratio of a country's share of private equity firms in the frame population to its share of firms in the survey sample. The type of private equity firm comprises venture capital (VC), buyout (BO), and *other*. VC includes eight firms of related firm types, such as "growth equity" and "business angel"; BO includes two firms of related firm types ("industry specific buyout" and "restructuring buyout"). M_{diff} denotes mean difference. Age is the number of years a respondent's firm has been in existence. Funds is the number of private equity funds a respondent's firm has raised. Capital is the rough total capital under management of a respondent's firm in € millions. Investments is the rough number of company investments managed by a respondent's firm. Investment Size is a respondent firm's rough typical investment size (equity stake) in € millions. Range specifications were replaced by their means, and amounts in other currencies were converted to € amounts using the averages of market exchange rates over the time of the survey. IRR is the rough average IRR (in %) that a respondent's firm has achieved across all funds. Some amounts were expressly specified as *gross*. One amount was specified as *net*; this value was divided by 0.8 to arrive at a rough approximation of gross return. Response data also include one forecast value and three minimum return specifications (implied by ">" as prefix or "+" as suffix). Multiple is the rough average multiple that a respondent's firm has achieved across all funds. Some figures were expressly specified as *gross*. Response data also include one forecast value and two minimum return specifications. Two extreme values (50 and 1300) were excluded from the analysis.

[a]Using independent samples t-tests for equality of means. All ps are two-tailed. Equal variances are only assumed for the variable Funds. $^{*}p < .10$. $^{**}p < .05$. $^{***}p < .01$.

[b]Mann-Whitney $U = 1{,}573$; p (two-tailed) = .008; mean rank VC = 57.3; mean rank BO = 74.8.

[c]Mann-Whitney $U = 494$; p (two-tailed) < .0005; mean rank VC = 33.1; mean rank BO = 58.7.

[d]An independent samples t-test for equality of means using ln IRR instead of simple IRR was also significant: p (two-tailed) = .001, equal variances not assumed, $M_{diff} = 0.64$, 95% CI [0.27, 1.00], $d = 0.88$.

The distribution of private equity firms in the sample is almost equally balanced between buyout firms and venture capital firms across all major geographical regions (see Table 6 in Chapter 2.2.3.5 for non-weighted country counts). Most private equity firms in the sample prefer a hands-on style of management and mostly manage their investments in closed-end funds. Buyout firms show a slightly stronger tendency than venture capital firms to obtain their fund capital from outside investors, whereas venture capital firms show a stronger tendency than buyout firms to obtain their fund capital from private families and from the government, state or a public institution.

Table 9
Key characteristics (nominal scale variables) of private equity firms in the survey sample by type

	Type			Type			VC vs. BO		
Characteristic	VC	BO	All	VC	BO	All	χ^2	p [a]	Φ
	Count			% within type					
Region									
US & Canada	48	45	98	76.0	73.4	71.9			
Europe	15	16	38	24.0	26.6	28.1			
Total	64	61	136	100.0	100.0	100.0			
Management Style									
Hands-on	39	40	88	62.8	65.5	65.8	0.1	.755	.03
Supportive	21	19	41	33.4	30.8	30.8	0.1	.758	-.03
Hands-off	0	1	1	0.0	1.8	0.8	1.1	.491 [b]	.10
Other	2	1	3	3.8	1.9	2.6	0.4	1.000 [b]	-.06
Total	62	61	134	100.0	100.0	100.0			
Closed-End Fund									
Yes	50	46	104	79.8	77.1	77.9	0.1	.716	-.03
No	13	14	30	20.2	22.9	22.1	0.1	.716	.03
Total	63	59	134	100.0	100.0	100.0			
Sources Of Fund Capital									
Outside investors	53	56	116	59.8	84.8	69.5	2.9	.087 *	.15
Private family	14	5	21	16.1	7.2	12.7	5.0	.026 **	-.20
Government, state etc.	12	1	14	13.4	1.6	8.2	9.5	.002 ***	-.28
Parent company	4	2	7	4.8	2.9	3.9	0.8	.680 [b]	-.08
Capital markets	1	1	3	1.6	1.1	1.5	0.2	1.000 [b]	-.04
Other	4	2	7	4.3	2.4	4.2	0.8	.680 [b]	-.08
Responses	88	67	167	100.0	100.0	100.0			
Total	64	61	136	72.1	91.1	81.1			

Note. All figures are based on country-weighted survey data. The weights reflect the ratio of a country's share of private equity firms in the frame population to its share of firms in the survey sample. The type of private equity firm comprises venture capital (VC), buyout (BO), and *other*. VC includes eight firms of related firm types, such as "growth equity" and "business angel"; BO includes two firms of related firm types ("industry specific buyout" and "restructuring buyout"). Region refers to the firms' headquarter locations. Because the data are country-weighted, the weight of a region in the sample reflects the weight of a region in the frame population. Closed-End Fund denotes whether a respondent's firm mostly manages its investments in (closed-end) funds with a fixed lifetime. Sources Of Fund Capital specifies the provider(s) of the majority of fund capital for a respondent's firm. In one case the information was manually researched.
[a] Using Chi-Square tests of homogeneity of proportions ($df = 1$). All ps are two-tailed. $^{*}p < .10$. $^{**}p < .05$. $^{***}p < .01$.
[b] Exact test applied because some cells had an expected count of less than 5.

The investment preferences of venture capital and buyout firms exhibit some general differences. Venture capital firms mostly target minority ownership stakes, whereas buyout firms mostly target majority stakes. Buyout firms also show a stronger tendency towards better-performing target companies than do venture capital firms. Many venture capital firms declared that they had no preference regarding target firms' performance; possibly because the performance of very early-stage companies is not considered to be a critical indicator for the future performance of such companies. Last, venture capital firms show a stronger tendency to specialise in industry sectors than buyout firms. One explanation for this difference might be the typical emphasis in venture capital on young, high-growth companies. Such companies are naturally more frequent in new and fast-growing industries.

Table 10

Key investment preferences (nominal scale variables) of private equity firms in the survey sample by type

	Type			Type			VC vs. BO		
Characteristic	VC	BO	All	VC	BO	All	χ^2	p[a]	Φ
	Count			% within type					
Preferred Ownership									
Majority	10	50	64	15.9	91.9	50.7	66.1	< .0005***	.76
Minority	41	1	47	68.5	1.3	37.2	55.4	< .0005***	-.70
Other	9	4	15	15.6	6.8	12.1	1.0	.317	-.09
Total	60	54	126	100.0	100.0	100.0			
Preferred Target Performance									
Well- or underperforming	35	54	100	59.7	94.4	79.1	19.6	< .0005***	.41
Loss-making	5	2	7	9.2	2.8	5.4	2.1	.272[b]	-.13
Other	18	2	20	31.1	2.8	15.4	16.4	< .0005***	-.38
Total	58	57	127	100.0	100.0	100.0			
Industry Specialisation									
Yes	50	30	84	78.9	50.3	62.5	11.0	.001***	-.30
No	13	30	51	21.1	49.7	37.5	11.0	.001***	.30
Total	63	60	135	100.0	100.0	100.0			
Geographic Specialisation									
Yes	45	45	98	71.4	73.9	72.2	0.1	.755	.03
No	18	16	38	28.6	26.1	27.8	0.1	.755	-.03
Total	64	61	136	100.0	100.0	100.0			

Note. All figures are based on country-weighted survey data. The weights reflect the ratio of a country's share of private equity firms in the frame population to its share of firms in the survey sample. The type of private equity firm comprises venture capital (VC), buyout (BO), and *other*. VC includes eight firms of related firm types, such as "growth equity" and "business angel"; BO includes two firms of related firm types ("industry specific buyout" and "restructuring buyout").

[a]Using Chi-Square tests of homogeneity of proportions ($df = 1$). All ps are two-tailed. $^{*}p < .10$. $^{**}p < .05$. $^{***}p < .01$.

[b]Exact test applied because some cells had an expected count of less than 5.

All firm characteristics were screened for large and significant levels of association with each other (see Appendix H). The closest levels of association exist between firm type (buyout or venture capital) and preferred ownership (majority or minority), between Age and Funds, and between Capital and Investment Size. In the following, the variable Preferred Ownership is omitted from tables and presentations, unless additional insights are offered by its inclusion.

3 Objectives and Minimum Return Requirements

3.1 Abstract

This part of the thesis concerns the objectives of private equity firms and the minimum rates of return they require from new investments. Following a review of existing literature, I develop exploratory survey questions and formulate testable hypotheses. The ensuing empirical analysis is based on the survey data of 136 private equity firms located in the United States of America, Canada, and Europe. The results show that private equity firms attach particularly high importance to the objective of delivering high returns to investors and to reputational objectives, the latter of which strengthens a central assumption of popular private equity theories and also supports the idea that at-stake reputation is a genuine incentive for private equity firms to align their interests with those of their investors and contract partners. The analysis reveals several statistically significant connections between respondents' importance ratings of objectives and the characteristics of their private equity firms. These suggest that a private equity firm's desire for reputation is linked to the degree of asymmetric information about the quality of the private equity firm between the private equity firm and its principal contract partners and that a private equity firm's appetite for risk is linked to its business focus. The data do not provide clear support for Lerner and Schoar's (2004) prediction of a (direct) link between the liquidity of investors' interests in the funds of a private equity firm and the intensity of asymmetric information about the quality of the private equity firm between inside investors and outside investors; instead, they appear to suggest that this relationship is moderated by reputation. If this holds true, Lerner and Schoar's theory on the causes of illiquidity should be extended to account for the effects of reputation. The survey data on minimum return requirements provide empirical evidence of their (expected) important role for investment decisions in private equity firms. Survey respondents attach particularly high importance ratings to minimum level internal rates of return and minimum level money multiples; in comparison, the sample of private equity firms attaches little importance to minimum level discount rates in discounted cash flow models. The survey results also provide information on determinants of the minimum return that private equity firms require for a particular investment: Factors such as investment stage and quality of management generated particularly high importance ratings from the sample of private equity firms. A comparison of mean importance ratings across all factors appears to support the idea that idiosyncratic risk plays an important part for a private equity firm's assessment of investment opportunities. Bivariate statistical tests show a number of significant relationships between characteristics of private equity firms and the importance ratings that private equity firm respondents assigned to various factors. I conclude from these results that a private equity firm's investment strategy and associated risk profile are important determinants of the levels of minimum return required from new investments and that the current degree of diversification plays a role for the importance that private equity firms attach to idiosyncratic risk when evaluating new investment opportunities. The results do not support the idea of Ruhnka and Young (1991, pp. 125–128) that a decline in the level of minimum return required from earlier to later stages of investment is caused by a decrease in internal risks.

3.2 Existing Literature

3.2.1 Objectives

There is almost no existing literature that explicitly discusses the objectives of private equity firms, but a number of studies make implicit assumptions about such objectives. These assumptions frequently refer to profitability objectives (e.g. Sahlman, 1990, p. 501), but they sometimes also refer to other aims. Gompers (1996), for example, hypothesizes that young venture capitalists take their portfolio companies public earlier than established venture capital firms in order to build a reputation (the grandstanding hypothesis). Black and Gilson (1998) also believe that reputation is important for private equity firms. They contend that reputational markets regulate implicit contracts over (future) control between venture capital firms and entrepreneurs (Black & Gilson, 1998, pp. 262–263).[34] Lerner and Schoar (2004) imply that private equity firms pursue liquidity objectives for the shares in their funds when they hypothesize that private equity firms impose transfer restrictions on the shares in their funds to attract "deep-pocket" investors and reduce the firm's cost of capital in follow-on fundraisings.[35]

Schefczyk (2006, pp. 18–21), on the other hand, discusses private equity firm objectives explicitly; he categorises (supposed) private equity firm objectives into original objectives ("originäre Ziele") and derivative objectives ("derivative Ziele"): Original objectives comprise market aims for fundraising ("Marktziele bei der Akquisition von Kapital"), efficiency aims for managing the private equity company ("Effizienzziele beim Betrieb der VCG [Venture Capital-Gesellschaft]"), and compensational aims for services rendered ("Vergütungsziele für die erbrachten Dienstleistungen"); derivative objectives comprise goals that are adopted from private equity investors, that is, high returns ("Rentabilitätsziel"), certainty ("Sicherheitsziel"), and liquidity ("Liquiditätsziel"). Schefczyk also maintains that some private equity investors, such as credit institutions, industrial firms, and governments, have additional aims (e.g. strategic or development aims). He speculates that investors who choose to invest in private equity generally place a higher emphasis on returns than on certainty and, especially, liquidity

[34] The importance of reputation in private equity is emphasized by many other authors, too (see, e.g. Fenn, Liang, & Prowse, 1997, pp. 43–46; Nahata, 2009; Neus & Walz, 2005, p. 255; Sahlman, 1990, p. 500)

[35] Of course, such reputational and liquidity objectives do not necessarily imply a multi-objective function and might also be regarded as a means to achieve a longer term profitability objective (as appears to be implied by Lerner and Schoar's reasoning)

interests (unless the private equity firm is listed). Paffenholz (2004) provides some information on the divestment objectives of private equity firms. In a survey of private equity firms located in Germany he finds that most firms in the sample (n = 108) rate the maximisation of sale proceeds ("Maximierung der Verkaufserlöse") as their primary divestment objective; reputational objectives generated a lower average rating (Paffenholz, 2004, pp. 156–161 and 219).

3.2.2 Minimum return requirements

One branch of research on the rates of return that private equity firms require from new investments has attempted to explain why private equity firms (and especially venture capital firms) use higher discount rates than might have been expected from applying the capital asset pricing model. Sahlman (1990), for example, suggests that high venture capital discount rates include a fudge factor, which compensates for overly optimistic financial projections of entrepreneurs:

> In theory the required rate of return on an entrepreneurial investment reflects the risk-free interest rates in the economy, the systematic risk of the particular asset and the market risk premium, the liquidity of the asset, and compensation for the value added by the supplier of capital (….) In practice, the use of high discount rates also reflects a well-known bias in financial projections made by entrepreneurs (p. 512).[36]

Others suggest that idiosyncratic risk could play a role. Manigart et al. (2002) observe that "the existence of huge market imperfections [in the market for venture capital investments] implies that idiosyncratic investment risk and other investment characteristics may be as important as market risk in determining required return (Rea,1989)" (p. 294). Jones and Rhodes-Kropf

---

36 Lerner, Hardymon and Leamon (2005, pp. 212–214) appear to take a similar view; they criticise the use of such a fudge factor in the venture capital method and recommend a thorough analysis (and adjustment, if necessary) of the financial projections, instead

(2003) suggest that the discount rates used by private equity firms are higher than beta-based discount rates, because "VCs take their compensation and compensation risk into account" (p. 3). They argue that observed excess alphas therefore do not represent excess returns, but rather "required returns both for the services performed by the VC [venture capitalist] and for the idiosyncratic risk borne by the VC" (p. 4). In a study of more than 1,200 U.S. private equity funds they were able to show that, consistent with their theory, buyout funds with fewer investments (proxied by the number of drawdowns) have higher average alphas than other buyout funds and that venture capital and buyout funds with lower (estimated) idiosyncratic risk have lower average alphas than other venture capital and buyout funds.[37]

Another branch of research has collated quantitative data on required rates of return and identified associations of these with characteristics of private equity firms and investments. One of these relations suggests that the average rates of return that private equity firms require from new investments declines from earlier to later stages of investment (Elango et al., 1995; Lockett et al., 2002, p. 1023; Manigart et al., 2002, pp. 301–302; Murray & Lott, 1995, p. 293; see also a review of three earlier studies by Ruhnka & Young, 1991, pp. 120–127). Ruhnka and Young (1991, pp. 125–128) suggest that this effect is caused by a decrease in *internal risks*, such as poor management quality, a high cash burn rate, or a lack of internal financial controls, as the investment continues to develop.[38] Murray and Lott (1995, p. 293) and Lockett, Murray and Wright (2002, p. 1023) identify a connection between required rates of return and the industry sector of target companies (technology or non-technology). And Manigart et al. (2002, pp. 303–306) find that independent venture capital firms require higher rates of return for their investments than captive venture capital firms do (early-stage investments excepted), that venture capital firms located in the United States of America or the United Kingdom require higher rates of return than those located in France, Belgium and the Netherlands, and that venture capital firms with a higher intensity of involvement (proxied by the number of investments per venture capital manager) require higher rates of return than those with a lower intensity of involvement. Dixon (1991) conducted a survey of 30 UK venture capital firms about factors that determine the risk premia of required rates of return. The factor *financing stage* generated the highest mean importance rating, whereas none of the sample firms appeared

---

[37] These results stand in some contrast with the results of a study of 73 investee (private equity) funds of one large U.S. institutional investor by Ljungqvist (2003a). In a cross-sectional regression analysis of excess fund IRRs, Ljungqvist does not find evidence that either idiosyncratic risk (proxied by various measures of concentration) or market risk (proxied by aggregated portfolio betas) have a statistically significant impact on excess fund IRR

[38] Ruhnka and Young (1991) contrast the internal risks with "*external* or market-determined risks such as the emergence of competitors, technological shifts, or economic downturns that slow market growth or prevent initial public offerings" (p. 125)

to employ beta coefficients of similar quoted companies. Dixon ascribes the former result to a link between the financing stage and rate of failure of investments (see Dixon, 1991, p. 341). An assumed link between financing stage and risk leads Vater (2003) to expect varying return requirements across private equity firms that are active in different markets. He finds empirical support for a predicted link between expected return and private equity firm type in the survey data of 56 private equity firms located in Germany; in particular, the sample data show that industry specialists and venture capital firms expected higher rates of return than buyout firms or generalist firms (Vater, 2003, pp. 124–126).

3.3 Development of Research Focus and Hypotheses

One of the fundamental conclusions of existing financial theory is that, given perfectly competitive capital markets, managers of firms will act in the best interests of their firm's shareholders if they undertake to maximise market value (Brealey, Myers, & Allen, 2011, pp. 37–43). This demand is the basis of two popular decision rules for capital investment: The *net present value rule* stipulates that managers should "accept [all] investments that have positive net present values", and the *rate-of-return rule* stipulates that managers should "accept [all] investments that offer rates of return in excess of their opportunity costs of capital" (Brealey et al., 2011, p. 53). These normative management policies of conventional finance theory are possibly reflected in mission statements of private equity firms, for example, when they declare that their objective is to "create value" (e.g. BC Partners) or to "generate superior returns" (e.g. Apax Partners).[39] Similarly, the rate-of-return rule from conventional finance theory could also be reflected in the minimum rates of return that private equity firms employ for the investment decision.

But private equity markets are far from being *perfect*; the simple instruction to maximise (net present) value might not be easy to apply in markets that are characterised by asymmetric (or absent)[40] information, illiquidity, and exposure to idiosyncratic risk. This thesis endeavours to investigate the objectives of private equity firms by directly asking executives of private equity firms, how much importance they attribute to various conceivable objectives and to different types of required minimum rates of return for new investments. Schefczyk's (2006, pp. 18–21) description of private equity firm objectives was used as a starting point for developing survey questions as it covers a wide range of potentially relevant objectives. For the survey questionnaire I make two changes to Schefczyk's categorisation: Firstly, I combine Schefczyk's *efficiency aims for managing the private equity company* and *compensational aims for services*

39 Statements sourced from the respective company websites (http://www.bcpartners.com/bcp/aboutus/ and http://www.apax.com/en/aboutus/index.html) as of August 2010

40 For example, lacking market prices for private company investments

rendered into a single income objective that is meant to represent the profit-seeking goals of private equity firms. Secondly, I replace Schefczyk's *market aims for fundraising* with reputational objectives. Reputation is a valuable asset for private equity firms (Fenn, Liang, & Prowse, 1997, pp. 43–46; Neus & Walz, 2005, p. 255; Sahlman, 1990, p. 500) and believed to be a "primary objective" for private equity firms (Nahata, 2009, p. 14). Empirical studies suggest that (venture capital firm) reputation has beneficial effects, not only on a firm's fundraising abilities, but also on its access to deal flow, and the contractual terms with investors and with entrepreneurs (see Nahata, 2009, for a comprehensive overview of empirical studies; see also Hommel & Schneider, 2006, on the effect of buyout firms' reputation on access to debt finance). Therefore, the survey form records the importance that private equity firms attribute to their reputation amongst various groups of contract partners.

One testable hypothesis is developed from a theory by Lerner and Schoar (2004) of the causes for the illiquidity of shares in private equity funds. Assuming asymmetric information about the quality of the private equity firm between existing investors and the market, Lerner and Schoar hypothesised that private equity firms impose transfer restrictions on the shares in their funds to attract "deep-pocket" investors and reduce the firm's cost of capital in follow-on fundraisings. They predicted that funds with a lower intensity of asymmetric information about the quality of the private equity firm between inside investors and outside investors (e.g. because of an existing track record of performance) should be associated with fewer transfer restrictions for investors. Using a sample of 243 U.S. private equity funds, they find that, consistent with their ideas, later funds of the same private equity firm have fewer transfer restrictions. The survey in this thesis records the importance that private equity firms attribute to generating high liquidity of investors' interests in their funds (the *liquidity objective*). If private equity firms can choose the degree of illiquidity for the shares in their funds (as hypothesized by Lerner and Schoar), the importance that private equity firms bestow on the liquidity objective should be a reasonable proxy for the actual liquidity of investors' interests in private equity firms' funds. It is therefore expected that the more funds a private equity firm has raised (i.e. the lower the intensity of asymmetric information), the more importance it tends to attribute to the liquidity objective (H1).

In an early study of 30 UK venture capital firms, Dixon finds that venture capital firms "made little use of current investment theory" in determining minimum return requirements (Dixon, 1991, p. 342). For a better understanding of private equity firms' investment decisions (and the role of conventional finance theory in these decisions), the survey also investigates the types of return requirements that private equity firms typically employ (i.e. multiples, IRRs, or discount rates) and the importance that private equity firms attribute to various factors that influence the level of minimum return required from a particular investment (*MRR factors*). Two testable hypotheses are derived from Ruhnka and Young's (1991, pp. 125–128) supposition that an observed decline in the levels of return requirements from earlier to later stages of investment is caused by a decrease in internal risks, such as poor management quality, a high cash burn rate, or a lack of internal financial controls, as the investment continues to develop. If their assumption holds true the internal risks of investments targeted by buyout firms should generally be lower than those targeted by venture capital firms, as buyout firms typically undertake investments in mature companies, whereas venture capital firm typically undertake investments in young, high-growth companies. Under the assumption that the importance private equity firms attach to a particular MRR factor is generally proportional to the amount of risk they associate with the determinant, it follows that the importance that buyout firms attribute to the MRR factor management quality is lower than the importance that venture capital firms attribute to the MRR factor management quality (H2a) and that the importance that buyout firms attribute to the MRR factor capital intensity is lower than the importance that venture capital firms attribute to the MRR factor capital intensity (H2b).

3.4 Results and Discussion

3.4.1 The importance of private equity firm objectives

Figure 5 shows the mean importance ratings that survey respondents attributed to various objectives for their private equity firms. The Returns objective stands out with the highest mean importance rating and a tight 95% confidence interval; paired samples tests of mean differences in importance ratings between the returns objective and each other objective in the survey questionnaire yielded statistically significant results in every instance ($p < .0005$, two-tailed).[41] Respondents also assigned high importance ratings to the reputation of their private equity firm among investors, to the reputation of their private equity firm among owners and entrepreneurs, and — to a lesser extent — to the reputation of their private equity firm among managers, and

41 The size of effect was smallest for the paired sample Returns and Reputation Among Investors ($d = 0.43$). The analysis of Wilcoxon signed ranks for this pair of objectives shows that roughly two thirds of respondents attributed equivalent importance ratings (tied ranks) to these two objectives

to Certainty. Reputation Among Financial Intermediaries yielded a moderate mean importance rating, with a 95% confidence interval above the midpoint of the rating scale. Income and Liquidity generated the lowest mean importance ratings, with 95 % confidence intervals around and just below the midpoint of the rating scale, respectively. Ten respondents specified an additional objective (besides those listed on the survey form) under *other* in the questionnaire: Four of these respondents (of which three are venture capital firms) attributed importance to their firm's reputation among co-investors. The remaining responses were varied.[42]

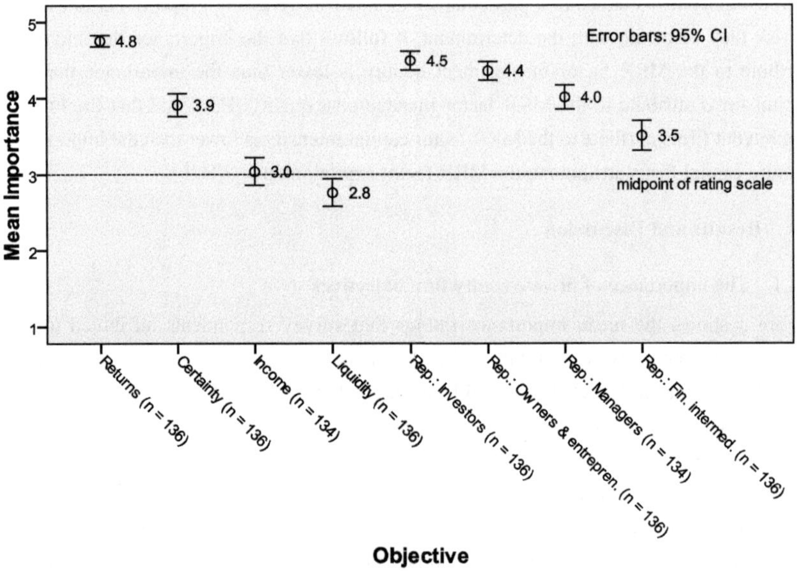

Figure 5. Importance of private equity firm objectives. Survey respondents' importance ratings were measured on numbered 5-point scales, ranging from 5 (*very important*) to 1 (*not important*). CI = confidence interval. Returns = "deliver high returns to investors". Certainty = "achieve high certainty of returns to investors". Liquidity = "generate high liquidity of investors' interests in your funds". Income = "generate high income for your firm". Rep.: Investors = "enhance your firm's reputation among investors". Rep.: Owners & entrepren. = "enhance your firm's reputation among company owners and entrepreneurs". Rep.: Managers = "enhance your firm's reputation among company managers". Rep.: Fin. intermed. = "enhance your firm's reputation among financial intermediaries". All figures are based on country-weighted survey data. The weights reflect the ratio of a country's share of private equity firms in the frame population to its share of firms in the survey sample.

42 Other responses were "[reputation in] political circles / interest groups", "build solid and high-performing companies", "make robust portfolio – [1 lucky investment not sufficient]", "[reputation] among staff of firm", and "[generate] high risk adjusted returns". One respondent noted that generating high *current* income is little important

The high mean importance of Returns and, to a somewhat lesser extent, of Certainty is consistent with the central role of returns and risk (conversely) in conventional finance theory (whereas the lower mean importance of Certainty could signify that private equity firms are prepared to assume a certain level of risk in their business undertaking). Nonetheless, the data clearly also exhibit the important role of reputation for private equity firms — a phenomenon that is incompatible with the perfect markets assumption of conventional finance theory, but coheres with ideas and theories from new institutional economics: Proponents of new institutional economics stipulate that information asymmetry and conflicting interests between market participants (e.g. between buyers and sellers or between investors and managers) can lead to market inefficiencies such as the "lemons" problem described by Akerlof (1970), the adverse selection problem portrayed by Myers and Majluf (1984), or agency costs described by Jensen and Meckling (1976).[43] Reputation is viewed as a mechanism that induces private equity firms to align their interests with those of private equity investors (Fenn et al., 1997, pp. 43–46; Megginson & Weiss, 1991, p. 881; Sahlman, 1990, p. 513). If this understanding of reputation is accurate, the importance that private equity firms assign to their reputation among investors could be linked to the degree of information asymmetry between investors and private equity firms (representing the degree of need for interest alignment); the results in the subsequent chapter appear to support this idea.

The data show that private equity firms seek to enhance their reputation not only with investors but also with other groups, such as company owners, entrepreneurs, and company managers. The high mean importance that the sample of respondents attributes to their reputation among investors and to their reputation among company owners and entrepreneurs appears to underline the strategic importance of these two groups for private equity firms. These findings are consistent with the assessment of Matz (2002, pp. 90–92) that private equity firms compete in two markets: the fundraising market ("Markt für anlagebereites Kapital") and the market for potential portfolio companies ("Markt für potentielle Beteiligungsunternehmen"). It is also consistent with Berg (2005, p. 25), who characterises the strategic challenge of buyout firms as a "double sourcing problem: On the one hand, they have to constantly source capital and on the other they have to continually source portfolio companies to conduct investments". The additional specifications provided by venture capital firm respondents suggest that venture capital firms also place high importance on the enhancement of their reputation among their

[43] The existence of such "market inefficiencies" is used to explain the existence of private equity firms: private equity firms can mitigate information asymmetry and reduce agency costs by "intensively scrutinizing firms before providing capital and then monitoring them afterward" (Lerner, et al., 2005, p. 5)

peers. This outcome is most probably a consequence of the common practise of syndication in venture capital finance.

Asymmetric information can also explain the importance attached to other reputational objectives. The sorting problem that company owners and entrepreneurs encounter when selecting a private equity firm as transaction partner is in some ways comparable to that of private equity investors when selecting a private equity fund for investment purposes. Before entering into a transaction, company owners and entrepreneurs are likely to be less informed about the quality of the private equity firm (and the associated likelihood of a successful project) than the managers of the private equity firm itself. Similar to the assumed role of reputation for the relationship between private equity firms and investors, the reputation of private equity firms among company owners and entrepreneurs could help to reduce adverse effects from such asymmetric information. This could explain the comparatively high mean importance of Reputation Among Owners and Entrepreneurs. Such an effect could also account for the comparatively high mean importance of Reputation Among Company Managers (in view of the importance for private equity firms of generating proprietary business leads from company managers; see Hommel et al., 2003, p. 326) and the lower mean importance of Reputation Among Financial Intermediaries: Financial intermediaries conduct repeat business with private equity firms and should accordingly be exposed to a lower degree of information asymmetry about the quality of private equity firms.

The remaining results are more likely caused by other effects. The comparatively low mean importance that the sample of private equity firm respondents assigned to the income objective is rather surprising given the profit-seeking nature of private equity firms. One possible explanation for this result is that private equity firms can secure their income indirectly by focussing on the returns objective: Metrick and Yasuda (2010) estimate that, on average, around 40% of private equity firm revenues are performance-related; Sahlman (1990) illustrates that, if successful, a private equity firm can achieve performance-related revenues that outweigh the management fee by an order of multiples. On the other hand, the responses in this thesis could also be affected by motivated misreporting: Some respondents might have been concerned about appearing too eager to increase their income because of a negative public sentiment against large rewards for fund managers (see Groves et al., 2004, pp. 224–225, on motivated misreporting; see Sender, 2007, for a critical view on the wealth of private equity firm partners). Last, the objective of generating high liquidity of investors' interests in private equity firms' funds generated the lowest mean importance rating of the eight objectives listed in the survey questionnaire. This result is largely in line with the hypothesis of Lerner and Schoar (2004) that private equity firms (intentionally) impose transfer restrictions on the shares in their funds to attract deep-pocket investors.

3.4.2 The influence of firm characteristics on the evaluation of objectives

Table 11 shows a number of significant relations between the dichotomous characteristics of private equity firms and their objectives. Strongest significant effects ($d > 0.50$ and $p < .05$, two-tailed) are associated with external funding (Outside Inv), preferred performance of target companies (Well/Under – Loss) and fund type (CEF). The results of the Spearman rank correlation tests between ordinal scale or continuous firm characteristic variables and private equity firm objectives are presented in Table 12. Strongest significant effects ($p < .05$, two-tailed) are associated with the characteristics Age, Funds, Capital and Investment Size. The significant correlation of Reputation Among Investors and Investment Size largely disappears when controlling for firm type.[44]

[44] Controlling for firm type, the relationship is significant only for venture capital firms at alpha = .10 ($r_s = .200$, $p = .085$, $n = 75$)

Table 11

Connections between firm characteristics (dichotomous variables) and respondents' importance ratings of objectives

Objective	EU - US/Can	BO - VC	GeoSpec	IndSpec	Outside Inv[a]	Well/Under - Loss[a]	Hands On - Supp	CEF[a]
Returns	-0.29^{b}	0.04	0.10	0.44^{**b+++}	0.67^{**b++}	-0.03	0.34^{*b++}	0.37^{b++}
Certainty	0.03	0.17	-0.03	-0.36^{**++}	0.03	0.97^{**+++}	-0.19	-0.15^{b}
Liquidity	-0.06	0.28^{+}	-0.19	-0.23^{+}	0.19	0.12	-0.10	-0.08
Income	0.08	-0.21^{+}	-0.44^{**++}	-0.12	0.11	0.22	-0.07	0.24
Rep.: Investors	-0.23	0.19	0.00	-0.27^{+++}	0.95^{**b++}	0.04	-0.09	$0.77^{***b+++}$
Rep.: Owners & entrepren.	-0.35^{*b+}	-0.13	0.21	0.04	0.43^{b}	0.37	-0.11	0.26
Rep.: Managers	-0.30^{*+}	0.27	0.13	-0.33^{*++}	0.16	-0.05	-0.20^{+}	0.30^{++}
Rep.: Fin. intermed.	0.02	0.11	0.13	-0.15	0.00	-0.12^{b}	0.15	-0.08

Note. The figures denote effect sizes (Cohen's *d*), which are calculated by dividing the differences in mean importance ratings of the two subsamples of a dichotomous column variable by the pooled standard deviation. Survey respondents' importance ratings were measured on numbered 5-point scales, ranging from 5 (*very important*) to 1 (*not important*). All figures, except those relating to EU - US/Can, are based on country-weighted survey data. The weights reflect the ratio of a country's share of private equity firms in the frame population to its share of firms in the survey sample. EU - US/Can denotes headquarter location: EU = Europe; US/Can = United States of America or Canada. BO - VC denotes firm type: BO = buyout; VC = venture capital; VC includes eight firms of related types, such as "growth equity" and "business angel"; BO includes two firms of related types ("industry specific buyout" and "restructuring buyout"). GeoSpec refers to firms, for which respondents specified whether or not they specialise in geographical areas. IndSpec refers to firms, for which respondents specified whether or not they specialise in industry sectors. Outside Inv refers to whether or not respondents specified that their firm sources the majority of its fund capital from outside investors. Well/Under - Loss refers to the preferred performance of target companies: Well/Under ="well-performing" or "underperforming"; Loss = "loss-making". Hands On - Supp denotes management style: Hands on = "hands-on"; Supp = "supportive". CEF refers to firms, for which respondents specified whether or not they mostly manage investments in (closed-end) funds with a fixed lifetime. Returns = "deliver high returns to investors". Certainty = "achieve high certainty of returns to investors". Liquidity = "generate high liquidity of investors' interests in your funds". Income = "generate high income for your firm". Rep.: Investors = "enhance your firm's reputation among investors". Rep.: Owners & entrepren. = "enhance your firm's reputation among company owners and entrepreneurs". Rep.: Managers = "enhance your firm's reputation among company managers". Rep.: Fin. intermed. = "enhance your firm's reputation among financial intermediaries".

$^{*}p < .10$. $^{**}p < .05$. $^{***}p < .01$. All *p*s are two-tailed and relate to independent samples *t*-tests for equality of means; in each case *df* (pairwise) ranges between 104 and 134. ^{+}p, ^{++}p, and ^{+++}p denote respective significance levels for the Mann-Whitney *U*-test.

[a]One of the subsamples has a data count of less than 30.

[b]Equal variances not assumed.

The data concerning respondents' evaluations of Reputation Among Investors support the idea mentioned in the preceding chapter of a link between information asymmetry and reputation: Respondents who had specified that outside investors — that is, investors with a high degree of information asymmetry — provide the majority of their firm's fund capital placed significantly higher importance ratings on the objective of enhancing their reputation among investors than respondents who had not specified that outside investors provide the majority of their firm's fund capital; the size of effect is large.[45] Further analyses suggest that other significant results are connected with this effect: When limiting the sample to respondents who had specified that outside investors provide the majority of their firm's fund capital (n = 116), the significant effects of variables CEF and Investment Size on Reputation Among Investors disappear (both parametric and non-parametric test results). On the other hand, the influence of the variable IndSpec on Reputation Among Investors is more pronounced for the reduced sample (mean difference = -0.27, t = -2.53, df [Welch-Satterthwaite] = 102, p = .013, two-tailed, equal variances not assumed, d = -0.45). This is consistent with the idea of a link between reputation and information asymmetry, too, if it is assumed that capital providers of industry-specialised private equity firms are generally more knowledgeable about the quality of private equity firms and investee companies in the respective industry sectors than investors in non-specialised private equity firms.

The significant connection between the importance of the returns objective and external funding is possibly caused by the intervening variable Reputation Among Investors: Reputation is believed to induce private firms to align their interests with those of their investors (Fenn et al., 1997, pp. 43–46; Megginson & Weiss, 1991, p. 881; Sahlman, 1990, p. 513). Hence, private equity firms that attribute higher importance to their reputation among investors might also attribute higher importance to the objective of generating high returns to their investors. This interpretation is supported by the statistically significant correlation of the two variables in the survey data (r = .36, p < .0005, two-tailed, n = 136). But the relationship could also signify a bias from motivated misreporting: Respondents from private equity firms that receive their fund capital mostly from outside investors may have attributed higher (than actual) importance to the returns objective out of a concern for their reputation among investors. Additional Chi-Square tests of independence between each of the two variables Returns and Reputation Among Investors and the variable Outside Inv, controlling for the other of the two variables, support the former interpretation and mitigate the concern of a bias in the data.[46]

Further analyses suggest that other significant relationships between the returns objective and firm characteristic variables are connected with these effects: For example, when limiting the

---

45 The group of respondents who had not specified that outside investors provided the majority of their firm's fund capital also includes one respondent who had specified that the majority of their firm's fund capital is provided by capital markets, as well as four respondents who had specified that the majority of their firm's fund capital is provided by other parties (e.g. institutionals and private investors). Exclusion of these respondents increases the effect size, but the subsample of 14 respondents for the group of firms without outside investors is rather small

46 It has to be noted that the validity of these additional test results are possibly compromised by the low counts of some cells in the respective contingency tables

data sample to respondents who had specified that outside investors provided the majority of their firm's fund capital (n = 116), the significant influences of the management style (Hands On – Supp), industry specialisation (IndSpec), fund type (CEF), and fund size (Capital) disappear (both parametric and non-parametric test results). Only one significant effect remains (and is even stronger) in the reduced sample: the negative association between Age and Returns. If Age is viewed as a proxy for reputation this result could suggest, either that the alignment effects of reputational incentives tend to loose strength as private equity firms achieve their reputational objectives, or that older private equity firms (with an established reputation) are less inclined to overstate (i.e. misreport) the importance of Returns.

Table 12

Spearman rank correlations between firm characteristics (ordinal scale and continuous variables) and respondents' importance ratings of objectives

Objective	Age (yrs)	Funds	Capital (€m)	Investments	Investment Size (€m)
Returns	-.16 **	.02	.21 **	.00	.13
Certainty	-.09	-.08	-.05	-.13	.03
Liquidity	.24 ***	.17 **	-.06	.00	.00
Income	.21 ***	.22 ***	.02	.12	.02
Rep.: Investors	-.02	.06	.12	.07	.18 **
Rep.: Owners & entrepren.	-.13	.00	.02	.16 *	-.05
Rep.: Managers	.05	.05	.03	.13	.05
Rep.: Fin. intermed.	-.10	-.08	-.04	-.03	.07

Note. Survey respondents' importance ratings were measured on numbered 5-point scales, ranging from 5 (*very important*) to 1 (*not important*). Correlations were tested pairwise, using country-weighted data. Weighted n ranges between 139 and 154. The weights reflect the ratio of a country's share of private equity firms in the frame population to its share of firms in the survey sample. Age is the number of years a respondent's firm has been in existence. Funds is the number of private equity funds a respondent's firm has raised. Capital is the rough total capital under management of a respondent's firm in € millions. Investments is the rough number of company investments managed by a respondent's firm. Investment Size is a respondent firm's rough typical investment size (equity stake) in € millions. Range specifications were replaced by their means, and amounts in other currencies were converted to € amounts using the averages of market exchange rates over the time of the survey. Returns = "deliver high returns to investors". Certainty = "achieve high certainty of returns to investors". Liquidity = "generate high liquidity of investors' interests in your funds". Income = "generate high income for your firm". Rep.: Investors = "enhance your firm's reputation among investors". Rep.: Owners & entrepren. = "enhance your firm's reputation among company owners and entrepreneurs". Rep.: Managers = "enhance your firm's reputation among company managers". Rep.: Fin. intermed. = "enhance your firm's reputation among financial intermediaries".

$^{*}p < .10$. $^{**}p < .05$. $^{***}p < .01$. All ps are two-tailed.

It was hypothesized that the more funds a private equity firm has raised, the more importance it tends to attribute to the liquidity objective (H1). Table 12 shows that, consistent with the hypothesis, the coefficient of Spearman rank correlation between the two variables is positive and statistically significant. But the multivariate test results presented in Table 13 do not support the predicted relationship.[47] Panel A shows a regression of Liquidity (dependent variable) against individual firm characteristics that match the independent variables used in Lerner and Schoar's (2004) analysis, plus a dichotomous location variable (the dataset used by Lerner and Schoar was limited to the United States of America). The regression model shown in Panel B includes Age as additional independent variable. Neither of the two models attaches statistical significance to the variable Funds; moreover, the point estimate of the regression coefficient for Funds is even negative in the model that includes firm age.

[47] Prior to the regression analyses, the data were screened for linearity, outliers, normality, multicollinearity, and homoscedasticity of residuals (see Appendix I for a table of correlations between predictor variables). Aside from a rather strong correlation between Ln Age and Funds, indicating a certain degree of multicollinearity, none of these analyses gave rise to serious concern. Additional tests, in which either one of the two correlated variables were removed, did not lead to changes in the statistical significance of the two coefficients

Table 13

Linear regression analysis of the importance of Liquidity (dependent variable) against selected firm characteristics

Variable	B	$SE\ B$	t	p	95% CI for B Lower	95% CI for B Upper
Panel A (n = 106)						
Constant	3.01	.46	6.5	< .0005 ***	2.10	3.92
EU - US/Can	-0.08	.24	-0.3	.750	-0.56	0.41
BO - VC	0.47	.23	2.0	.043 **	0.01	0.93
Ln Capital	-0.08	.10	-0.9	.392	-0.28	0.11
Funds	0.01	.04	0.3	.751	-0.06	0.08
Panel B (n = 106)						
Constant	2.58	.47	5.5	< .0005 ***	1.65	3.50
EU - US/Can	-0.01	.24	-0.1	.953	-0.48	0.46
BO - VC	0.32	.23	1.4	.163	-0.13	0.78
Ln Capital	-0.15	.10	-1.6	.118	-0.35	0.04
Funds	-0.05	.04	-1.2	.243	-0.13	0.03
Ln Age	0.48	.16	3.0	.003 ***	0.17	0.80

Note. Panel A: $R^2 = .04$, $F(4, 101) = 1.09$, $p = .368$. Adjusted $R^2 < .01$. Panel B: $R^2 = .35$, $F(5, 100) = 2.76$, $p = .022$. Adjusted $R^2 = .08$. The importance of the liquidity objective was measured on a numbered 5-point scale, ranging from 5 (*very important*) to 1 (*not important*). All figures are based on country-weighted survey data. The weights reflect the ratio of a country's share of private equity firms in the frame population to its share of firms in the survey sample. Independent variables were entered together in one block. EU - US/Can denotes headquarter location: EU = Europe; US/Can = United States of America or Canada (reference). BO - VC denotes firm type: BO = buyout; VC = venture capital (reference); VC includes eight firms of related types, such as "growth equity" and "business angel"; BO includes two firms of related types ("industry specific buyout" and "restructuring buyout"). Ln Capital is the natural logarithm of the rough total capital under management of a respondent's firm in € millions. Funds is the number of private equity funds a respondent's firm has raised. Ln Age is the natural logarithm of the number of years a respondent's firm had been in existence. Range specifications were replaced by their means, and amounts in other currencies were converted to € amounts using the averages of market exchange rates over the time of the survey.
$^{*}p < .10$. $^{**}p < .05$. $^{***}p < .01$.

Subject to the limitations of the regression models (the tests will not reliably detect statistical significance, if the effect is small;[48] some of the independent variables employed in Lerner and Schoar's model were not available for the regression model in this thesis) it is concluded that the results do not provide clear support for Lerner and Schoar's (2004) prediction of a (direct) link between the number of funds a private equity firm has raised and the liquidity of investors' interests in its funds (proxied by the importance that private equity firms attributed to the

48 At a sample size of $n = 106$, a chosen alpha level of .05 and required statistical power of .80, the tests will reliably detect significant models with medium and large effect sizes, that is, $f^2 > .128$ (or $R^2 > .113$) for the model in Panel A, and $f^2 > .118$ (or $R^2 > .106$) for the model in Panel B

objective of generating high liquidity of investors' interests in their funds). Instead, the results appear to suggest a link between the importance attributed to the liquidity objective and firm age — just like Lerner and Schoar's own results. Lerner and Schoar discarded this effect in their analysis (although they believed it to be consistent with their hypothesis), arguing that the sequence number of a fund is a better proxy of information asymmetry than firm age, because the fund sequence number "reflects the amount of prior information that is available for each fund" (p. 23). But the regression model in Panel B shows a significant partial effect for the variable Age, not for the variable Funds. It is possible that Lerner and Schoar overlooked a factor: Investors might view a private equity firm's age as a rough indicator of the firm's quality — independent of the amount of prior information that is available from previous funds. If reputation (proxied by firm age) can reduce the adverse effects of information asymmetries between market participants, the respective contribution of the fund sequence in the multivariate model to the overall effect might have been reduced below the detectable threshold by the influence of Age.

Other effects appear to have varied causes. The importance that respondents attributed to the certainty objective appears to be connected with the riskiness of their firms' investment strategy: Respondents from private equity firms with higher-risk investment strategies (e.g. a strategy of industry specialisation or a focus on turnaround situations) assigned significantly lower importance to the certainty objective than respondents with lower-risk investment strategies (e.g. no industry specialisation or a focus on well- and underperforming target companies). Assuming that a private equity firm's appetite for risk corresponds to the inverse of the importance it attaches to the certainty objective, these results suggest that a private equity firm's appetite for risk is linked to its business focus. The importance of the income objective is significantly positively correlated with variables Age and Funds. This could indicate that older private equity firms (with an established reputation) are less inclined to understate (i.e. misreport) the importance of the income objective. No plausible explanation was found for the link between Income and Geographic Specialisation.

3.4.3 The importance of MRR types for the investment decision

Figure 6 shows the mean importance that survey respondents attributed to various types of minimum return requirements for investment decisions at their firms (*MRR types*). The MRR types IRR and Multiple generated comparatively high mean importance ratings, whereas the discount rate generated a mean importance rating well below the midpoint of the rating scale. Further analyses showed that 91.8% of respondents (95% CI [85.7%, 95.5%]) attributed an importance rating of at least 4 (on a scale with five numbered steps ranging from 5 [*very important*] to 1 [*not important*]) to either IRR or Multiple and that almost all respondents who had attributed an importance rating of 3 or higher to the discount rate, had rated (at least) one of the two other MRR types as equally or more important than the discount rate. Altogether 70.9% of respondents (95% CI [62.4%, 78.2%]) attributed an importance rating of at least 4 to two or more MRR types. Only three respondents specified a different MRR type under *other* in the questionnaire; two of these emphasized the importance of limiting the maximum investment duration.

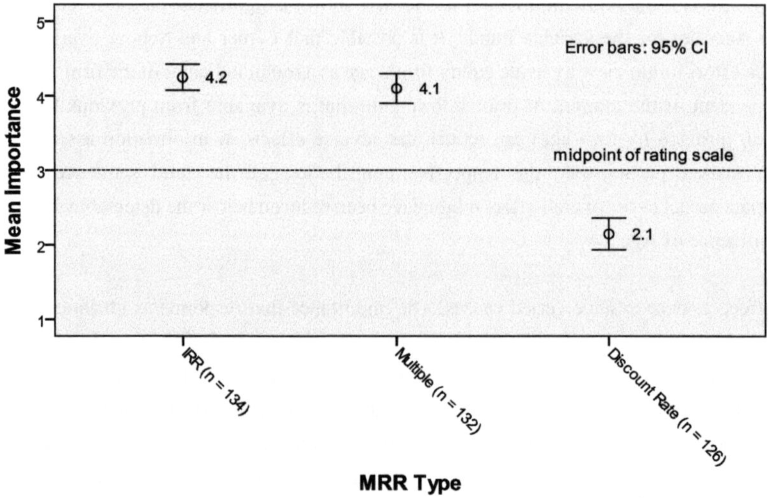

Figure 6. Importance of minimum return requirement types (MRR types). Survey respondents' importance ratings were measured on numbered 5-point scales, ranging from 5 (*very important*) to 1 (*not important*). CI = confidence interval. IRR = "minimum level IRR". Multiple = "minimum level money multiple". Discount Rate = "minimum level discount rate in discounted cash flow (*DCF*) model". All figures are based on country-weighted survey data. The weights reflect the ratio of a country's share of private equity firms in the frame population to its share of firms in the survey sample.

The results provide empirical evidence for the (expected) important role that minimum return requirements play for investment decisions in private equity firms. Most respondents appear to state their minimum return requirements as IRRs or money multiples; minimum level discount rates are regarded as considerably less important by the sample of respondents. These data points are consistent with the importance levels that the sample attaches to corresponding metrics for measuring the success of company investments (see Chapters 4.5.1 and 4.5.2) and strengthen the view that metrics based on modern portfolio theory and the capital asset pricing model do not play an important role for investment decisions in private equity firms.

3.4.4 The influence of firm characteristics on the evaluation of MRR types

Table 14 shows a number of significant relations between dichotomous firm characteristics and respondents' importance ratings of MRR types. One noteworthy outcome is the connection between firm type and the evaluation of the MRR type Discount Rate: The subgroup of respondents from venture capital firms placed significantly higher mean importance on this MRR type ($M = 2.4$, $SD = 1.19$, $n = 57$) than the subgroup of respondents from buyout firms ($M = 1.8$, $SD = 1.10$, $n = 58$). This effect is possibly a result of increased employment of the *venture capital method* by venture capital firms. According to this method, the present value of a target company is calculated by applying a high discount rate (e.g. between 40% and 60%) to the estimated value of the company at the time of exit; the result is then used as a basis for calculating the share in the target company's equity that is demanded in return for a capital investment (see Lerner, Hardymon, & Leamon, 2005, pp. 212–213, and Sahlman, 1990, p. 511, for more detailed descriptions of the venture capital method).

Table 14

Connections between firm characteristics (dichotomous variables) and respondents' importance ratings of minimum return requirements

MRR type	EU - US/Can	BO - VC	GeoSpec	IndSpec	Outside Inv[a]	Well/Under - Loss[a]	Hands On - Supp	CEF[a]
IRR	-0.09	0.09	0.44 ** +++	0.01	-0.08	0.30	0.10	-0.25 ++
Multiple	0.05	0.09	0.00	0.09	-0.14	-0.01	-0.11	0.21
Discount Rate	-0.11	-0.58 *** +++	-0.39 * ++	0.33 * +++	-0.43 * +	0.43	-0.11	-0.14

Note. The figures denote effect sizes (Cohen's *d*), which are calculated by dividing the differences in mean importance ratings of the two subsamples of a dichotomous column variable by the pooled standard deviation. Survey respondents' importance ratings were measured on numbered 5-point scales, ranging from 5 (*very important*) to 1 (*not important*). All figures, except those relating to EU - US/Can, are based on country-weighted survey data. The weights reflect the ratio of a country's share of private equity firms in the frame population to its share of firms in the survey sample. EU - US/Can denotes headquarter location: EU = Europe; US/Can = United States of America or Canada. BO - VC denotes firm type: BO = buyout; VC = venture capital; VC includes eight firms of related types, such as "growth equity" and "business angel"; BO includes two firms of related types ("industry specific buyout" and "restructuring buyout"). GeoSpec refers to firms, for which respondents specified whether or not they specialise in geographical areas. IndSpec refers to firms, for which respondents specified whether or not they specialise in industry sectors. Outside Inv refers to whether or not respondents specified that their firm sources the majority of its fund capital from outside investors. Well/Under - Loss refers to the preferred performance of target companies: Well/Under ="well-performing" or "underperforming"; Loss = "loss-making". Hands On - Supp denotes management style: Hands on = "hands-on"; Supp = "supportive". CEF refers to firms, for which respondents specified whether or not they mostly manage investments in (closed-end) funds with a fixed lifetime. MRR = minimum return requirement. IRR = "minimum level IRR", Multiple = "minimum level money multiple", Discount Rate = "minimum level discount rate in discounted cash flow (*DCF*) model".

$^{*}p < .10$. $^{**}p < .05$. $^{***}p < .01$. All *p*s are two-tailed and relate to independent samples *t*-tests for equality of means; in each case *df* (pairwise) ranges between 96 and 133. ^{+}p, ^{++}p, and ^{+++}p denote respective significance levels for the Mann-Whitney *U*-test.
[a]One of the subsamples has a data count of less than 30.

The results of the Spearman rank correlation tests between ordinal scale or continuous firm characteristic variables and importance ratings of MRR types are presented in Table 15. The strongest significant effects ($p < .05$, two-tailed) are associated with the characteristics Capital and Funds. No plausible explanation was found for these relationships.

Table 15

Spearman rank correlations between firm characteristics (ordinal scale and continuous variables) and respondents' importance ratings of minimum return requirements

MRR type	Age (yrs)	Funds	Capital (€m)	Investments	Investment Size (€m)
IRR	.00	.14	.07	.01	.08
Multiple	-.05	.01	-.29 ***	-.15 *	-.13
Discount Rate	.16 *	.18 **	-.04	.18 (**)	-.17 (**)

Note. Survey respondents' importance ratings were measured on numbered 5-point scales, ranging from 5 (*very important*) to 1 (*not important*). Correlations were tested pairwise, using country-weighted data. Weighted *n* ranges between 131 and 152. The weights reflect the ratio of a country's share of private equity firms in the frame population to its share of firms in the survey sample. Age is the number of years a respondent's firm has been in existence. Funds is the number of private equity funds a respondent's firm has raised. Capital is the rough total capital under management of a respondent's firm in € millions. Investments is the rough number of company investments managed by a respondent's firm. Investment Size is a respondent firm's rough typical investment size (equity stake) in € millions. Range specifications were replaced by their means, and amounts in other currencies were converted to € amounts using the averages of market exchange rates over the time of the survey. MRR = minimum return requirement. IRR = "minimum level IRR", Multiple = "minimum level money multiple", Discount Rate = "minimum level discount rate in discounted cash flow (*DCF*) model".

$^{*}p < .10$. $^{**}p < .05$. $^{***}p < .01$. All *p*s are two-tailed. Parentheses denote that the respective Spearman rank correlations within the buyout and venture capital subsamples were not significant at alpha = .05.

3.4.5 The importance of MRR factors

Figure 7 shows the mean importance that survey respondents attributed to various factors that determine required levels of minimum return requirements for particular investments for their firms (*MRR factors*). MRR factors Investment Stage and Quality Of Management generated the overall highest mean importance ratings. Inflation Rates and Beta Coefficient generated the overall lowest importance ratings. Only four respondents specified an additional factor (besides those listed on the survey form) under *other* in the questionnaire, whereas the comments varied between respondents.[49] Four buyout firm respondents and three venture capital firm respondents (altogether 5.4% of valid responses to this item) checked the item on the questionnaire specifying "none – same level for all investments".

[49] Other responses were "private placement memorandum", "overall risk of investment", "competitive environment and barriers to entry", and "acquisition price preferred of less than $20 million"

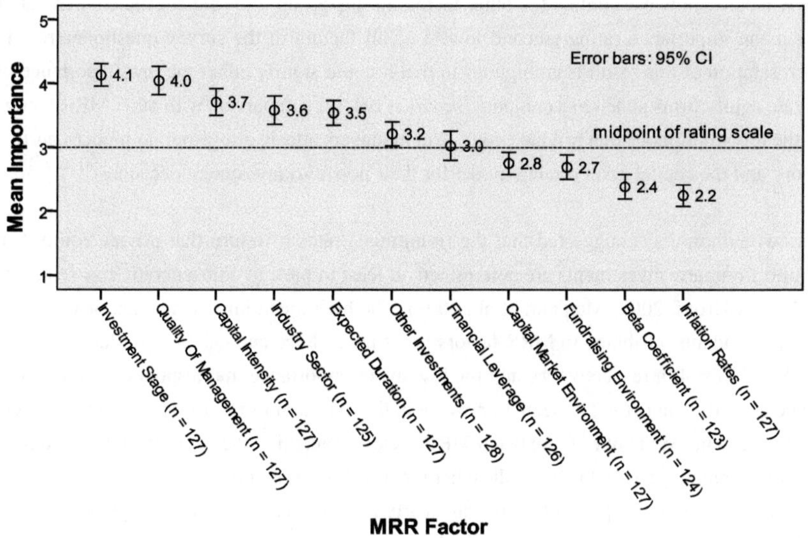

Figure 7. Importance of factors that determine required levels of minimum return requirements for particular investments (MRR factors). Survey respondents' importance ratings of MRR factors were measured on numbered 5-point scales, ranging from 5 (*very important*) to 1 (*not important*). CI = confidence interval. Other Investments = "profile of other investments already undertaken by the same fund". All figures are based on country-weighted survey data. The weights reflect the ratio of a country's share of private equity firms in the frame population to its share of firms in the survey sample.

Altogether, the sample of respondents attributes importance to a fairly wide range of MRR factors: Six of the eleven factors queried in the survey generated mean importance ratings with 95% confidence intervals above the midpoint of the rating scale. The MRR factors can be grouped into three categories arranged in descending order of mean importance: Firstly, MRR factors that describe a target company's business and managers; these include Investment Stage, Quality Of Management, Capital Intensity, and Industry Sector. Secondly, MRR factors that concern the period of ownership by the private equity firm; these include Expected Duration, Other Investments, and Financial Leverage. And thirdly, MRR factors that relate to capital markets, that is, Capital Market Environment, Fundraising Environment, and Inflation Rates.[50] A notable exception to this pattern is the factor Beta Coefficient. The *beta* of an investment is a measure of its market risk and specifies "the extent to which the value of the investment is affected by a change in the *aggregate* value of all the assets in the economy" (Brealey et al., 2011, p. 901). As a company attribute the beta coefficient should belong to the first category of

50 These findings are largely consistent with earlier results of Dixon (1991)

MRR factors; however, unlike the other factors in this group, the beta coefficient generated a low mean importance rating (second lowest of all factors in the survey questionnaire). The interpretation of this result is ambiguous in that it could signify either the low importance that private equity firms attach to a company's market risk (in comparison with other MRR factors), or, the low importance that private equity firm managers attach, altogether, to modern portfolio theory and the capital asset pricing model for their portfolio investment decisions.[51]

Various authors have suggested that the (minimum) rates of return that private equity firms require from new investments are determined, at least in part, by idiosyncratic risk (e.g. Jones & Rhodes-Kropf, 2003; Manigart et al., 2002). The high mean importance that private equity firm respondents attributed to MRR factors Investment Stage and Quality Of Management (M = 4.1 and M = 4.0, respectively), and the low mean importance that respondents attributed to the beta coefficient (M = 2.4) seem to provide indicative support for this idea. But the evidence is not clear-cut. At the outset, the listed MRR factors (excepting the beta coefficient) cannot be allocated unambiguously to either idiosyncratic or market risk. For example, the success of an investment with high capital intensity can clearly be sensitive to unique management errors as well as to market-wide shocks; similarly, an early investment stage or a low quality management team can also make a company more vulnerable to market-wide shocks. Besides, the importance that respondents assign to MRR factors might be affected by determinants that are unrelated to risk. The high importance rating of the MRR factor Quality Of Management could, for example, signify the importance that respondents attribute to a premium that compensates for overly optimistic financial projections made by entrepreneurs (the "fudge factor" suggested by Sahlman, 1990, p. 512).

Last, and perhaps most surprisingly, a small percentage of private equity firms specify that they require a fixed minimum rate of return from all investments; this matches earlier results of Lockett, Murray and Wright (2002), who observe that such policy is "bizarre as it suggests that risk is removed as a consideration from the pricing/selection equation" (p. 1023). But this must not necessarily be the case: These private equity firms might simply have a narrow investment focus; that is, the investment risk of their target companies might be limited by their investment strategy. For example, a buyout firm might target only established, well-performing companies within a particular industry sector. These companies will tend to have similar levels of operational risk, and market conditions will determine the maximum amount of leverage that

---

51 Additional exploratory analyses show significant connections between the MRR type Discount Rate and CAPM-relevant MRR factors, such as Beta Coefficient ($r_s = .34$, $p < .0005$, two-tailed, $n = 134$), Inflation Rates ($r_s = .24$, $p = .005$, two-tailed, $n = 137$), and Industry Sector ($r_s = .22$, $p = .01$, two-tailed, $n = 134$), suggesting that at least some private equity firms attach importance to the capital asset pricing model

can be attached to an investment, thus setting an upper limit for leverage risk. In view of theoretical and practical issues in estimating the levels of opportunity cost for each investment (see Chapter 4.3.2), such a buyout firm might decide that a fixed minimum return requirement is sufficiently precise for its investment appraisals.

3.4.6 The influence of firm characteristics on the evaluation of MRR factors

Table 16 shows a number of significant relations between dichotomous firm characteristic variables and MRR factors. Many of the strongest significant effects ($d > 0.50$ and $p < .05$, two-tailed) are associated with firm type (BO - VC) and investment strategy (e.g. Well/Under – Loss and IndSpec).The results of the Spearman rank correlation tests between ordinal scale or continuous firm characteristic variables and MRR factors are presented in Table 17.

Table 16

Connections between firm characteristics (dichotomous variables) and respondents' importance ratings of MRR factors

MRR factor	EU - US/Can	BO - VC	GeoSpec	IndSpec	Outside Inv[a]	Well/Under - Loss[a]	Hands On - Supp	CEF[a]
Investment Stage	-0.10	-0.76 $^{***b+++}$	0.25 ^{b}	0.26	0.03	-0.18	0.18	0.03
Industry Sector	-0.28	-0.34 $^{*++}$	-0.18	0.48 $^{**++}$	-0.07	0.66 $^{++}$	-0.01	-0.09
Capital Intensity	-0.33	-0.10	-0.26	-0.05	-0.08	-0.18	0.02	-0.01
Beta Coefficient	0.19	-0.05	-0.28	-0.30 $^{+}$	-0.36 $^{+}$	1.35 $^{***b+++}$	-0.40 $^{**++}$	-0.11
Financial Leverage	0.01	0.71 $^{***b+++}$	-0.08	-0.59 $^{***+++}$	-0.18	0.85 $^{**+}$	0.23	-0.16
Quality Of Management	-0.09	-0.19	0.15	0.08	-0.04	0.61 $^{++}$	0.01	-0.42 $^{*+++}$
Expected Duration	0.07	-0.89 $^{***b+++}$	0.16 ^{b}	0.25	-0.34	0.08	-0.08	0.08
Capital Market Environm.	-0.05	0.17	0.05	-0.10	-0.07	0.81 $^{**++}$	0.03	-0.38 *
Inflation Rates	0.15 $^{++}$	0.14	0.18	-0.14	-0.14	0.93 $^{**++}$	0.16 ^{b}	0.18
Fundraising Environment	-0.18	-0.49 $^{**+++}$	-0.06	0.09	-0.07	-0.27	0.13	-0.29
Other Investments	0.16	-0.18	-0.36 *	-0.12	0.22	-0.48	0.01	0.65 $^{***+++}$

Note. The figures denote effect sizes (Cohen's *d*), which are calculated by dividing the differences in mean importance ratings of the two subsamples of a dichotomous column variable by the pooled standard deviation. Survey respondents' importance ratings of factors that determine required levels of minimum return requirements for particular investments (MRR factors) were measured on numbered 5-point scales, ranging from 5 (*very important*) to 1 (*not important*). All figures, except those relating to EU - US/Can, are based on country-weighted survey data. The weights reflect the ratio of a country's share of private equity firms in the frame population to its share of firms in the survey sample. EU - US/Can denotes headquarter location: EU = Europe; US/Can = United States of America or Canada. BO - VC denotes firm type: BO = buyout; VC = venture capital; VC includes eight firms of related types, such as "growth equity" and "business angel"; BO includes two firms of related types ("industry specific buyout" and "restructuring buyout"). GeoSpec refers to firms, for which respondents specified whether or not they specialise in geographical areas. IndSpec refers to firms, for which respondents specified whether or not they specialise in industry sectors. Outside Inv refers to whether or not respondents specified that their firm sources the majority of its fund capital from outside investors. Well/Under - Loss refers to the preferred performance of target companies: Well/Under ="well-performing" or "underperforming"; Loss = "loss-making". Hands On - Supp denotes management style: Hands on = "hands-on"; Supp = "supportive". CEF refers to firms, for which respondents specified whether or not they mostly manage investments in (closed-end) funds with a fixed lifetime. Other Investments = "profile of other investments already undertaken by the same fund".

$^{*}p < .10$. $^{**}p < .05$. $^{***}p < .01$. All *p*s are two-tailed and relate to independent samples *t*-tests for equality of means; in each case *df* (pairwise) ranges between 97 and 127. ^{+}p, ^{++}p, and ^{+++}p denote respective significance levels for the Mann-Whitney *U*-test.
[a]One of the subsamples has a data count of less than 30.

Assuming that investment risk is a key determinant of the minimum levels of return that private equity firms require from new investments (Dixon, 1991, pp. 341–342; Murray & Lott, 1995, p. 293), many of the observed effects can be explained by differences in the typical levels of investment risk between private equity firms with varying investment strategy. For example, the higher mean importance that managers of venture capital firms assigned to the MRR factor Investment Stage could be a result of a higher variance of risk from this MRR factor for venture capital investments: The investment stage (and the associated risk) of venture capital investments can vary widely, for example, between seed and later stage, whereas the investment stage of buyout investments is generally limited to mature, established companies.[52] Similarly, the importance that managers of buyout firms assign to the MRR factor Financial Leverage could be higher than the importance that managers of venture capital firms assign to this MRR factor, because the financial leverage (and the associated risk) of buyout investments varies, whereas the financial leverage of venture capital investments is mostly zero.

The same could apply to a number of other effects, such as the significantly lower mean importance that respondents from private equity firms with an industry specialisation strategy attributed to the MRR factor Financial Leverage compared to respondents from private equity firms without an industry specialisation strategy, or the significantly higher mean importance that respondents from private equity firms with an industry specialisation strategy attributed to the MRR factor Industry Sector compared to respondents from private equity firms without an industry specialisation strategy.[53] Similarly, managers of venture capital firms might have assigned higher mean importance to the MRR factor Expected Duration than managers of buyout firms did because the typical duration of their investments (and the associated risk) is more variable than that of buyout firms. Ljungqvist and Richardson (2003b, Table 5) have already presented evidence that venture capital investments have significantly longer average holding periods than buyout investments. A higher variability in the duration of venture capital investments seems plausible when considering the high risk of such investments and the industry practise of staged financing.[54] Last, the significant positive Spearman rank correlation between respondents' importance ratings of the MRR factor Inflation Rates and the number of funds a respondents' private equity firm has raised could be caused by the increased likelihood of a private equity firm that has raised many funds to have managed at least one fund in a currency zone that is exposed to high inflation rates.

---

52 Such an effect would possibly be compounded by the generally lower risk of mature investments in comparison with early stage investments

53 Assuming that the associated variance of risk is larger for private equity firms with an industry specialisation strategy than for private equity firms without an industry specialisation strategy, because private equity firms without an industry specialisation strategy only rarely venture into high-risk industry sectors, such as internet or bio-tech

54 Gompers and Lerner (2004, pp. 160–161) describe staged financing as "the meting out of financing in discrete stages over time"; staged financing reduces the financing risk for venture capital firms and "keeps the owner/manager on a 'tight leash'". As a consequence of staged financing, the total duration of a venture capital firm's commitment to a portfolio company investment can vary (by definition) in discrete steps

Table 17

Spearman rank correlations between firm characteristics (ordinal scale and continuous variables) and respondents' importance ratings of MRR factors

MRR factor	Age (yrs)	Funds	Capital (€m)	Investments	Investment Size (€m)
Investment Stage	-.07	-.01	-.28 (***)	.14	-.26 (***)
Industry Sector	.03	.07	-.12	-.09	-.13
Capital Intensity	.00	.10	-.13	-.17 **	-.16 *
Beta Coefficient	.17 **	.18 **	.00	.08	-.03
Financial Leverage	-.08	-.10	-.11	-.33 ***	.11
Quality Of Management	-.03	.06	-.16 *	-.21 **	-.06
Expected Duration	-.09	.00	-.21 (**)	.14 *	-.31 (***)
Capital Market Environment	.01	-.01	-.01	-.09	.10
Inflation Rates	.10	.23 ***	.16 *	-.01	.13
Fundraising Environment	.10	.12	-.18 **	.06	-.17 (**)
Other Investments	.01	.00	-.22 **	-.09	-.27 ***

Note. Survey respondents' importance ratings of factors that determine required levels of minimum return requirements for particular investments (MRR factors) were measured on numbered 5-point scales, ranging from 5 (*very important*) to 1 (*not important*). Correlations were tested pairwise, using country-weighted data. Weighted *n* ranges between 126 and 145. The weights reflect the ratio of a country's share of private equity firms in the frame population to its share of firms in the survey sample. Age is the number of years a respondent's firm has been in existence. Funds is the number of private equity funds a respondent's firm has raised. Capital is the rough total capital under management of a respondent's firm in € millions. Investments is the rough number of company investments managed by a respondent's firm. Investment Size is a respondent firm's rough typical investment size (equity stake) in € millions. Range specifications were replaced by their means, and amounts in other currencies were converted to € amounts using the averages of market exchange rates over the time of the survey. Other Investments = "profile of other investments already undertaken by the same fund".

$^{*}p < .10$. $^{**}p < .05$. $^{***}p < .01$. All *p*s are two-tailed. Parentheses denote that the respective Spearman rank correlations within the buyout and venture capital subsamples were not significant at alpha = .05.

Some groups of respondents might have attributed low importance ratings to a particular MRR factor, because they view the level of risk associated with the factor as small in comparison with other risk factors. For example, respondents from private equity firms that target loss-making companies (i.e. *turnarounds*) may have attributed lower importance to MRR factors Industry Sector, Beta Coefficient, Financial Leverage, Quality Of Management, Capital Market Environment and Inflation Rates than respondents from private equity firms that target well-performing or underperforming companies, because respondents from private equity firms that target loss-making companies regard the risks associated with these factors as small in comparison with the risks involved in a turnaround situation. In this context, the higher emphasis that respondents from private equity firms mostly managing their investments in closed-end funds with a fixed lifetime placed on the MRR factor Other Investments in comparison with private equity firms not mostly managing their investments in closed-end funds with a fixed lifetime appears to suggest that the former place more importance on actively managing the total risk of their portfolio of investments than the latter. This is plausible because an open-ended fund is not capital restricted and has more flexibility to adjust portfolio risk at any time by adding further investments.

Some effects might be attributable to market conditions at the time of the survey and to diversification. A temporarily more challenging market for venture capital funds may have caused respondents from venture capital firms to attribute higher mean importance to the MRR factor Fundraising Environment than respondents from buyout firms (Table 8 in Chapter 2.3 shows that the specified average return across all funds of venture capital firms in the sample was considerably lower than the specified average return across all funds of buyout firms in the sample).[55] And the tendency of the importance ratings of MRR factors Capital Intensity, Financial Leverage, Quality Of Management, and Other Investments to decrease as the number of investments increases could be explained by a corresponding decrease in the contribution of idiosyncratic risk to total risk.

It was hypothesized that the importance that buyout firms attribute to the MRR factor management quality is lower than the importance that venture capital firms attribute to the MRR factor management quality (H2a) and that the importance that buyout firms attribute to the MRR factor capital intensity is lower than the importance that venture capital firms attribute to the MRR factor capital intensity (H2b). Table 18 shows that, for each factor, the difference between the mean importance rating of venture capital firm respondents and the mean importance rating of buyout firm respondents is small, whereas the direction of the difference is consistent with the prediction; but the statistical tests are not significant. Subject to the limitations of the analysis (moderate sensitivity of statistical tests, no multivariate statistical analysis, and the assumed proportionality of the importance attached to MRR determinants and the amount of risk associated with the determinant),[56] it is concluded that the results do not support Ruhnka and Young's (1991, pp. 125–128) idea that an observed decline in the level of minimum return required from earlier to later stages of investment is caused by a decrease in internal risks, such as poor management quality or a high cash burn rate, as the investment continues to develop.

---

55 An additional test result supports this reasoning: Respondents from venture capital firms with comparatively high IRRs (equal to or higher than 30%) rated the importance of the MRR factor Fundraising Environment significantly lower than other venture capital firm respondents ($M_{\text{diff}} = .88$ $t = 2.22$, $df = 31$, $p = .034$, two-tailed, $d = 0.88$; Mann-Whitney $U = 80$; p [exact, two-tailed] = .025)

56 The data did not permit meaningful multivariate statistical analyses due to non-normal distributions (multiple regression) and low cell counts (logistic regression). A post-hoc power analysis shows that, based on a minimum required statistical power of .80 and an alpha level of .05 (one-tailed), the independent samples t-tests were sensitive enough to detect at least medium effect sizes ($d > 0.46$ and $d > 0.47$ for Capital Intensity and Quality Of Management, respectively)

Table 18

The importance of MRR factors Capital Intensity and Quality Of Management across firm types

	Type		Type		Type		VC - BO				
							Equality of means			Mann-Whitney	
MRR factor	VC	BO	VC	BO	VC	BO	M_{diff}	p	d	U	p
	Mean (Median)		Standard deviation		Subsample size						
Capital Intensity	3.8 (4.0)	3.7 (4.0)	1.3	1.1	59	57	0.1	.297	0.10	2,097	.204
Quality Of Management	4.1 (5.0)	3.9 (4.0)	1.2	1.4	58	57	0.2	.161	0.19	2,167	.300

Note. Survey respondents' importance ratings of factors that determine required levels of minimum return requirements for particular investments (MRR factors) were measured on numbered 5-point scales, ranging from 5 (*very important*) to 1 (*not important*). All figures are based on country-weighted survey data. The weights reflect the ratio of a country's share of private equity firms in the frame population to its share of firms in the survey sample. *Venture capital* (VC) also includes eight firms of related firm types, such as "growth equity" and "business angel". *Buyout* (BO) also includes two firms of related firm types ("industry specific buyout" and "restructuring buyout"). M_{diff} denotes mean difference. All *p*s are one-tailed; equal variances assumed.

3.5 Conclusions

3.5.1 Objectives

The survey data show that the underlying population of private equity firms attaches particularly high importance to the objective of delivering high returns to investors, to the objective of enhancing their firm reputation among investors and to the objective of enhancing their firm reputation among company owners and entrepreneurs. An exploratory analysis of connections between respondents' importance ratings of individual objectives and characteristics of their private equity firms yields a number of statistically significant relationships. These include a link between the importance of the objective to enhance firm reputation among investors and the extent of funding by outside investors, a link between the importance of the objective to achieve a high certainty of returns to investors and the extent of industry specialisation, and a link between the importance of the objective to achieve a high certainty of returns to investors and the preferred performance of target companies. Additionally, the importance levels of some objectives are associated with firm age and experience.

These results lead to a number of observations. Firstly, the data provides empirical evidence for the high importance that private equity firms assign to reputational objectives. This strengthens a central assumption of popular private equity theories, such as Gompers's (1996) grandstanding hypothesis and Black and Gilson's (1998) implicit contract over control-theory; it also supports the idea that at-stake reputation is a true incentive for private equity firms to align their interests with those of their investors (e.g. Fenn et al., 1997, pp. 43–46; Megginson

& Weiss, 1991, p. 881; Sahlman, 1990, p. 513) and contract partners. The results also show for the first time that (and to what extent) private equity firms seek to enhance their good name with contract partners and audiences other than private equity investors.

Secondly, the exploratory results regarding the influence of particular characteristics of private equity firms on the importance that respondents from these private equity firms attached to enhancing their firm reputation among investors seem to support the idea put forward in this thesis that the degree of information asymmetry about the quality of the private equity firm between the private equity firm and its principal contract partners is a key determinant of the value a private equity firm attaches to its reputation among these contract partners. Such a link is plausible, if it is assumed that at-stake reputation can help to reduce adverse effects of an information gap between private equity firms and their contract partners, such as agency and transaction costs.

Thirdly, assuming that a private equity firm's appetite for risk corresponds to the inverse of the importance it attaches to the Certainty objective, the results suggest that private equity firms have a certain appetite for risk, the degree of which is linked to a firm's business focus. In the survey data, private equity firms place considerably less importance on the Certainty objective than they place, for example, on the Returns objective or on key reputational objectives, and, the importance they attribute to the Certainty objective is linked to the general risk of their business focus: Respondents from private equity firms with higher-risk strategies (i.e. a strategy of industry specialisation, or, a focus on turnaround situations) assigned significantly lower importance to the Certainty objective than respondents with the corresponding lower-risk investment strategies (i.e. no industry specialisation, or a focus on well- and underperforming target companies).

Finally, the comparatively low importance levels that respondents assigned to the objective of generating high liquidity of investors' interests in private equity firms' funds is largely in line with the hypothesis of Lerner and Schoar (2004) that private equity firms impose transfer restrictions on the shares in their funds to attract deep-pocket investors. The data do not, however, provide clear support for Lerner and Schoar's prediction of a (direct) link between the liquidity of investors' interests in the funds of a private equity firm (proxied by the importance that private equity firms attributed to generating high liquidity of investors' interests in their funds) and the intensity of asymmetric information about the quality of the private equity firm between inside investors and outside investors (proxied by the number of funds a private equity firm has raised). Instead, the data in this study (as well as some of the results in Lerner and Schoar's own study) seem to indicate that the effects of information asymmetry on the liquidity of interests in private equity funds are moderated by reputation. Such an effect would also be consistent with the suggestion further above, that reputation can help to reduce adverse effects of asymmetric information. If this holds true, Lerner and Schoar's theory should be extended to account for the effects of reputation.

3.5.2 Minimum return requirements

The survey data show that in their investment decisions private equity firms attach (on average) high importance to minimum return requirements that are stated as IRRs or money multiples; minimum level discount rates in discounted cash flow models are regarded as considerably less important.[57] The data also show the importance that the sample of private equity firms attribute to eleven factors that determine required levels of minimum return requirements for particular investments. The factors Investment Stage and Quality Of Management generated the overall highest mean importance ratings, whereas Inflation Rates and Beta Coefficient generated the overall lowest importance ratings — these results are consistent with earlier findings of Dixon (1991). A bivariate exploratory analysis of connections between respondents' importance ratings of individual factors and the characteristics of their private equity firms yielded a number of statistically significant relationships. The importance that private equity firm respondents assigned to individual factors is frequently associated with firm type (buyout or venture capital), investment focus (preferred performance of target companies and whether or not a private equity firm specialises in industry sectors), fund horizon (whether or not a private equity firm's investments are mostly managed in closed-end funds), and the number of investments, and is generally not associated with the age, geographical location, geographical specialisation, management style and source of funding of private equity firms. The results do not support the two hypotheses that were derived from Ruhnka and Young's (1991, pp. 125–128) idea that an observed decline in the level of minimum return required from earlier to later stages of investment is caused by a decrease in internal risks, such as poor management quality or a high cash burn rate, as the investment continues to develop.

The following conclusions are drawn from these results: Firstly, the results provide empirical evidence for the (expected) important role that minimum return requirements play for investment decisions in private equity firms. Survey respondents attached particularly high importance ratings to minimum level IRRs and minimum level money multiples. In comparison, the sample of private equity firms attached very little importance to minimum level discount rates in discounted cash flow models. These results are consistent with the sample's rating of respective success measures (see Chapters 4.5.1 and 4.5.2) and provide additional

57 This difference is less pronounced for the subsample of venture capital firms – this is most probably a result of the widespread use of the venture capital method for evaluating investments in the venture capital industry

support for the idea that metrics based on modern portfolio theory and the capital asset pricing model do not play an important role in private equity firms.

Secondly, the data show that private equity firms regard a number of factors as important determinants of the minimum return they require for a particular investment. Particularly high importance ratings were generated by factors that are associated with the stand-alone risk of the investment, such as the investment stage and the quality of management. This in conjunction with the low importance levels that respondents attributed to the factor Beta Coefficient seems to support the idea that idiosyncratic risk plays an important part in the assessment of investment opportunities.

Thirdly, the data show numerous significant connections between respondents' importance ratings of the factors that determine required levels of minimum return and the key characteristics of their private equity firms. Many of these effects can be attributed to variances in risk between differing investment strategies of private equity firms. This underlines the importance of risk as a determinant of the levels of minimum return that are required from new investments. The tendency of importance ratings of some factors to decrease significantly as the number of investments increases is possibly explained by diversification effects.

4 Success Measures and Decision Metrics

4.1 Abstract

This part of the thesis explores the metrics that private equity firms use to measure and manage the performance of portfolio investments. Following a review of existing literature and an examination of known private equity performance measures, I describe theoretical and practical challenges that private equity firms encounter when attempting to apply metrics from conventional finance theory to private equity investments. I also review the quality of the multiple and the internal rate of return (IRR) for performance measurement in private equity firms and find defensible arguments for their popularity. The theoretical discussion is followed by an analysis of survey data from 136 private equity firms located in the United States of America, Canada, and Europe. The empirical data offer strong support for the expected prominent role that the money multiple and IRR play in private equity firms — both in terms of measuring investment success (ex post) and as criteria for key decisions regarding portfolio investments (ex ante). In comparison to these metrics, success measures that are based on modern portfolio theory and the capital asset pricing model received, on average, far lower importance ratings. One deficiency of both the IRR and the multiple is their unreliability (in comparison to the net present value) for ranking and selecting investment projects that are mutually exclusive. As the data suggest that most private equity firms do have to decide between mutually exclusive investment opportunities, I conclude that at least some private equity firms forfeit better performance by inappropriately employing the IRR and multiple for the appraisal of mutually exclusive investment opportunities. In the survey, item non-response was particularly high for measures of risk or risk-return for individual investments; the available data suggest that private equity firms generally employ a range of methods for such purpose, whereas only few firms employ beta-based metrics. I attribute these results to the widespread use of risk-adjusted minimum return requirements and to market imperfections in private equity markets. Otherwise, the importance that private equity firms assigned to individual success measures is frequently associated with firm type, external funding, and fund horizon and is generally not associated with the age, size, geographical location, and investment focus of private equity firms. I ascribe the former results to a tendency of private equity firms to select metrics that offer a high measurement quality for the average investment and to a streamlining influence of external funding on a firm's choice of metrics.

4.2 Existing Literature

Literature has hitherto placed little emphasis on the landscape of metrics used by private equity firms to measure and manage the performance of their investments. Two existing studies have investigated measures and methods that venture capital firms use to evaluate new investment projects. Using survey data from a sample of 30 UK venture capital firms, Dixon (1991, pp. 339–340) finds that almost all firms reporting the use of financial ratios for evaluating investment projects employ the IRR for such purpose; only one interview partner reported the use of net present values. Dittmann, Maug, and Kemper (2004) conduct a survey of 53 German venture capital funds that engage in early stage and seed financing. Their data suggest that venture capital firms typically employ several valuation methods, whereas the market multiples method and the discounted cash flow-method (DCF-method) are the ones most frequently reported (Dittmann et al., 2004, p. 620). Using additional interview data, Dittmann et al. infer that only about one third of the respondents who claim to use the DCF-method truly do follow textbook recommendations (involving, e.g. CAPM or WACC) to arrive at "objectifiable" estimates of the discount rate. They present test results suggesting that venture capital firms that employ the DCF-method in conjunction with objectifiable discount rates have significantly lower write-off rates (on average 5.4% less) than venture capital firms that do not employ the DCF-method in this way.

One related strand of research is concerned with private equity firms' reporting to investors. Kemmerer and Weidig (2005), for example, find in a sample of private equity firms located in Europe that frequencies, aggregation levels, and delivery times of reporting are associated with fund characteristics such as experience ("first time fund or not"), stage (i.e. "venture capital" or "mid market"), and focus (i.e. "regional" or "non-regional", "technology" or "non technology"). Cumming and Walz (2010) present empirical evidence for the assumption that the reporting of fund performance (in particular unrealised IRRs) to institutional investors is systematically inflated. They also show that the degree of bias is linked to the legal and accounting environment as well as to proxies for the degree of information asymmetry between institutional investors and private equity firms (see also Phalippou & Gottschalg, 2009, on overstated performance reporting). Other data points on private equity reporting are provided in a non-academic study of private equity firms and investors on private equity reporting and performance measurement practices conducted by the Private Equity Industry Guidelines Group (PEIGG, 2004).[58] Their data provide indicative evidence for the prominent role of the IRR and multiple in the private equity industry: Almost all investors participating in the survey desired to be supplied with such information in private equity firm reports, whereas around two thirds of partaking private equity firms stated that these metrics were already included in their

[58] The PEIGG study was conducted as an online survey and distributed to "the membership of the Institutional Limited Partners Association (ILPA), Private Equity CFO Association, National Venture Capital Association's (NVCA) CFO Task Force, the VCBC network and to various other individuals and entities on an ad-hoc basis" (PEIGG, 2004, p. 2). The sample comprises 55 private equity firms (mostly venture capital), 28 investors, and 7 fund of funds. The study report includes an explicit notice that the results are "not scientific and should not be interpreted as a statistical representation of the private equity industry" (PEIGG, 2004, p. 1)

reporting. On the other hand, the PEIGG survey data are inconclusive as to the need or feasibility of (traditional) risk and risk-return measures in private equity reporting. Although many of the partaking investors expressed a desire to be supplied with measures such as standard deviation, beta, alpha, or the Sharpe ratio, some investors "questioned the usefulness of the non-traditional performance measures [i.e. performance measures other than IRRs or multiples]" (PEIGG, 2004, p. 15), and most private equity firm respondents declared such measures "difficult or impossible to provide" (PEIGG, 2004, p. 16).

Another related strand of research is concerned with quantifying the performance of and the private equity asset class. Some studies in this field of research also address general issues of measuring private equity performance (especially investment risk) that possibly affect the choice of metrics by practitioners at private equity firms.[59] Chiampou and Kallett (1989), for example, question the suitability of the conventional *standard deviation of annual returns* for measuring the risk of venture capital investments on account of issues such as the illiquidity and long-term horizons of these investments, and also the "spiked return profile" (p. 5) of venture capital portfolios.[60] Reyes (1990) describes more generally how the lack of market prices for investments gives rise to considerable challenges for the employment of risk measures from modern portfolio theory and the capital asset pricing model in venture capital. Jones and Rhodes-Kropf (2003) suggest that venture capital firms are not well diversified and

59 As this part of the thesis is concerned with performance measurement in private equity firms, issues of performance calculation that are particular to external parties (e.g. because they do not have access to detailed cash flow information) are not addressed here (see Kaplan & Schoar, 2005, and Kaserer & Diller, 2004b, on problems of survivorship bias and the accurateness of reported net asset values)

60 Chiampou and Kallett propose the use of alternative methods for evaluating venture capital risk. For example, they compare the percentage distribution of venture capital partnerships across defined return categories with the percentage distribution of securities in an equity capital market across the same return categories, or, they compare the respective percentage of funds and securities in each asset class that were in default at a certain date. These measures are clearly less suitable for measuring the risk of a single portfolio investment

thus exposed to "considerable" idiosyncratic risk (see also Müller, 2011).[61] Assuming that such risk is priced by investors, they predicted that private equity returns (net of fees) should increase with the level of idiosyncratic risk. In a study of more than 1,200 U.S. private equity funds they were able to show that, consistent with their theory, buyout funds with fewer investments (proxied by the number of drawdowns) had higher average alphas than other buyout funds and that venture capital and buyout funds with lower estimated idiosyncratic risk (estimated) had lower average alphas than other venture capital and buyout funds. Ljungqvist and Richardson (2003a, pp. 3 and 20–21) argue that time-series correlations with the market return (used for example by Jones et al., 2003) are unsuitable for measuring the risk of private equity funds because of too few cash flow-based data points for fund returns.[62] Instead, they estimate market risk of private equity funds by assigning capital market industry betas to portfolio companies and aggregating these for each fund. For a sample of 73 private equity funds from the records of one large U.S. institutional investor, they found that, on average, the sample funds were not well diversified, displaying low average numbers of investments and substantial industry concentration. A cross-sectional regression of the excess fund IRRs against various fund characteristics did not yield significant results for idiosyncratic risk (proxied by various measures of concentration) or market risk (proxied by aggregated portfolio betas).[63] Cochrane

[61] The idea that private equity firms may be exposed to idiosyncratic risk was not new. In their study on the determinants of required return in venture capital investments, Manigart et al. (2002) declared that "the existence of huge market imperfections [in the market for venture capital investments] implies that idiosyncratic investment risk and other investment characteristics may be as important as market risk in determining required return (Rea,1989)" (p. 294). Using survey data from 209 venture capital firms in five countries, they found that mean required rates of return varied across investment stages and that the return required for early-stage investments was significantly higher than the return required for later-stage investments. They concluded that "contrary to the expectations of conventional finance theory, diversification by investment stage does not appear a significant risk-reduction strategy of VCCs" (Manigart et al., 2002, p. 292)

[62] Fund returns based on actual cash flow data can of course only be calculated after the fund has been liquidated. The use of net asset values (i.e. accounting information) to calculate private equity fund returns is often considered as problematic because net asset values include estimates of the value of unrealised investments (e.g. Ljungqvist & Richardson, 2003a, p. 4; Phalippou & Gottschalg, 2009, p. 2)

[63] In a related study, Groh, Baule, and Gottschalg (2008) use a Contingent Claims Analysis to calculate implied idiosyncratic risk of individual leveraged-buyout transactions, but do not assess the aggregate risk of the private equity firm

(2005) argues that "private equity could be just like public equity" (p. 4) and finds similarities between the risk return profile of venture capital investments (derived from a sample of venture capital financing rounds) and a sample of Nasdaq stocks with a market capitalisation of less than $2 million. He suggests that high empirical mean returns in the sample are a result of "large idiosyncratic volatility of (…) individual firm returns" (p. 5) and that systematic risk might only be a "small component of the risk of an individual venture capital investment" (p. 18). Groh and Gottschalg (2006) conclude from their comparison of 199 U.S. buyout fund investments with matching public market investments that — ignoring idiosyncratic risk — leverage risk and systematic risk are important determinants for the performance of buyout transactions. They speculate that outperformance of buyout investments "beyond what investors could demand as illiquidity premia" could be the result of "some kind of mispricing" (p. 27), which they associate with information asymmetries, or could arise from "the efforts of active investors in private companies and from the burden of debt" (p.27) in line with the free cash flow hypothesis. Phalippou (2009) points out that the simple average IRR and IRR spread in a portfolio of private equity investments could be exaggerated because deviations of individual investment IRRs from the "effective" rates of return are (positively and negatively) overstated. He also suggests that the use of the IRR could provide managers with incentives to time their cash flow strategically (e.g. by exiting good investments early or by paying early dividends, pp. 6–7) or to otherwise inflate IRRs in ways that are harmful to effective investor returns.[64] He proposes the employment of modified IRRs to avoid such issues. Peterson, Kasarda, and Grier (in press) also believe that the IRR overstates fund performance and put forward an alternative PME methodology. Harris, Jenkinson, and Kaplan (2012) demonstrate that money multiples and IRRs of buyout and venture capital funds can be reliable predictors of the respective funds' PMEs; based on their results, they argue that multiples are generally better measures of fund performance (by the standards of the PME) than are IRRs.

64 Phalippou does point out that such "strategic activity" would also negatively affect a private equity firm's income from carried interest and that the additional analysis of money multiples can help (external parties) to uncover such distortions (pp. 7–8)

4.3 Performance Measurement in Private Equity

4.3.1 Review of private equity performance measures

4.3.1.1 Investment multiple

The *investment multiple* (also referred to as *money multiple* or just *multiple*[65]) is a simple measure of return that is defined as the ratio between cumulative payments received from an investment and cumulative payments paid into the investment:[66]

$$Multiple = \frac{\sum_{t=0}^{T} D_t}{\sum_{t=0}^{T} I_t},$$

whereas D_t represents payments received from the investment (*distributions*) in period t, I_t represents payments into the investment (*investments*) in period t, and T represents investment duration. When the multiple is calculated before the investment has been realised, an estimate of the unrealised portion of the investment (*residual value*) is sometimes added to the sum of payments received from the investment. Both the *Global Investment Performance Standards* (GIPS®) of the CFA Institute and the *EVCA Reporting Guidelines* of the European Private Equity and Venture Capital Association (EVCA) require private equity firms to include multiples for their funds and portfolios in reports to investors.[67] The investment multiple is a simple and easy to understand metric that is popular among private equity practitioners (Bader, 1996, p. 310; Ellis, Pattni, & Tailor, 2012; Ljungqvist & Richardson, 2003b, p. 21). But the metric does not take the timing of an investment's cash flows into account; this is clearly a

65 Industry practitioners also use other terms, such as *cash multiple*, *cash on cash return*, or *cash on cash multiple* (e.g. 3i Group, 2006; Craigs Investment Partners, 2009; Grabenwarter, 2007; Soulignac, 2002)

66 The definition here is general in that it can be used for individual investments or entire funds. Some authors use other definitions that vary from this one in terminology or scope (e.g. Bader, 1996, p. 314; Grabenwarter & Weidig, 2005, p. 22; Ljungqvist & Richardson, 2003b, p. 21); see also the definitions in the EVCA Reporting Guidelines, 2006, and the Global Investment Performance Standards of the CFA Institute, 2010

67 Required multiples include distributions to paid-in capital (*DPI* or *realised multiple*), residual value to paid-in capital (*RVPI* or *unrealised multiple*), and the total value to paid-in capital (*TVPI* or *investment multiple*). Note that the guidelines do not require these ratios to be reported for the underlying investments (the *EVCA Reporting Guidelines* recommend the inclusion of a market-to-book ratio, i.e. *fair value to cost*, for individual investments; see CFA Institute, 2010, and EVCA, 2006)

disadvantage because, as an investment project that, for example, doubles the investment outlay in one year (i.e. generates a multiple of 2) is preferable to an investment project that achieves the same result over a period of, for example, ten years. The investment multiple also does not take into consideration investment properties such as risk or liquidity.

The *annualised multiple* adjusts the investment multiple to account for time.[68] It can be thought of as the geometric mean of a (hypothetical) string of period multiples over the duration of the investment:

$$Annualised\ multiple = multiple^{\frac{1}{T}}.$$

The annualised multiple takes into account the total duration of an investment, but it disregards the timing of interim cash flows: Whether an investment generates an early interim distribution or a late one does not affect the metric — provided that the amount of the distribution is the same.

The example calculations in Table 19 show that an evaluation of projects A and B using the annualised multiple can lead to a different outcome than an evaluation of the two projects using the ordinary multiple. It also shows that the values of the two metrics for pooled investments are not necessarily intuitive: The multiple of the pooled investments does not equal the mean average of multiples of each investment in the pool, and the annualised multiple of the pooled investment is in fact lower than the annualised multiple of either investment in the pool.

68 In private equity literature Ljungqvist and Richardson (2003b) and Sudarsanam and Nwaghodoh (2005), for example, use annualised multiples or related metrics

Table 19

Example calculations of the multiple (m) and the annualised multiple ($m^{[1/T]}$)

	Period (t)							
Amount	0	1	2	3	4	Σ	m	$m^{1/T}$
Project A								
Payments received (D_t)				135	30	165		
Payments made (I_t)	100	10				110		
							1.5	1.11
Project B								
Payments received (D_t)					36	36		
Payments made (I_t)				30		30		
							1.2	1.20
A & B pooled								
Payments received (D_t)				135	66	201		
Payments made (I_t)	100	10		30		140		
							1.4	1.09

Note. $m = \Sigma D_t / \Sigma I_t$.

4.3.1.2 Internal rate of return

The *internal rate of return* (IRR, sometimes also referred to as dollar-weighted or capital-weighted rate of return) is defined as the discount rate of cash flow that makes net present value equal zero (Brealey et al., 2011, p. 136; Franke & Hax, 2004, p. 172):

$$\sum_{t=0}^{T} \frac{C_t}{(1+IRR)^t} = 0\,,$$

whereas C_t represents cash flow in period t, and T represents investment duration. IRR figures are typically expressed in per cent. Their calculation requires no information other than a complete cash flow profile, that is, the amounts and dates of all cash events of an investment. In particular, their calculation does not require external parameters, such as interest rates or the weighted average cost of capital. Like the investment multiple, the IRR can be computed for single investments, investment portfolios, and funds. It can also be calculated prior to, during, or after an investment, using estimates of future cash flow or residual values, as required.

The IRR is frequently held to be the most common measure of return in private equity (e.g. Fenn et al., 1997; Grabenwarter & Weidig, 2005, p. 23; Phalippou, 2009, p. 2; Reyes, 2003, p. 32). Unlike the investment multiple and the annualised multiple, the IRR takes into account the timing of all cash events: In the IRR equation, cash flows that are generated early carry more weight than cash flows that are generated later.[69] Reyes (2003) reasoned that the IRR is the "best measure of returns for private equity fund managers in that it takes timing (time value of money) into account", thus appropriately accounting for effects from capital drawdowns and distributions that are controlled by the private equity firm (p. 32).[70] This point of view appears to be shared by at least one major industry association, which advocates the IRR as "the most accurate measure of performance for an individual private equity manager" (CFA Institute, Investment Performance Council, 2003, calculation methodology section, para. 1). Industry reporting standards such as the *Global Investment Performance Standards* of the CFA Institute and the *EVCA Reporting Guidelines* accordingly promote the use of the IRR in reports to investors (see CFA Institute, 2010; EVCA, 2006).

The hazards of using IRRs for evaluating investment performance and for investment selection decisions are well documented (e.g. Brealey et al., 2011, pp. 137–143; Franke & Hax, 2004, pp. 172–185 and pp. 193–201). Popular criticism frequently points out the mathematical possibility of multiple solutions or no solution to the IRR equation, the lack of distinction between investing and financing returns, and the unreliability of the metric in comparison to the net present value for ranking and selecting investments. Another, perhaps more subtle hazard of the IRR lies in its rather deceptive appeal as a percentage rate that can be seemingly easily compared to other percentage rates of return, such as stock market returns. It was perhaps on account of this deceptive characteristic that Brealey and Myers (1991) once criticized the IRR so harshly as

69 Note that this characteristic is only true for positive, non-zero IRRs as the monotonic exponential function $(1+IRR)^t$ increases with t, only if IRR > 0. In cases where the IRR is zero, the simple sum of all cash flows is equal to zero – hardly an attractive investment proposition. In cases where the IRR is below zero, the IRR equation in fact attributes lower weightings to early cash flows than to later ones

70 Reyes (2003) concedes that the IRR is less suitable for comparing private equity returns to public market returns; he maintains that, in this case, "the IRR becomes problematic and either a TWR or Index Method PME approach may be used" (p. 33)

a derived figure without any simple economic interpretation. If we wish to define it, we can do no more than say that it is the discount rate which applied to all cash flows makes NPV = 0 (….) The problem here is not that the IRR is a nuisance to calculate but that it is not a very useful number to have. (p. 87)

The example IRR calculations in Table 20 (coincidentally) yield the same ranking of projects as the annualised multiple. As with the investment multiple, the IRR of the aggregate pool of investments (14.4%) does not equate the mean average of the IRRs of each investment in the pool (17.0%).[71]

Table 20
Example calculations of the IRR (continued example)

	Period (t)								
Amount	0	1	2	3	4	Σ	m	$m^{1/T}$	IRR
Project A									
Payments received (D_t)				135	30	165			
Payments made (I_t)	100	10				110			
Aggregate cash flow (C_t)	-100	-10	0	135	30	55	1.5	1.11	0.14
Project B									
Payments received (D_t)					36	36			
Payments made (I_t)				30		30			
Aggregate cash flow (C_t)				-30	36	6	1.2	1.20	0.20
A & B pooled									
Payments received (D_t)				135	66	201			
Payments made (I_t)	100	10		30		140			
Aggregate cash flow (C_t)	-100	-10	0	105	66	61	1.4	1.09	0.14

Note. $m = \Sigma D_t / \Sigma I_t$. IRR = internal rate of return.

The *excess IRR* is sometimes used for evaluating the performance of an investment compared to a public market benchmark. It is calculated as the difference between the IRR of an investment and the compound annual growth rate of a public market index over a matched

[71] Some authors recommend the use of duration-weighted means (e.g. Phalippou, 2009) or capital-weighted means (e.g. Bader, 1996, p. 324) for approximating pooled IRRs. In the example, the capital-weighted mean of investment IRRs amounts to 15.3%. For some purposes it may also be suitable to calculate the *simultaneous IRR* of a portfolio (i.e. the hypothetical pooled IRR, assuming all investment projects having commenced in the same year); in the example simultaneous IRR amounts to 14.5%. See Bader (1996, pp. 318–325) and Kraft (2001, pp. 297–302) for additional information on methods of aggregation

period of time (see Kaserer & Diller, 2004a, pp. 404–405, and Ljungqvist & Richardson, 2003a, pp. 18–20, for definitions and examples of usage). The simplicity of the approach is appealing, but it is also potentially misleading because the comparable public market rate of return does not reflect possible interim cash flows of the private equity investment. Neither does the measure account for other investment properties, such as risk or liquidity. Judging by the excess IRR values in the example calculations in Table 21, both projects are unattractive; once again, the rank order of the two projects is reversed.

Table 21

Example calculations of the excess IRR (continued example)

	Period (t)							Excess
Amount	0	1	2	3	4	IRR	CAGR	IRR
Project A								
Aggregate cash flow (C_t)	-100	-10	0	135	30	0.14		
Public market index	1.00	1.15	1.44	1.39	1.74		0.15	
								-0.01
Project B								
Aggregate cash flow (C_t)				-30	36	0.20		
Public market index				1.39	1.74		0.25	
								-0.05
A & B pooled								
Aggregate cash flow (C_t)	-100	-10	0	105	66	0.14		
Public market index	1.00	1.15	1.44	1.39	1.74		0.15	
								-0.01

Note. CAGR = compound annual growth rate. IRR = internal rate of return.

Some of the problems associated with the IRR (e.g. the mathematical possibility of multiple solutions or no solution to the IRR equation, the lack of distinction between investing and financing returns) can be avoided by using the *modified IRR* (MIRR; see, e.g. Busse von Colbe & Laßmann, 1990, pp. 118–127, or Kierulff, 2008, for a detailed overview of this methodology).[72] The MIRR requires an estimate of the discount rate that is used to compound payments received from the investment to end value (the *reinvestment rate*). A second discount rate is sometimes required for adding to the initial investment outlay the present value of any

[72] Kierulff (2008, pp. 327–328) additionally demonstrates that the MIRR resolves the ranking problem of the IRR for mutually exclusive projects — provided that the projects do not differ in size

additional payments into the investment. The MIRR is calculated by determining the IRR of the two point values:

$$MIRR = \sqrt[T]{\frac{\sum_{t=0}^{T} D_t \prod_{i=t+1}^{T}(1+j_i)}{\sum_{t=0}^{T} I_t \prod_{i=0}^{t}(1+k_i)^{-1}}} - 1,$$

whereas D_t represents payments received from the investment (*distributions*) in period t, I_t represents payments into the investment (*investments*) in period t, j_i is the reinvestment rate for payments received in period I, k_i is the discount rate of cash outflow in period I ($k_0 = 0$), and T represents investment duration.

For appraising independent investment projects, the (expected) MIRR is typically compared to the reinvestment rate. For appraising mutually exclusive investment projects, the respective MIRRs are ranked, provided that they yield at least the reinvestment rate. Mutually exclusive investment projects with differing investment amounts or differing useful lives require additional calculations (Busse von Colbe & Laßmann, 1990, p. 119; Kierulff, 2008, pp. 327–328; Phalippou, 2009, pp. 10–11). In the example in Table 22, the MIRR (13.9%) is coincidentally almost equivalent to the ordinary IRR (14.4%). The MIRR is lower than the assumed reinvestment rate of the firm (20%), suggesting that the investment proposition is unattractive.

Table 22
Example calculations of the modified IRR (continued example)

		Period (t)							
Amount		0	1	2	3	4	Σ	IRR	MIRR
Payments received (D_t)					135	66	201		
Payments made (I_t)		100	10		30		140		
Aggregate cash flow (C_t)		-100	-10	0	105	66	61	0.14	
End value of D_t at	20%				162	66	228		
Present value of I_t at	5%	100	10		26		135		
									0.14

Note. IRR = internal rate of return. MIRR = modified internal rate of return.

Literature is undecided about what constitutes *adequate* reinvestment or discount rates. Busse von Colbe and Laßmann (1990, p. 119), for example, state rather vaguely that, instead of the firm's average return rate as proposed by Baldwin, the discount rate ("Kalkulationszinsfuß")[73] or interest rates of explicit investment opportunities ("explizite Verzinsungsmöglichkeiten") can be employed.[74] Kierulff (2008) proposes "a chosen reinvestment rate that represents expected future opportunities with risks equal to the investment risk" for compounding positive cash flows and "a hurdle rate that fairly represents the investment risk" (p. 327) for discounting negative cash flow. For private equity investments, Phalippou (2009, p. 9) appears to suggest either a reinvestment rate of 8% because "most funds charge carried interest (incentive fees) with a 8% hurdle rate" or the return rate of "a fairly universal market index such as the S&P 500". He suggests using the same rate for discounting investment outlays (Phalippou, 2009, pp. 11–12). Some criticise the use of MIRRs as a tool for evaluating fund manager performance on the grounds that reinvestment and discount rates are outside of their control (e.g. Ellis, Pattni, & Tailor, 2012, p. 12). Moreover, the MIRR can be confusing for practitioners who are accustomed to working with net present values, which typically decrease as the discount rate increases: As can be seen from the MIRR formula, the use of high reinvestment and discount rates increases the ratio of final value to present value, and thus increases the MIRR. In this context, the use of the term *hurdle rate* by Kierulff (2008) and Phalippou (2009) for the discount rate that applies to negative cash flow seems rather unfortunate.

4.3.1.3 Time-weighted rate of return

Time-weighted rates of return (TWRs) are presumably not often employed by private equity firms for measuring investment performance. They are nevertheless included in this overview, because they are a standard measure of performance in the asset management industry, used for example by the *Global Investment Performance Standards* of the CFA Institute. TWR is calculated as the geometric mean of all period returns over the entire duration of the investment. Effects from capital flows into and out of funds (i.e. contributions and withdrawals) are eliminated from the calculation, for example, by adjusting the time intervals in such a way that capital flows always occur at the beginning or end of an interval.

$$TWR = \left(\prod_{t=1}^{N}(1 + R_t)\right)^{\frac{1}{N}} - 1\,,$$

whereas R_t is the holding-period return in period t, and N is the total number of (equidistant) time periods.

[73] Busse von Colbe and Laßmann appear to imply the opportunity cost of capital (see Busse von Colbe & Laßmann, 1990, p. 53)

[74] A note of caution is required here. As pointed out by Eagle, Kiefer, and Grinder (2008), the incremental principle (and therefore the underlying assumption of independent investments) may be breached if the discount rate reflects a particular investment opportunity

Time-weighted returns are used to measure the performance of mutual funds because they disregard effects of capital contributions and withdrawals — cash flow events that are outside the control of mutual fund managers (Bodie, Kane, & Marcus, 2008, pp. 137–138; Reyes, 2003, p. 32). As private equity firms typically do control the capital flows into and out of their funds (i.e. fundraisings, drawdowns, and distributions), the IRR is frequently viewed as the more adequate performance measure for private equity (e.g. Grabenwarter & Weidig, 2005, pp. 23–24; Reyes, 2003; Rouvinez, 2003). Moreover, the calculation of time-weighted returns for private equity investments is challenging, because typically, market prices are only available at rare events throughout the lifetime of an equity investment.[75] TWRs for private equity investments are therefore sometimes computed by replacing market prices with accounting figures, such as net asset values. An extension of the example calculation presented in Table 23 shows that this can lead to rather unsatisfactory results: If circumstances at the end of period 3 had required a write-down of the investment's net asset value to 1 (instead of 85), TWR would have amounted to 182% instead of 8%.; the IRR would have remained unaffected by this accounting change.[76]

Table 23

Example calculations of the time-weighted rate of return (continued example)

	Period (t)						
Amou nt	0	1	2	3	4	IRR	TWR
Aggregate cash flow (C_t)	-100	-10	0	105	66	0.14	
Net asset value	100	108	134	85	0		
Holding-period return		-.02	.24	.42	-.22		
Cumalative growth factor		.98	1.22	1.72	1.34		0.08

Note. TWR = time-weighted return. The TWR is calculated by raising the cumulative growth factor in the final year to the power of 1/4 and subtracting 1. Net asset values are used as proxy for market values.

4.3.1.4 Public market equivalent

The *public market equivalent* emerged some 20 to 30 years ago as a method for comparing private equity IRRs with public market returns.[77] An early methodology (frequently referred to as the method of Long and Nickels[78]) calculates the hypothetical IRR of a fictitious investment

[75] This is less of an issue for open-ended or evergreen funds, which is reflected in the fact that they are treated differently in industry reporting guidelines (see, e.g. the Global Investment Performance Standards of the CFA Institute, 2010)

[76] See also Footnote 62 on the use of net asset values for calculating private equity fund returns

[77] See Reyes (2003) and Long (2008) for a more detailed account of the metric's early development

[78] Long and Nickels provided a detailed description of this methodology in an unpublished working paper presented at the AIMR Conference in 1996 on venture capital investing (see Long, III & Nickels, 1996)

in a public market index, whereas the cash flow profile of the fictitious investment matches that of the private equity investment, excepting the final cash flow (or end value), which is determined by the resultant value of the fictitious investment. This hypothetical IRR — representing the equivalent public market performance — is then compared to the IRR of the private equity investment.

This early method received much criticism for its characteristic of frequently yielding (hypothetical) short positions in the public market index, and sometimes also delivering a hypothetical IRR of -100% (e.g. Thomas Kubr in Bushrod, 2004, p. 51; Grabenwarter & Weidig, 2005, pp. 24–25; Reyes, 2003, p. 33). In the last couple of years, scholars and practitioners have put forward alternative methodologies that overcome these deficiencies (e.g. Rouvinez, 2003). One calculation method was described by Kaplan and Schoar (2003) and (only marginally different) Kaserer and Diller (2004a). Their method compares the end value of all payments received from the private equity investment (cash inflows) to the end value of all payments into the private equity investment (cash outflows), using the rate of total return of a public market index (e.g. S&P 500) as compounding rate:[79]

$$PME = \frac{\sum_{t=0}^{T} D_t \prod_{i=t+1}^{T}(1 + R_i)}{\sum_{t=0}^{T} I_t \prod_{i=t+1}^{T}(1 + R_i)},$$

whereas D_t represents payments received from the investment (*distributions*) in period t, I_t represents payments into the investment (*investments*) in period t, R_i is the total index return in period I, and T represents investment duration.

The public market equivalent enables a comparison of private equity returns with a public market index and therefore appears to be particularly suitable for institutional investors who undertake investments in public markets *and* private equity. Its utility for performance measurement and for the appraisal of investment opportunities in private equity firms is, however, limited by a number of factors. Its computation is cumbersome and the outcome is not intuitively understood — what is the profit if the PME metric yields 1.03? From a theoretical point of view, Kaplan and Schoar (2003, pp. 8–9; 2005, p. 1797) point out that the metric will not accurately reflect "true risk-adjusted returns" if the beta of the investment is unequal to one.[80] They speculate that "the systematic risk for LBO funds exceeds 1 because these funds invest in highly leveraged companies" (Kaplan & Schoar, 2005, p. 1803). For practical purposes, Harris, Jenkinson, and Kaplan (2012) find that in their sample of around 1,400 U.S.

---

79 Formula of Kaserer and Diller (2004a, p. 405), adjusted for the notation used in this paper

80 More recent extensions to the PME method have tried to address this issue (see, e.g. Peterson, Kasarda, & Grier, in press)

private equity funds fund-level PMEs are largely insensitive to variations in the assumed beta. Lastly, the public market equivalent does not take into account idiosyncratic risk or liquidity of private equity investments.

In the example shown in Table 24, the public equivalent IRR according to the methodology of Long and Nickels (12.9%) is lower than the IRR of the private equity investment (14.4%), indicating that the private equity investment outperformed the public market index (note that in this example the excess IRR would have led to the opposite conclusion because the simple IRR of the public market index is higher than the IRR of the private equity investment). The methodology described by Kaplan and Schoar (2003) and Kaserer and Diller (2004) implies the same outcome as the methodology of Long and Nickels (1996). The public market equivalent of 1.03 denotes that the end value of all payments received from the private equity investment (compounded using the return rate of the public market index) is 3% higher than the end value that matching investments in the public market index would have achieved.

Table 24

Example calculations of the public market equivalent (continued example)

	Period (t)							
Amount	0	1	2	3	4	Σ	IRR	PME
Payments received (D_t)				135	66	201		
Payments made (I_t)	100	10		30		140		
Aggregate cash flow (C_t)	-100	-10	0	105	66	61	0.14	
Public market index	1.00	1.15	1.44	1.39	1.74		0.15	
Methodology of Long & Nickels (1996)								
No. of shares purchased	100	9		-75				
Value of shares held	100	125	156	47	58			
Index comparison cash flow	-100	-10	0	105	58		0.13	
Methodology of Kaplan & Schoar (2003) and Kaserer & Diller (2004)								
End value of payments received				169	66	235		
End value of payments made	174	15		38		227		
								1.03

Note. IRR = internal rate of return. PME = public market equivalent. PME methodologies sourced from: Long, A. M., III & Nickels, C. J. (1996). *A private investment benchmark*. Retrieved November 16, 2011, from http://www.alignmentcapital.com /pdfs/research/icm_aimr_benchmark_1996.pdf; Kaplan, S. N. & Schoar, A. (2003). *Private equity performance: Returns, persistence and capital flows*. MIT Sloan Working Paper No. 4446-03. Retrieved from http://ssrn.com/abstract=473341; Kaserer, C., & Diller, C. (2004). Cash-flows und Performance von europäischen Private Equity-Fonds. *Finanz Betrieb*, *6*(5), 400–407.

4.3.1.5 Profitability index

The profitability index, defined as the present value of cash flow received from an investment divided by the present value of cash flow paid into the investment,[81] effectively represents an investment multiple that takes into account the time value of cash flow. The metric is very similar to the public market equivalent described by Kaplan and Schoar (2003) and Kaserer and Diller (2004a), the only material difference being the employment of a discount factor that represents the cost of capital rather than the return of a public market index.[82] Ljungqvist and Richardson (2003a), for example, use profitability indices to investigate the relative performance of a sample of private equity funds, adopting the risk-free rate (proxied by the yield to maturity on ten-year treasuries at the time the fund was raised) to discount cash outflows and adopting capital market industry betas and returns on public market indices (S&P 500, Nasdaq Composite) to calculate the discount rate for distributions.

$$PI = \frac{\sum_{t=0}^{T} D_t \prod_{i=0}^{t}(1+j_i)^{-1}}{\sum_{t=0}^{T} I_t \prod_{i=0}^{t}(1+k_i)^{-1}},$$

whereas D_t represents payments received from the investment (*distributions*) in period t, I_t represents payments into the investment (*investments*) in period t, j_i is the cost of capital of payments received in period i ($r_0 = 0$), k_i is the cost of capital of cash outflow in period I ($k_0 = 0$), and T represents investment duration.

The profitability index appears to be a more adequate measure of private equity performance than the previous metrics because it takes into account the investment's cost of capital. But in the absence of a satisfactory theoretical model for estimating the cost of capital in private equity (see Chapter 4.3.2 on theoretical and practical challenges of measuring performance in private equity) its practical benefit is limited.

In the example calculation in Table 25, the profitability index at 0.99 shows that the present value of returns from the private equity investment, discounted at the return rate of the public market index is 1% lower than the present value of the payments into the investment, discounted at the risk-free rate. Note that the implied order of preference in this example calculation is different to the implied order of preference in the PME example calculation (see Table 24),

---

81 The definitions of the profitability index sometimes vary (see Brealey et al., 2011, pp. 143–144)

82 A formal difference is that the public market equivalent sets end values in relation to each other, whereas the profitability index sets present values in relation to each other. As can easily be shown by extending the PME formula with the factor $\frac{\prod_{i=1}^{T}(1+R_i)^{-1}}{\prod_{i=1}^{T}(1+R_i)^{-1}}$, the ratio of end values is equivalent to the ratio of present values, and, for practical purposes, is possibly more a matter of preference; perhaps depending upon whether the metric is being used ex ante, for investment decisions, or ex post, for evaluation purposes

because the investment outlays in year 1 and year 3 are discounted at lower discount rates than the respective cumulative return rates of the public market index.

Table 25
Example calculations of the profitability index (continued example)

	Period (t)						
Amount	0	1	2	3	4	Σ	PI
Payments received (D_t)				135	66	201	
Payments made (I_t)	100	10		30		140	
Public market index	1.00	1.15	1.44	1.39	1.74		
Risk-free rate index (at $r_f = 5\%$)	1.00	1.05	1.10	1.16	1.22		
Present value of D_t				97	38	135	
Present value of I_t	100	10		26		135	
							0.99

Note. The profitability index (PI) is calculated using the return of the public market index as discount rate for cash inflows and the risk-free rate as discount rate for cash outflows.

4.3.1.6 Other metrics

A variety of other metrics are also conceivably employed for the task of evaluating private equity investments: Practitioners frequently refer to the *capital gain* of an investment, roughly defined as the sale value of the investment above its purchase cost. Capital gains are rather similar to investment multiples, but measure absolute rather than relative gains.[83] Due to their simplicity and similarity with investment multiples, they are not separately described in this thesis. Neither does this review include popular pricing and valuation methods, such as net present value (NPV), discounted cash flow valuation (DCF), and adjusted present value (APV), as these methods are widely discussed in existing literature. The ensuing chapter highlights some of the issues that arise when applying these methods to private equity investments (one additional practical consideration is that, for the purposes of performance measurement, private equity firms are likely to prefer metrics that measure the value-add of an investment over the holding period to ones that value the investment at a particular moment in time). A number of scholars have adopted more complex methodologies to measure overall private equity performance. For example, Cochrane (2005) and Groh and Gottschalg (2006) calculate Jensen alphas, adjusting for various factors, such as financial leverage and selection bias. These methods are clearly too cumbersome for day-to-day management purposes, and they also do

[83] Let $I_A \dots I_n$ be contributions to an investment and $D_A \dots D_m$ be distributions from the investment, then the capital gain equates to $\sum_{i=1}^{m} D_i - \sum_{j=1}^{n} I_j$ and the investment multiple is $\frac{\sum_{i=1}^{m} D_i}{\sum_{j=1}^{n} I_j}$

not resolve theoretical issues relating to idiosyncratic risk and illiquidity. Last, existing literature rarely alludes to specific measures of investment risk that private equity firms might employ. Reyes (1990, p. 25) suggests that private equity firms are more concerned with the default risk of investments than with traditional risk measures. He and Schefczyk (1998, p. 169; 2006, p. 156) mention the use of default ratios and win-loss ratios (relative numbers, or book values, of successful and unsuccessful transactions in a fund).[84]

4.3.2 Theoretical and practical challenges of measuring performance in private equity

For the appraisal of investments, many finance textbooks promote the use of metrics that are based on modern portfolio theory and the capital asset pricing model. This chapter is concerned with theoretical and practical challenges that private equity firms encounter when attempting to measure investment performance using such "traditional" metrics. A review of the existing literature on performance measurement in private equity (see Chapter 4.2) suggests that the key challenges might be i) the illiquidity of private equity investments, ii) their lack of market prices, and iii) the exposure of private equity firms to idiosyncratic risk.

Firstly, private equity investments are illiquid. At investor level, illiquidity (of private equity partnership interests) is caused by contractual transfer restrictions imposed by the private equity firm (Lerner & Schoar, 2004).[85] A number of authors have suggested that investors require a return premium to compensate for the illiquidity of private equity investments (e.g. Fenn et al., 1997, p. 42; Ljungqvist & Richardson, 2003a; see also Amihud and Mendelson, 2012, for a

---

84 Schefczyk points out that he does not regard the default ratio as a satisfactory measure: "Die Ausfallquote kann aber keinen exakten und finanzwirtschaftlich befriedigenden Risikomaßstab darstellen, da sie letztlich nur eingetretene Misserfolge anstelle des Risikos im eigentlichen Sinne abbildet [the default ratio cannot, however, constitute an exact and financially satisfactory risk measure, because, in the end, it represents only unsuccessful investments rather than risk in the true sense]" (Schefczyk, 1998, p. 169; 2006, p. 156; reiterated by Kraft, 2001, p. 307; and Vater, 2003, p. 38)

85 In the past, illiquidity of private equity partnership interests was also attributed to a lack of vibrant secondary markets (e.g. Ljungqvist & Richardson, 2003b, p. 4). More recent data from practitioner reports suggest that these markets have experienced strong growth over the last years and have now reached a sizeable proportion of the primary private equity market (e.g. Lüchinger & Schnyder, 2009)

more general discussion of the cost of illiquidity).[86] Such an effect would imply, ceteris paribus, higher cost of capital for private equity firms (see Bodie et al., 2008, pp. 317–322, for a description of the effect of asset liquidity on the capital asset pricing model). At the level of the private equity firm, portfolio company investments are illiquid because of high transaction costs in markets for private business holdings (Damodaran, 2005). Like investors, private equity firms might also expect to receive a return premium to compensate for the illiquidity of portfolio company investments. Illiquidity of private equity investments is a challenge for the application of traditional performance measures because the equilibrium of the capital asset pricing model assumes perfect markets — illiquidity is not priced.[87]

Secondly, market prices for private equity assets are only available at rare occasions during their lifetimes, for example, at purchase, re-financing and exit. In traditional finance, investment risk is specified as the statistical dispersion (typically standard deviation or variance) of investment returns around expected return (e.g. Bodie et al., 2008, p. 134). For traded securities these parameters — and the beta from the capital asset pricing model — are frequently estimated using historical data (see Bodie et al., 2008, pp. 138–139 and 260–270, on the methodology of time-series analysis). The typically very limited amount of historical market prices for private equity investments raises substantial issues for the calculation and estimation of such measures in private equity. Alternative approaches such as the use of net asset values instead of market prices for calculating standard deviation or the use of industry betas from public companies for estimating the market risk of private companies bear their own issues (see Ljungqvist & Richardson, 2003a; Reyes, 1990; Woodward, 2009, for a discussion of the challenges of calculating risk measures in private equity and for an overview of alternative approaches).

Thirdly, private equity firms are not always fully diversified and therefore can be exposed to idiosyncratic risk. Conventional finance theory divides investment risk into idiosyncratic risk, which can be eliminated through portfolio diversification, and market risk, which cannot be eliminated through diversification. In the equilibrium of the capital asset pricing model, investors receive returns that correspond with the degree of market risk borne by them — idiosyncratic risk is not priced. A number of scholars argue that in private equity idiosyncratic risk is priced, both at the level of the private equity firm (Manigart et al., 2002; Müller, 2011;

86 In a recent study, Franzoni, Nowak, and Phalippou (2011) provide evidence for the pricing of liquidity risk in private equity returns

87 Bodie, Kane, and Marcus (2008, pp. 317–322) also discuss extensions of the standard capital asset pricing model that incorporate liquidity costs and liquidity risk. These extensions are rather complex and require data that are typically not available for private equity investments

Rea, 1989) and at investor level (Jones & Rhodes-Kropf, 2003). Empirical evidence from Manigart et al. (2002), Jones and Rhodes-Kropf (2003), and Müller (2011) supports these views, whereas a study by Ljungqvist and Richardson (2003a) does not find a significant association between private equity fund returns and idiosyncratic risk (see Chapter 4.2). Idiosyncratic risk could be an issue for CAPM-based performance measurement because these measures do not account for the idiosyncratic risk that is possibly borne by the private equity firm.

4.3.3 The quality of IRRs and multiples as measures of performance

4.3.3.1 Criteria for evaluating the quality of performance measures

The utilisation of IRRs and multiples in private equity is largely unaffected by the theoretical and practical challenges described in the previous chapter; on the one hand because their validity does not depend on the more demanding assumptions of modern portfolio theory and the capital asset pricing model, on the other hand because their calculation requires no information other than a cash flow profile. Of course, this does not imply that IRRs and multiples are appropriate performance measures for private equity investments. For the purpose of evaluating the quality of IRRs and multiples as measures of performance for private equity firms, it is perhaps necessary to take a step back and look into what characterises *good* performance measures.

A number of scholars have suggested criteria for assessing the quality of measures used in areas such as accounting, productivity management, or business research (e.g. Emory, 1985; Hannula, 1999; Sink, 1985).[88] Emory applies quality standards from the field of psychology and education to business research. He suggests that sound measures should be valid, reliable

[88] In his discussion of criteria for assessing the quality of measures, Hannula (1999, pp. 69–79) refers to a 1979 dissertation by Vehmanen on accounting measures. Unfortunately, a copy of Vehmanen's work was not available to the author of this paper

and practical (Emory, 1985, pp. 94–101).[89] In broad terms, Emory specifies that a measure is *valid* if it accurately measures what it is intended to measure,[90] *reliable* if it invariably produces the same results under the same conditions (some refer to this as *consistency*), and *practical* if it is cost and resource efficient (*economic*), easy to use (*convenient*), and easy to understand (*interpretable*). Hannula (1999) proposes a framework of "sound productivity measurement criteria" (p. 78)[91] that comprises Emory's criteria (albeit with slightly differing definitions) and includes a fourth criterion, *relevance,* which he defines as "the value and usefulness of the measurement results for the users of the measure" (p. 78). Rouse and Putterill (2003) find it important that performance measures "must relate to organisational goals and strategy" (p. 802) and require *comparatives* for evaluation purposes. Lebas and Euske (2007) also emphasize the importance of comparability: "Performance measures and the underlying performance must be qualified as good or bad. No signal of performance is intrinsically either. There must always be a comparison to qualify the performance" (p. 135).

The criteria are summarised in Table 26. Rouse and Putterill's (2003) goal conformity criterion and Hannula's (1999) relevance criterion are grouped together.[92] Lebas and Euske's (2007) comparability criterion is integrated into a wide definition of validity. Performance measures cannot be expected to meet all criteria simultaneously. Lönnqvist and Hannula (2000, pp. 1–2) state that "(...) useful performance measures are always compromises between different criteria" and that "extremely valid measures are not always very practical". The criteria listed in Table 26 are used as a framework for discussing the quality of IRRs and multiples in the following chapter.

---

89 Sink (1985) put forward a list of quality criteria very similar to that of Emory. Sink's criteria included among others *validity* and *reliability* as well as *comprehensibility* and *cost effectiveness*

90 More precisely, this description of validity is what Emory refers to as *internal* validity, which he sets in contrast to *external* validity, defined as the "ability [of a measure] to be generalized across persons, settings, and times" (Emory, 1985, p. 94)

91 In later publications, Hannula labels his quality criteria for productivity measurement more generally as a "framework for the criteria of sound performance measurement" (Lönnqvist & Hannula, 2000, p. 1)

92 The implicit assumption here is that the interests of private equity firms and their managers are highly aligned with each other so that the "value and usefulness" of measures for the "users" (i.e. investment managers of private equity firms) are principally determined by their ability to measure the attainment of "organisational goals and strategy"

Table 26

Framework of criteria for evaluating the quality of performance measures

Criterion	Description
Relevance / goal conformity	Metric is useful, linked to the corporate objectives and strategy
Validity	Metric accurately measures what it was intended to measure, metric is comparable
Reliability	Metric invariably produces the same results under the same conditions
Practicality	Metric is cost- and resource-efficient, easy to use and understand

Note. The criteria presented in the table are based on criteria suggestions from Emory, C. W. (1985). *Business research methods* (3rd ed.). Homewood, IL: Irwin; Hannula, M. (1999). *Expedient total productivity measurement* (Doctoral dissertation, Tampere University of Technology, Finland). Espoo, Finland: Finnish Academy of Technology; Rouse, P., & Putterill, M. (2003). An integral framework for performance measurement. *Management Decision, 41*(8), 791–805. doi:10.1108/00251740310496305; Lebas, M., & Euske, K. (2007). A conceptual and operational delineation of performance. In A. Neely (Ed.), *Business performance measurement: Theory and practice* (2nd ed., pp. 125–139). Cambridge, UK: Cambridge University Press.

4.3.3.2 Discussion

4.3.3.2.1 Relevance and goal conformity

The widespread utilisation of IRRs and multiples in the private equity industry makes it evident that private equity firms consider these measures as relevant. The two metrics also clearly relate to an objective of private equity firms: the aim of generating high returns to investors (see Chapter 3 for more detail on private equity firm objectives). Whilst the investment multiple delivers information about an investment's total capital efficiency, the IRR reports information about capital efficiency per unit of time. In addition, the two measures might also be used as indicators of the degree to which an investment contributes to other private equity firm objectives, such as reputation and income: As investors use IRRs and investment multiples to assess the quality of private equity firms,[93] fund managers who generate superior investment performance by the standards of these measures can expect to enhance their reputation with investors (and thus facilitate future fundraising).[94] Moreover, a substantial component of private equity firm income — *carried interest* — is typically linked to the positive difference between fund profit and committed capital (sometimes involving a premium; see, e.g. Gompers & Lerner, 1999; Litvak, 2004; Metrick & Yasuda, 2010, on private equity firm compensation). Assuming that a fund is expected to call upon most of its committed capital for portfolio investments before the end of its lifetime, the investment multiple provides information on whether, and to what extent, an investment contributes to the carried interest generated by a fund.[95]

4.3.3.2.2 Validity and reliability

There is a long history of academic debate regarding the utility of the IRR as a measure of investment return. Criticism of the IRR frequently centres on the mathematical possibility of multiple solutions or no solution to the IRR equation, the lack of distinction between investing and financing returns, and the unreliability of the metric in comparison to the net present value for ranking and selecting investments. In the area of private equity, some of these issues are possibly mitigated by the typical characteristics of private equity investments. Firstly, most private equity firm investments should satisfy the conditions put forward by Norstrøm (1972) that secure a unique non-negative solution to the IRR equation. Norstrøm required that i) the investment should begin with a cash outflow, ii) the sum of all cash flows should be positive,

---

93 This is a general notion in the private equity industry; indicative evidence for its validity is the promotion of IRRs and multiples as standard measures of performance in major industry reporting guidelines (see chapters 4.3.1.1 and 4.3.1.2)

94 This is not a circular argument because private equity firms compete with each other for investor capital and because fund managers have incentives to attract investors by offering purposeful information — thus lowering information asymmetries and agency conflicts (Kemmerer & Weidig, 2005, pp. 5, 9, and 23)

95 Example: Let carried interest be 20% of all distributions exceeding a threshold of 108% of capital contributions. In rough terms, an investment will contribute (proportionately) to the achievement of carried interest by the private equity firm if its investment multiple exceeds the level of 1.08. The proportionate amount of carried interest roughly equates 20% of the positive difference between the investment multiple and 1.08 (disregarding possible catch-up provisions, repayments of management fees, and taxes etc.)

and iii) there should be only one change of sign in the stream of cash flows. Ex ante, at the time of the investment decision, virtually all private equity investment opportunities contemplated should satisfy these conditions so that the investment decision will typically not be affected by this issue. Secondly, the typical cash flow profile of private equity firm investments also serves to characterise them as investing activity rather than borrowing activity. Interpreting whether an IRR is being earned or paid should present no difficulty for most private equity investments. This is evident, for example, for investments that satisfy Norstrøm's conditions and also for unsuccessful investments that do not meet the second condition of Norstrøm. Finally, it is criticised that the IRR can be misleading when ranking and selecting between investment projects, which are mutually exclusive (Brealey et al., 2011, pp. 139–141). In the field of private equity it seems rather unlikely that attractive and attainable investment opportunities are so abundant that private equity firms should be required to choose between competing investment propositions very often.[96] Whenever such competition does not occur, the IRR rule (to only accept investment projects with an IRR equal to or higher than the respective opportunity cost of capital;[97] Brealey et al., 2011, p. 137) should not be affected by this criticism.[98] In analogy, the points discussed here for the investment appraisal should largely also apply to ex post evaluations of investment success.

Concluding, the IRR — used in concert with the opportunity cost of capital — should in many instances be a reasonably valid and reliable performance measure for private equity firms. The discussion also makes it evident that its use requires great caution. As sole criterion, the IRR can fail to be a valid and reliable measure of performance, for example when deciding on

---

96 Moreover, top performing private equity firms can also hardly be considered to be capital constrained (Gompers & Lerner, 2001, p. 152)

97 As a matter of convenience the rule is here formulated as a rule of acceptance, rather than as a rule of rejection

98 In this context, (Brealey et al., 2011, pp. 141–142) point out another source of error: Computation of the opportunity cost of capital (i.e. the benchmark for the IRR) can be challenging if the opportunity cost of capital is not the same for all cash flows, for example, when short-term interest rates are different from long-term rates. This is indeed a concern, especially for investments with sizeable interim cash flows. But the issue should not be a problem for investments that consist of only two cash flows (i.e. investment and exit cash flow)

mutually exclusive investments or when evaluating unsuccessful investments that did not return capital investment (and therefore do not satisfy Norstrøm's conditions). The IRR rule can also be inaccurate, if the cash flow profile comprises sizeable interim cash flows (see Footnote 98). More generally, the IRR can be misleading whenever it is used as criterion for comparing and ranking the return of investments without taking into account the corresponding opportunity cost of capital.[99]

Unfortunately, in cases where the IRR fails to be a valid and reliable measure of return the investment multiple hardly offers improvement. Generally, the investment multiple can be expected to be less reliable than the IRR because it does not take into account the timing of cash flows.[100] On the upside, the investment multiple is so simple that it can almost always be computed and is probably less deceptive than the IRR.[101] In fact, if the investment multiple is set in comparison with a hurdle that truly reflects opportunity cost of capital over the investment's duration, it is not necessarily less valid or reliable than the IRR. For example, the multiple of an investment that consists of only two cash flows (a frequent scenario in private equity) can be calculated by compounding its IRR plus one over the duration of the investment.[102] Thus, if the hurdle rate that is used in connection with the investment multiple equates to one plus the hurdle rate that is used in connection with the IRR, compounded over

---

99 Indeed, this should be a concern for investors who rank private equity firms and funds using IRRs and multiples

100 Contrary to this expectation, Harris, Jenkinson, and Kaplan (2012) present results suggesting that the investment multiple is a more reliable indicator of (fund-level) PME than is the IRR

101 On the latter point, Phalippou (2009) points out that comparing multiples and IRRs can help investors to identify "distorting" IRR effects that are potentially a result of "strategic" behaviour of private equity firms (i.e. private equity firms seeking early exits or dividends from investments in order to boost reported IRR, although additional returns above opportunity cost of capital could have been achieved by waiting longer), because investment multiples are not affected by timing of cash flows and because they are lower if the investment is exited at a lower price than might have been achieved, for example, by waiting longer

102 The relationship between the investment multiple (m) and IRR for an investment with only two cash flows $C_0 < 0$ and $C_T > 0$ can be described as follows: $\frac{-C_0}{(1+IRR)^0} + \frac{C_T}{(1+IRR)^T} = 0; m = \frac{C_T}{C_0} \Leftrightarrow m = (1 + IRR)^T$

the investment's duration, the resulting signal from the two metrics should be equivalent (assuming positive, non-negative investment multiple and IRR hurdle rate).

4.3.3.2.3 Practicality

One great practical advantage of the investment multiple is its simplicity — it is quick and easy to calculate and should be effortlessly understood. The IRR is perhaps not quite as straightforward as the multiple, but it is clearly less complicated than a number of metrics that have been proposed as improved measures of private equity performance, such as the MIRR, the public market equivalent, and the profitability index. The IRR possibly appeals to practitioners because it is conveniently expressed as a percentage rate — although this can be misleading (see Chapter 4.3.1.2). Perhaps the biggest practical advantage of the two metrics is that their calculation does not require a discount rate – determining adequate discount rates for private equity investments is challenging (see Chapter 4.3.2) and can introduce an element of arbitrariness.[103] A clear separation of benchmark and return metric (as in the IRR rule) increases transparency and enables practitioners to assess the effect of changes to either number (e.g. due to uncertainties about their precise levels) at a glance.[104] Last, IRRs and multiples offer a strategic advantage: Private equity firms will probably favour reporting a low positive IRR or multiple to investors than having to report a negative net present value.

4.3.3.3 Preliminary observations

The foregoing discussion of the quality of the investment multiple and the IRR identifies a number of defensible arguments for their popularity: The IRR is a comparatively simple metric, its calculation does not require a discount rate (whose estimation can be challenging and contentious), and it is conveniently expressed as a percentage rate (though this can sometimes be deceptive). In addition, some of the IRR's most criticised deficiencies, that is, no solution or multiple solutions to the IRR equation, no differentiation between lending and borrowing, and the unreliability of the metric in comparison to the net present value for ranking and selecting investments, appear to be less troubling in a typical private equity environment. The investment multiple complements the IRR in that it provides information on total investment return rather than return per unit of time. Like the IRR, its calculation does not require a discount rate. Its greatest advantage is perhaps its simplicity: It is very easy to calculate and to understand. On the other hand, the investment multiple can generally be expected to be less valid and reliable than the IRR because it does not account for time (unless used in connection with a benchmark

---

[103] This should be a particularly sensitive issue for the purposes of external reporting, as investors and private equity firms may well have different views on the appropriate level of discount rate

[104] Practitioners sometimes refer to the difference between expected return and minimum return requirement (the hurdle rate) as *headroom*. The headroom gives a feel for the extent that the constituent amounts can change adversely before the investment criterion is breached

that reflects the time profile of cash flow). Additionally, the investment multiple can convey a rough idea of an investment's contribution to firm income. Nonetheless, it must be emphasized that the two metrics can be misleading when used to rank (and select between) mutually exclusive investment opportunities, to compare performance across investments, to evaluate unsuccessful investments or investments with complex cash flow streams, or when used to evaluate investments with sizeable interim cash flows.

I have pointed out that the MIRR can overcome some of the issues associated with the IRR. Some researchers therefore recommend the MIRR for measuring private equity performance (e.g. Phalippou, 2009). But the MIRR's superiority for practical purposes is far from certain: The MIRR requires the estimation of — and agreement upon — up to two discount rates, the adequate levels of which literature is yet unclear about. The metric is arguably not any easier to understand than the IRR, and it is doubtful to what extent the use of the MIRR would actually enable private equity firms to enhance their decision quality: According to Eagle, Grinder, and Kiefer (2008), the MIRR offers no improvement on the IRR rule for appraising independent investment projects without capital constraints and can be misleading if the *reinvestment assumption* is misinterpreted. At the same time, attractive investment opportunities are supposedly rare, so that it seems unlikely that private equity firms should encounter mutually exclusive investment projects that are both attractive and attainable very often.

4.4 Development of Research Focus and Hypotheses

This part of the thesis explores the metrics that private equity firms use to measure and manage the performance of portfolio investments. Clearly, the choice of metrics can affect firm success — both measured and actual: Measured success can be affected because different metrics can lead to different measurements; actual success can be affected because different measurements can lead to different management action.[105] For the appraisal of investments, many finance textbooks promote the use of metrics that are based on modern portfolio theory and the capital asset pricing model. But Chapter 4.3.2 has described how in the field of private equity illiquidity, lack of market prices, and chunky investment portfolios raise considerable theoretical and practical challenges for the employment of such metrics. Anecdotal evidence suggests that instead of following textbook recommendations, the private equity industry has widely adopted the use of "practitioner metrics", such as money multiples and IRRs, which are also promoted by industry reporting guidelines. Measures of risk appear to be largely absent (Schefczyk, 2006, p. 156).[106]

The confusion over actual industry practice is illustrated by conflicting opinions in existing literature. For example, Fenn, Liang, Prowse (1997), Reyes (2003, p. 32), Grabenwarter and Weidig (2005, p. 23), and Phalippou (2009, p. 2) believe that the IRR is the metric most commonly used. Ljungqvist and Richardson (2003b, p. 21) maintain that it is the multiple, and Bader (1996, p. 310), Kraft (2001, pp. 290–308), and Weidig and Mathonet (2004, p. 6) are of the opinion that the IRR and multiple are both typical metrics in private equity. For a better understanding of how private equity firms manage their investment portfolio, and for an evaluation of the quality of their decisions, it appears necessary to explore what metrics private

---

105 Consider a private equity firm that needs to decide between investment projects A and B. Both projects require immediate investment of 100. Project A is expected to generate proceeds of 200 at the end of the first year, whereas project B is expected to generate proceeds of 300 at the end of the second year (no interim cash flow in either project). As sole decision criterion, the multiple would lead to a preference of project B ($Multiple_B$ = 300/100 = 3.0 is larger than $Multiple_A$ = 200/100 = 2.0). The IRR as sole decision criterion would lead to a preference of project A (IRR_A = 200/100 – 1 = 1 is larger than $IRR_B = [300/100]^{1/2} - 1$ = .73). Net present values would yield a preference of project B for any discount rate below 50% and a preference of project A for any discount rate above 50%

106 This is particularly evident in private equity reporting: Private equity reporting standards and guidelines typically do not require private equity firms to report measures of risk or risk-return to investors; in fact, the word *risk* occurs only twice in a 32 page document on reporting guidelines issued by the European Private Equity & Venture Capital Association (EVCA, 2006) and not at all in the respective 22-page document issued by the Private Equity Industry Guidelines Group (PEIGG, 2005). The Global Investment Performance Standards of the CFA Institute (2010) have only recently included provisions that relate to risk

equity firms use to measure and manage the performance of portfolio investments. The foregoing discussion suggests that IRRs and money multiples offer private equity firms a unique compromise between a high degree of practicality on the one hand and reasonable validity and reliability on the other. Based on this and on the existing anecdotal evidence of these metrics in industry practise it is hypothesized that private equity firms generally view money multiples and IRRs as more important than other metrics for measuring the success of portfolio company investments (H3).

4.5 Results and Discussion

4.5.1 The importance of success measures

Figure 8 shows considerable differences in the averages of the importance ratings that survey respondents attributed to various metrics for measuring the success of company investments.[107] The multiple and the IRR stand out prominently, with high mean importance ratings and comparatively tight 95% confidence intervals. Further analyses shows that 98.8% of the survey respondents attributed an importance rating of at least 4 (on a scale with five numbered steps ranging from 5 [*very important*] to 1 [*not important*]) to either multiple or IRR. The metric capital gain takes a middle position with a moderate mean importance rating. All other metrics generated lower mean importance ratings, with 95% confidence intervals well below the midpoint of the rating scale. Only two respondents specified an additional success measure (besides those listed on the survey form) under *other* in the questionnaire.[108]

[107] A glossary of success measure definitions from the survey package is included in Appendix B

[108] One buyout respondent specified "profit increase and amount of deleveraging". One venture capital respondent specified "internal key performance indicators" as important for the firm

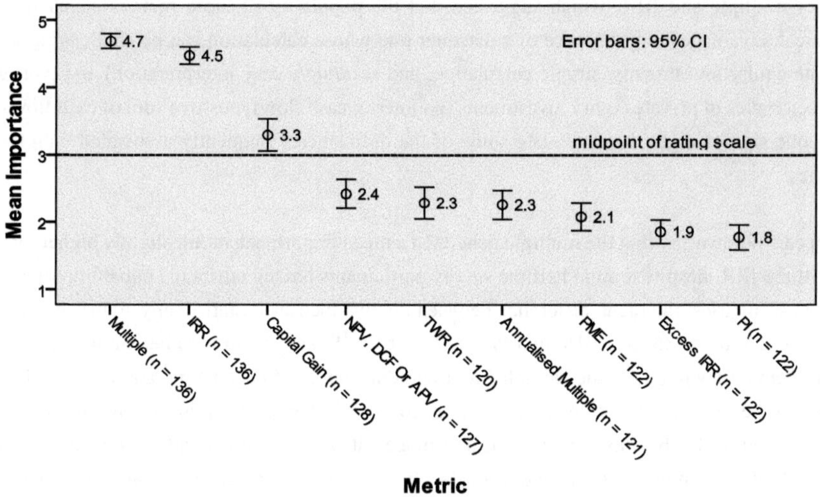

Figure 8. Importance of metrics for measuring the success of company investments. Survey respondents' importance ratings were measured on numbered 5-point scales, ranging from 5 (*very important*) to 1 (*not important*). CI = confidence interval. IRR = internal rate of return. NPV = net present value. DCF = discounted cash flow. APV = adjusted present value. TWR = time-weighted return. PME = public market equivalent. PI = profitability index. All figures are based on country-weighted survey data. The weights reflect the ratio of a country's share of private equity firms in the frame population to its share of firms in the survey sample.

It was hypothesized that private equity firms generally view money multiples and IRRs as more important than other metrics for measuring the success of portfolio company investments (H3). The results of paired samples tests of mean differences in importance ratings between the multiple, the IRR, and each other metric in the survey questionnaire offer strong support for the hypotheses: All differences are statistically significant and the size of effect is large in every instance.[109] These results are consistent with the foregoing discussion of the quality of the

[109] The results of the paired samples tests are available from the author upon request

money multiple and IRR, which suggested that the popularity of these metrics stems from practical advantages (e.g. absence of a discount rate whose calculation can be challenging for private equity investments, simple calculation, and *seemingly* easy interpretation) and typical characteristics of private equity investments (no interim cash flows, positive sum of cash flows, only one sign change) that attenuate some of the deficiencies frequently associated with the metrics.

It appears noteworthy that the multiple generated a mean importance rating slightly higher than that of the IRR, despite around half the survey participants having attributed equal importance to the two metrics; the mean difference between the two metrics is statistically significant (n = 136, t = -2.4, df = 135, p = .018, two-tailed, d = -0.30).[110] This result is rather surprising from an academic viewpoint, as the "simple" multiple does not account for time and can therefore generally be expected to be less reliable than the IRR. This shortcoming of the multiple is possibly believed to be outweighed by its advantages: It was highlighted in Chapter 4.3.3.3 that the multiple is simple, robust, and can also be used as an indicator for an investment's contribution to firm income; if employed appropriately (i.e. in connection with a hurdle that reflects opportunity cost of capital over the duration of the investment), the multiple can deliver results that are as valid and reliable as those of the IRR.

All other metrics show considerably lower mean importance ratings. Capital Gain achieved an overall moderate importance rating; further analysis reveals that none of the survey participants attributed their highest importance rating exclusively to this metric (see Table 27 in Chapter 4.5.2). These results suggest that private equity firms regard the metric as a supplementary measure, which might be used to assess absolute gain or for tax purposes. It is notable that measures and methodologies frequently recommended in finance textbooks, such as the NPV, DCF or APV, and occasionally the profitability index, generated mean importance ratings well below the midpoint of the rating scale. In the earlier discussion it was pointed out that the application of metrics that are based on modern portfolio theory and the capital asset pricing model to private equity investments gives rise to considerable theoretical and practical challenges; these results provide empirical evidence for the low import of such metrics in private equity firms.

[110] A Wilcoxon signed ranks test with all respondents who had assigned differing (paired) importance ratings to the IRR and multiple also yielded a significant preference for the multiple (z = 2.25, p = .024, two-tailed, n - ties = 75)

4.5.2 A ranking of success measures by importance

Further analysis of the data shows that 92 survey respondents (67.6% of the sample) attributed an importance rating of at least 4 to three or more success measures. For a better understanding of how many success measures a sample firm would typically regard as important for measuring the success of company investments, respondents' importance ratings were ranked by arranging the importance ratings of the nine metrics in descending order for each survey respondent. The metric with the highest rating was assigned rank number one and the following metrics were assigned increasing rank numbers. Metrics with equal importance ratings were attributed the same ranking number and a corresponding gap was left in the following rank numbers. For example, a respondent's importance ratings of the nine success measures listed in the questionnaire could yield a sequence of ranks, such as "1 – 2 – 2 – 4 – 5 – 5 – 5 – 8 – 9".

Table 27

Respondents' highest ranking success measures

Highest rank assigned to	MM	IRR	CG	NPV, DCF or APV	TWR	Ann. MM	PME	PI	eIRR	MM and/ or IRR	MM and IRR	All metrics	
	Count												%
1 metric	33	11	0	2	0	0	1	2	0	44		48	35.3
2 metrics	57	51	12	2	2	3	0	0	0	63	45	63	46.3
3 or more metrics	23	25	18	6	7	6	4	2	2	25	25	25	18.4
Total	112	86	30	10	9	9	4	4	2	131	70	136	100.0
% of all metrics	82.5	63.6	22.1	7.0	6.6	6.5	3.2	2.9	1.8	96.8	51.2	100.0	

Note. Survey respondents' importance ratings were measured on numbered 5-point scales, ranging from 5 (*very important*) to 1 (*not important*). The metrics with the highest importance ratings per respondent were assigned a number one rank. The figures in the table show counts of number one rankings for each metric, broken down by the number of highest ranking metrics that each private equity firm assigned. MM = multiple. IRR = internal rate of return. CG = capital gain. NPV = net present value. DCF = discounted cash flow. APV = adjusted present value. TWR = time-weighted return. Ann. MM = annualised multiple. PME = public market equivalent. PI = profitability index. eIRR = excess IRR. All figures are based on country-weighted survey data. The weights reflect the ratio of a country's share of private equity firms in the frame population to its share of firms in the survey sample.

An analysis of these rankings (see Table 27) shows that most private equity firms attach highest importance ratings to two or more success measures, rather than to one single metric: Roughly two thirds of sample firms (64.7%, or 88 respondents, 95% CI [56.3%, 72.3%]) assigned their highest importance rating to two or more success measures, and just over three quarters of these firms attributed their highest scores to (at minimum) the multiple and the IRR. Overall, around 96.8% of respondents attributed their highest importance rating (exclusively or non-exclusively) to the multiple, the IRR or to both metrics together.[111] One possible explanation for this phenomenon is that private equity firms endeavour to counterbalance known limitations or defects of individual measures by basing their evaluations on a mix of complementary measures. The multiple, for example, provides information on total return of an investment ("cash-on-cash") but does not account for time; the IRR provides information on the capital efficiency per unit of time but does not specify total investment return. Consequentially, existing literature often recommends that the two measures be used together (Grabenwarter & Weidig, 2005, pp. 48–49; Phalippou, 2009, p. 8). Another possible explanation for this phenomenon is that private equity firms apply different measures for different purposes. For example, a private equity firm might use the multiple for managing its investment portfolio and the IRR and TWR for reporting to investors. Alternatively, a private equity firm might use different measures for measuring an investment's contribution to the achievement of different firm objectives.[112] Last, a small number of private equity firms (roughly 3% of the sample) attached their highest importance rating (exclusively or non-exclusively) to newer and more complex metrics, such as the public market equivalent and the profitability index. This could signify a new trend in private equity performance measurement.

4.5.3 The importance of IRRs and multiples as decision criteria

Figure 9 shows that the multiple and the IRR are not only employed for measuring and reporting investment success, but that they are also important decision criteria for managing the private equity investment portfolio: All means and associated 95% confidence intervals are well above the mid-point of the rating scale.[113] As inappropriate employment of these metrics can impair firm performance, practitioners need to be cautious about the respective limitations of the two metrics: One deficiency of both the IRR and the multiple is their unreliability (in comparison to the net present value) for ranking and selecting investment projects that are mutually exclusive (see Chapters 4.3.1.2 and 4.3.3.2.2). The survey results do not provide conclusive evidence on the magnitude of potential error from this deficiency. But they do show that respondents attributed higher average importance to the multiple and IRR for purposes of investment decisions than for any other type of decision listed in the survey questionnaire. It was speculated in the earlier discussion of the IRR and multiple that attractive and attainable private equity investment opportunities might not be so abundant that private equity firms are

111 The five exclusive number one ranks that were not assigned to the multiple or IRR (see Table 27), are distributed among NPV, DCF Or APV, profitability index, and PME

112 It is also conceivable that private equity firms use different success measures for different geographic areas, investment stages or perhaps investment types — this would make comparing or aggregating performance very cumbersome

113 Consistent with respondents' evaluations of individual success measures (see Chapter 4.5.1), the multiple was generally attributed a little more importance than the IRR

required to choose between competing investment propositions very often (see Chapter 4.3.3.2.2). In order to investigate this idea, the survey form requested participants to specify on a rating scale with five numbered steps ranging from 5 (*very often*) to 1 (*never*) how often their firms were forced to reject acceptable investment opportunities because of limited capacities (*rejection frequencies*).

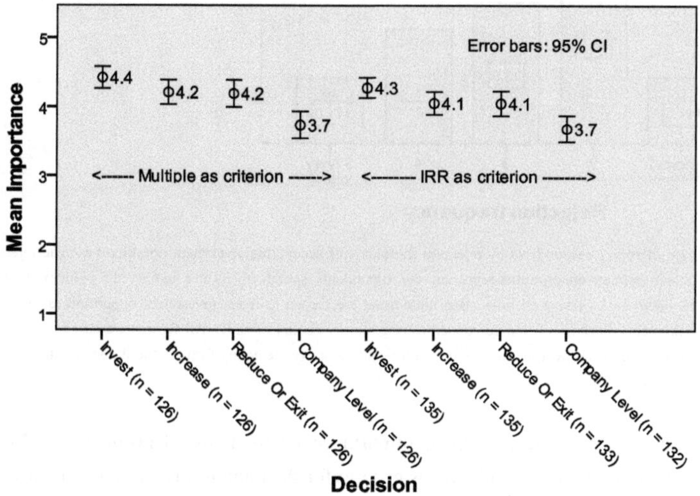

Figure 9. Importance of the multiple and the IRR as criteria for decisions regarding portfolio company investments. Survey respondents' importance ratings were measured on numbered 5-point scales, ranging from 5 (*very important*) to 1 (*not important*). All figures are based on country-weighted survey data. The weights reflect the ratio of a country's share of private equity firms in the frame population to its share of firms in the survey sample. CI = confidence interval. IRR = internal rate of return. Invest = decision to invest in a portfolio company. Increase = decision to increase the investment in a portfolio company. Reduce Or Exit = decision to reduce or exit a portfolio company investment. Company Level = major decisions at portfolio company level (e.g. acquisitions, restructuring, expansion programmes).

Figure 10 shows a concentration of responses around lower and mid-range rejection frequencies, but also a sizeable amount of higher rejection frequencies. This seems to suggest that many private equity firms are, at times, required to select between mutually exclusive investment opportunities. But the interpretation of the data requires some caution: As a strong deal flow is an important investment criterion for investors in private equity funds (Groh & von Liechtenstein, 2011), respondents might have been reluctant to suggest in a personalised survey that their firm receives only few attractive investment opportunities, thus causing a bias in the data towards higher rejection frequencies (see Groves et al., 2004, pp. 224–225, on motivated misreporting). Notwithstanding such a potential bias, the data imply that at least *some* private equity firms are possibly forfeiting better performance by inappropriately using the multiple or the IRR as criterion for mutually exclusive investment decisions.[114]

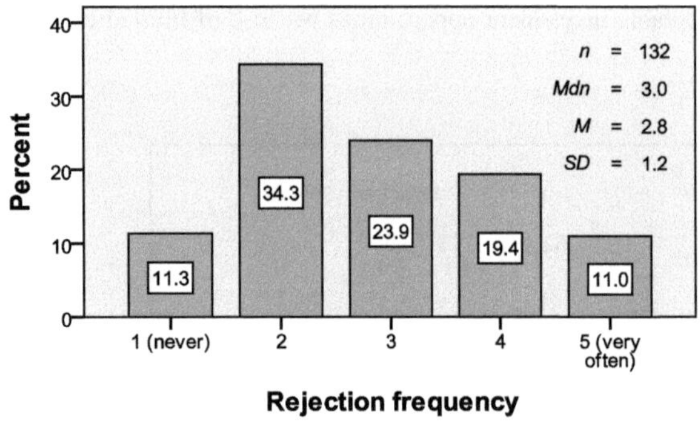

Figure 10. Distribution of survey respondents by rejection frequency of acceptable investment opportunities. The rejection frequency of acceptable investment opportunities represents the respondents' specifications on a numbered 5-point rating scale, ranging from 5 (*very often*) to 1 (*never*) on how often their firms are forced to reject investment opportunities that meet minimum return requirements, because of limited capacities (e.g. equity capital or staff). All figures are based on country-weighted survey data. The weights reflect the ratio of a country's share of private equity firms in the frame population to its share of firms in the survey sample.

Figure 9 also shows a recurring pattern of importance levels across decision types: Mean importance ratings of the multiple and IRR as criteria for deciding to invest in a company are significantly higher than mean importance ratings of the multiple and IRR for any other type of decision (alpha = .01, two-tailed). At the other end of the scale each metric was assigned significantly lower mean importance as criterion for considering major decisions at portfolio company level than as criterion for any other decision (alpha = .01, two-tailed).[115] For major decisions at portfolio company level private equity firms might favour decision metrics that are used within their portfolio companies; alternatively private equity firms could have attributed less importance to these decisions because their degree of involvement in such decisions is lower than it is for portfolio decisions.[116]

114 Additional statistical tests of the relationship between rejection frequencies and IRR importance (both as success measure and as decision criterion) did not yield significant results (alpha = .05, two-tailed)

115 Detailed information on these statistical tests are available from the author upon request

116 This ambiguity of interpretation is unfortunately the result of an ill-defined survey question (see Appendix B for the exact wording), making it impossible to distinguish between the importance that respondents attribute to each decision type and the importance they attribute to the respective metrics for these decisions

4.5.4 The influence of firm characteristics on the evaluation of success measures

A review of the statistical test results in Table 28 shows that respondents' importance ratings of success measures for company investments are particularly frequently negatively associated with external funding (Outside Inv): Respondents who had declared that their firms receive a majority of funds from outside investors rated six metrics (out of nine listed in the survey questionnaire) significantly lower than respondents who had not declared that their firm receives a majority of funds from outside investors (alpha = .05, two-tailed); the evaluations of the IRR and the multiple appear to be largely unaffected by this. One interpretation of these results is that major funding by outside investors has a streamlining effect on the importance that private equity firms attribute to success measures; such an effect could be explained by the need for outside investors to compare performance across funds, resulting in an impetus for the implementation of industry reporting guidelines in private equity firms.

Table 28

Connections between firm characteristics (dichotomous variables) and respondents' importance ratings of success measures

Metric	EU - US/Can	BO - VC	GeoSpec	IndSpec	Outside Inv[a]	Well/Under - Loss[a]	Hands-On - Supp	CEF[a]
IRR	-0.27^{++}	-0.31^{*+}	0.10	-0.16^{b}	-0.22	0.79^{**++}	-0.17	-0.17
Multiple	0.00	0.46^{**b+++}	0.27^{b+}	0.15	0.33^{b}	-0.24	-0.01	0.35^{*++}
Annualised Multiple	0.26	-1.13^{b+++}	-0.19	0.37^{**b++}	-0.60^{**++}	-0.17	0.10	-0.23
Capital Gain	$0.52^{***b+++}$	0.06	0.01	0.03	-0.48^{*++}	-0.25	0.25	-0.03
TWR	-0.15	-0.31	0.13	-0.13	-0.60^{**+++}	-0.02	0.11	-0.14
DPV, DCF Or APV	-0.03	$-0.65^{***b+++}$	-0.07^{b}	0.09	-0.42^{++}	0.00	-0.05	-0.42^{**++}
PI	0.24	-0.11	0.07	-0.02	-0.56^{**+++}	0.11	0.18	-0.45^{**+}
PME	0.15	-0.40^{**++}	0.11	0.17	-0.36^{++}	-0.12	0.17	-0.67^{***+++}
Excess IRR	0.22	-0.27^{++}	0.18	-0.15	-0.35^{+}	-0.24	0.14	-0.13

Note. The figures denote effect sizes (Cohen's *d*), which are calculated by dividing the differences in mean importance ratings of the two subsamples of a dichotomous column variable by the pooled standard deviation. Survey respondents' importance ratings were measured on numbered 5-point scales, ranging from 5 (*very important*) to 1 (*not important*). All figures, except those relating to EU - US/Can, are based on country-weighted survey data. The weights reflect the ratio of a country's share of private equity firms in the frame population to its share of firms in the survey sample. EU - US/Can denotes headquarter location: EU = Europe; US/Can = United States of America or Canada. BO - VC denotes firm type: BO = buyout; VC = venture capital; VC includes eight firms of related types, such as "growth equity" and "business angel"; BO includes two firms of related types ("industry specific buyout" and "restructuring buyout"). GeoSpec refers to firms, for which respondents specified whether or not they specialise in geographical areas. IndSpec refers to firms, for which respondents specified whether or not they specialise in industry sectors. Outside Inv refers to whether or not respondents specified that their firm sources the majority of its fund capital from outside investors. Well/Under - Loss refers to the preferred performance of target companies: Well/Under ="well-performing" or "underperforming"; Loss = "loss-making". Hands On - Supp denotes management style: Hands on = "hands-on"; Supp = "supportive". CEF refers to firms, for which respondents specified whether or not they mostly manage investments in (closed-end) funds with a fixed lifetime. IRR = internal rate of return. TWR = time-weighted return. NPV = net present value. DCF = discounted cash flow. APV = adjusted present value. PI = profitability index. PME = public market equivalent.

$^{*}p < .10$. $^{**}p < .05$. $^{***}p < .01$. All *p*s are two-tailed and relate to independent samples *t*-tests for equality of means; in each case *df* (pairwise) ranges between 90 and 134. ^{+}p, ^{++}p, and ^{+++}p denote respective significance levels for the Mann-Whitney *U*-test.

[a]One of the subsamples has a data count of less than 30.

[b]Equal variances not assumed.

The strongest effects in Table 28 are associated with firm type: The mean importance that the group of venture capital firm respondents attached to the listed metrics is higher than the mean importance that the group of buyout firm respondents attached to these metrics for every metric excepting the time-insensitive metrics Multiple and Capital Gain. Many of these differences are statistically significant ($p < .05$, two-tailed). One explanation for this phenomenon could be a higher emphasis on the factor *time* by venture capital firms: Venture capital firms might generally place more emphasis on time than do buyout firms, because the typical duration of their investments is (comparatively) more variable than that of buyout firms. This seems plausible, when taking into account the high uncertainties of early stage investments and the common practice of staged financing (see Footnote 54 on staged financing).

More generally, it seems possible that private equity firms' preferences for success measures are (roughly) matched to the general characteristics of their investments in a way that increases the average quality of performance measurement. In order to explore this idea a little further, a couple of additional analyses were undertaken: One item on the questionnaire recorded the importance of various factors that influence a respondent firm's level of minimum return required for particular investments (*MRR factors*). Assuming that respondents' importance ratings of these factors are associated with the degree to which their private equity firms are typically exposed to variance in the respective conditions,[117] a number of MRR factors were used as proxy indicators for the typical investment characteristics of these private equity firms. The results of correlation tests between the importance ratings of success measures and the selected MRR factors are presented in Table 29.

117 For example, a high importance rating of the factor *inflation rate* would suggest that the respective private equity firm is accustomed to undertaking investments that are exposed to varying inflation rates

Table 29

Spearman rank correlations between respondents' importance ratings of success measures and respondents' importance ratings of MRR factors

Metric	Capital Intensity	Leverage (debt to equity)	Expected Duration (yrs)	Inflation Rates
IRR	.15 *	.09	.02	-.01
Multiple	-.07	-.02	-.31 ***	-.11
Annualised Multiple	.15 *	.00	.26 ***	.29 ***
Capital Gain	.10	.17 *	.15 *	.05
TWR	.06	.03	.35 ***	.24 ***
NPV, DCF Or APV	.09	.24 ***	.19 **	.14
PI	.12	.08	.21 **	.40 ***
PME	-.10	-.06	.10	.22 **
Excess IRR	-.03	.01	.09	.27 ***

Note. Survey respondents' importance ratings of success measures and of factors that influence a respondent firm's level of minimum return required for particular investments (MRR factors) were measured on numbered 5-point scales, ranging from 5 (*very important*) to 1 (*not important*). The importance that respondents attributed to MRR factors is used as proxy for the typical degree to which the private equity firms' investments are exposed to variance of these factors. Correlations were tested pairwise, using country-weighted data. Weighted *n* ranges between 128 and 145. The weights reflect the ratio of a country's share of private equity firms in the frame population to its share of firms in the survey sample. IRR = internal rate of return. TWR = time-weighted return. NPV = net present value. DCF = discounted cash flow. APV = adjusted present value. PI = profitability index. PME = public market equivalent.
$^{*}p < .10$. $^{**}p < .05$. $^{***}p < .01$. All *p*s are two-tailed.

The data appear to support the idea of a connection between success measure preferences and supposed investment conditions. For example, the more a private equity firm is exposed to variance in expected duration, the more the respective respondent tends to emphasize time-sensitive metrics, such as Time-Weighted Return, Annualised Multiple, Profitability Index, and NPV, DCF Or APV, and the less they tend to value the (time-insensitive) Multiple.[118] The

[118] The results for (time-insensitive) Capital Gain point in the opposite direction; however, both the level of significance and the strength of correlation are low

inflation factor is significantly positively correlated with metrics Profitability Index, Annualised Multiple, Excess IRR, Time-Weighted Return and Public Market Equivalent; all of these metrics can easily take into account changing inflation rates by adjusting the respective discount rate or reference rate. And finally, the MRR factor Leverage is significantly positively correlated with leverage-sensitive metrics NPV, DCF Or APV.

Another review of the data in Table 28 and a review of the results for ordinal scale and continuous firm characteristic variables in Table 30 show that, controlling for the above effects, other characteristics, such as age and size, location, geographical focus, strategic focus, and preferred management style, only rarely have a significant influence on respondents' importance ratings.[119] [120] One exception is the higher importance that respondents from private equity firms located in Europe attributed to Capital Gain in comparison with respondents from private equity firms located in the United States of America or Canada; this effect could stem from differences in tax systems and languages.

119 These results stand in some contrast to findings of Kemmerer and Weidig (2005) regarding the effect of fund experience and focus on reporting characteristics

120 The influence of the variable CEF on respondents' evaluations of success measures is possibly caused by a link between the variables CEF and Outside Inv: $\chi^2 = 16.9$, $\Phi = .36$, $df = 1$, $p < .0005$, two-tailed, $n = 133$ (one cell in the contingency table had an expected cell count lower than 5; p is the value of Fisher's exact test)

Table 30

Spearman rank correlations between firm characteristics (ordinal scale and continuous variables) and respondents' importance ratings of success measures

Metric	Age (yrs)	Funds	Capital (€m)	Investments	Investment Size (€m)
IRR	.01	.10	.10	-.04	-.11
Multiple	.01	.12	.20 (**)	-.10	.29 ***
Annualised Multiple	-.04	.08	-.08	.21 (**)	-.30 (***)
Capital Gain	.07	-.01	-.10	.03	-.11
TWR	-.09	-.22 (**)	-.15 (*)	-.01	-.15 (*)
NPV, DCF Or APV	-.06	-.08	-.11	.08	-.13
PI	-.11	-.13	-.15 (*)	-.14 *	-.02
PME	-.12	-.07	.01	.01	.11
Excess IRR	.04	-.07	.01	.03	.00

Note. Survey respondents' importance ratings of success measures were recorded on numbered 5-point scales, ranging from 5 (*very important*) to 1 (*not important*). Correlations were tested pairwise, using country-weighted data. Weighted *n* ranges between 125 and 154. The weights reflect the ratio of a country's share of private equity firms in the frame population to its share of firms in the survey sample. Age is the number of years a respondent's firm has been in existence. Funds is the number of private equity funds a respondent's firm has raised. Capital is the rough total capital under management of a respondent's firm in € millions. Investments is the rough number of company investments managed by a respondent's firm. Investment Size is a respondent firm's rough typical investment size (equity stake) in € millions. Range specifications were replaced by their means, and amounts in other currencies were converted to € amounts using the averages of market exchange rates over the time of the survey. IRR = internal rate of return. TWR = time-weighted return. NPV = net present value. DCF = discounted cash flow. APV = adjusted present value. PI = profitability index. PME = public market equivalent.

$^{*}p < .10$. $^{**}p < .05$. $^{***}p < .01$. All *p*s are two-tailed. Parentheses denote that the respective Spearman rank correlations within the buyout and venture capital subsamples were not significant at alpha = .10.

4.5.5 Measures of investment risk or risk-return

Non-response for this item in the questionnaire was exceptionally high, comprising more than half of the survey sample (see Table 31). Due to the fact that the wording of the question required a response only in the event of a private equity firm actually employing measures of investment risk or risk-return,[121] the high non-response could be viewed as an indication that most private equity firms do not typically calculate such measures for their company investments. This interpretation is underscored by the high percentage of participants (29%) that actually did respond to this item in the questionnaire, declaring that their firm does not calculate any, or, any quantitative, measures of investment risk or risk-return. It also agrees

121 Because the question was formulated as an open question it is not possible to discern whether respondents who had left the response field blank had been unwilling to respond to this item on the questionnaire, or had meant to imply that their firm did not use any measure of risk or risk-return (see Appendix B for the exact wording of the question)

with findings of a survey on private equity reporting, in which most sample firms declared measures such as standard deviation, beta, alpha or Sharpe ratio "difficult or impossible" to provide to investors (PEIGG, 2004).

Table 31

Measures of investment risk or risk-return that private equity firms calculate for individual company investments

Responses (grouped into categories)	Count	% of sample	% of responses
IRRs, multiples, return rates	12	8.5	21.5
Scenarios, sensitivities, risk models, monte carlo	9	6.5	16.4
Beta-based measures	5	4.0	10.2
Sharpe ratio, expected shortfall	5	3.5	9.0
Other measures and methods	7	5.4	13.8
None, not quantitative	16	11.4	29.0
Total responses	53	39.3	100.0
No response	82	60.7	
Total sample	136	100.0	

Note. All figures are based on country-weighted survey data. The weights reflect the ratio of a country's share of private equity firms in the frame population to its share of firms in the survey sample. IRR = internal rate of return.

In their investment decisions, private equity firms might account for risk by using minimum rates of return rather than calculating specific measures of risk or risk-return (Murray & Lott, 1995, p. 293). This view receives general support from the study results on minimum return requirements presented in Chapter 3. Additional support is derived from the fact that around 21.5% of respondents to this item in the questionnaire declared that their firm employs IRRs, multiples or return rates for the purpose of measuring risk or risk-return; a number of these responses specifically implied the use of these metrics as minimum rates of return. The remainder of responses suggest that these private equity firms employ a variety of alternative methods to evaluate the risk of individual company investments, ranging from simple heuristics and "gut feeling" to sensitivities and scenarios as well as more complex methods and models, such as Monte Carlo simulations and the calculation of expected shortfalls. Only 10.2% of valid responses (exclusively buyout firms) refer to beta-based measures (e.g. "CAPM", "EVA", "WACC", and "Beta"). Again, these results appear to reflect the minor role that metrics based on modern portfolio theory and the capital asset pricing model play for private equity firms.

4.6 Conclusions

In a foregoing discussion of the quality of the money multiple and the IRR for private equity firms I find that these metrics have many practical advantages, and can deliver reasonably valid and reliable results if used appropriately: They are comparatively simple measures that do not require a discount rate and whose calculation can be challenging (and contentious); some of their most criticised deficiencies (i.e. no solution or multiple solutions to the IRR equation, no differentiation between lending and borrowing, and the unreliability of the metrics in comparison to the net present value for ranking and selecting investments) appear to be less troublesome in a private equity environment. The two metrics also appear to complement each other as measures of efficiency — measuring total return on the one hand (money multiple) and return per unit of time on the other (IRR). At the same time, the discussion also points out that the two metrics are generally unreliable when used to rank (and select between) mutually exclusive investment opportunities, when used to compare performance across investments, as well as when used to evaluate unsuccessful investments or investments with complex cash flow profiles.

The survey data strongly suggest that the underlying population of private equity firms regards the multiple and the IRR as more important than other metrics for measuring the success of company investments. The metric Capital Gain yielded a moderate mean importance rating, whereas all other metrics generated lower mean importance ratings, with 95% confidence intervals well below the midpoint of the rating scale. The data also show that most respondents attributed highest importance ratings to two or more success measures, rather than to one single metric and that private equity firms evaluate the multiple and the IRR as important criteria for major decisions regarding their portfolio company investments. A bivariate exploratory analysis of connections between respondents' importance ratings of individual metrics and the characteristics of their private equity firms yielded a number of statistically significant relationships. The importance that private equity firm respondents assigned to success measures is frequently associated with firm type (buyout or venture capital), external funding (whether or not a private equity firm sourced the majority of fund capital from outside investors), and fund horizon (whether or not a private equity firm's investments are mostly managed in closed-end funds), and is generally not associated with the age, size, geographical location, and investment focus of private equity firms.

The survey question on measures of risk and risk-return for individual company investments appears to have been rather unpopular among respondents: Almost three quarters of participants either did not respond to this item on the survey questionnaire, or declared that their private equity firm did not calculate such (quantitative) measures. Many of the participants that did respond to this item on the survey questionnaire stated that their private equity employed minimum rates of return or calculated models, scenarios and sensitivities for the purpose. This ties in with the results in Chapter 3, which document the high importance that private equity firms attach to minimum return requirements for the investment decision and which suggest that risk is an important determinant of the level of return required for a particular investment. Only very few participants (exclusively from buyout firms) specified that their firm applied beta-based measures of risk or risk-return.

From these results I draw the following conclusions. Firstly, the analysis provides strong support for the expected prominent role that the money multiple and IRR play in private equity firms — both in terms of measuring investment success (ex post) and as criteria for key decisions regarding portfolio investments (ex ante).[122] In comparison to these metrics, success measures that are based on modern portfolio theory and the capital asset pricing model play a very much smaller part for measuring investment success in private equity firms.

Secondly, the survey results show that private equity firms generally attribute high importance to the multiple and the IRR when deciding to invest in a company; at the same time they suggest that most private equity firms typically encounter a moderate number of investment opportunities that are mutually exclusive. In combination, these results seem to indicate that at least some private equity firms forfeit better performance by inappropriately employing the IRR and multiple for the appraisal of mutually exclusive investment opportunities.

Thirdly, the pattern of effects associated with firm type and the results of additional tests appear to indicate that private equity firms are capable of choosing success measures that are better suited to their investment strategy, that is, to prefer such metrics that increase the average quality of performance measurement for the firm.

Fourthly, the pattern of effects associated with external funding and fund horizon suggest that major funding by outside investors has a streamlining influence on private equity firms' preferences of success measures. Such an effect could be explained by the need for outside investors to compare performance across funds, resulting in an impetus for the implementation of industry reporting guidelines in private equity firms.

Fifthly, instead of using specific measures of risk or risk-return to account for investment risk, private equity firms appear to employ (risk-adjusted) minimum return requirements or calculate scenarios, sensitivities, or risk models for the purpose. The limited use of beta-based metrics

122 In Chapter 4.4 a number of conflicting opinions on the relative importance of the IRR and the multiple for industry practice were presented. The empirical results of the survey offer support for the views of Bader (1996, p. 310), Kraft (2001, pp. 290–308), and Weidig and Mathonet (2004, p. 6), who had suggested that the IRR and multiple are both typical metrics in private equity

for the evaluation of investment risk is possibly a consequence of issues that arise from asymmetric (or absent) information, illiquidity, and exposure to idiosyncratic risk.

Finally, the results also show that a small number of private equity firms attach highest importance (exclusively or non-exclusively) to the newer and more complex metrics public market equivalent and profitability index; this could signify a new trend in private equity performance measurement.

5 Exit Decisions

5.1 Abstract

This part of the thesis investigates three aspects of the exit decisions of private equity firms: the exit decision power of private equity firms in relation to the portfolio company, the decision rules that private equity firms employ for deciding when to begin an exit process, and the principal determinants of the exit channel decision. Following a review of existing literature, I develop exploratory survey questions and formulate testable hypotheses. The ensuing empirical analysis is based on the survey data of 136 private equity firms located in the United States of America, Canada, and Europe. I find that private equity firms are mostly not prepared to let the decision on exit time or channel be dominated by portfolio company management or a third party — even though a considerable proportion of private equity firms are generally prepared to share exit decision power with portfolio company management. I also find that venture capital firms commonly share significantly more exit decision power with portfolio company management than buyout firms do and ascribe this effect to the existence of implicit contracts over control in the venture capital industry. The survey data do not support the assumption of Wright, Robbie, Thompson et al. (1994) that smaller buyout portfolio companies have more exit decision power than larger buyout portfolio companies. As regards rules for deciding when to begin the exit process for performing and for underperforming investments, the data show that the sample of private equity firms attaches a mean or high frequency rating of usage to a wide range of rules and that most private equity firms attach high frequency ratings to at least two decision rules. I conjecture from this that private equity firms typically choose the decision rule for a particular exit decision and investment from a selection of heuristics, rather than relying on one single decision rule for all exit decisions. Further analysis shows that the decision rules that are most popular with private equity firms are – under certain conditions — consistent with a policy to maximise net present value. But the survey data make it doubtful that the respective conditions are met. Otherwise, I find only weak empirical support for an early culling of poor quality investments — instead, I detect a contrasting tendency of buyout firms to procrastinate the exits of such investments. I also find that, for exiting underperforming investments, a private equity firm's usage of the simpler decision heuristics tends to increase with its age, experience, and size. Last, the survey data show that private equity firms attach importance to a wide range of criteria for the exit channel decision. Price stands out as the most important criterion, followed by the related criteria form of payment, and timing until, and certainty of achieving a full (100%) exit. Reputational concerns also play an important role, whereas the importance attached to these concerns appears to be linked to the degree of asymmetric information between the private equity firm and its contract partners. The data also suggest that, overall, buyout firms devote more attention to the choice of exit channel than do venture capital firms.

5.2 Existing Literature

5.2.1 Early contributions

The first academic publications to focus on private equity exits emerged in the United States of America and the United Kingdom in the early 1990s — perhaps not coincidentally — during the period of subdued private equity activity that followed the first major surge of private equity business volumes in these countries. At this time, literature on buyouts — mostly referred to as *leveraged buyouts* or *management buyouts* and *buy-ins* — and on venture capital developed largely independent of each other.[123]

Early contributions in the buyout area (e.g. Kaplan, 1991, in the United States of America; Wright, Robbie, & Thompson, 1991; Wright et al., 1994, in the United Kingdom) arose from the debate that had been instigated by Jensen (1989) and Rappaport (1990) about the longevity of leveraged buyouts as an organisational form (see Kaplan, 1991, pp. 287–289, for a brief summary of the respective positions). These works collated first data on holding periods and preferred exit routes and began to explore the reasons for the time and channel of exits. Initial publications in the venture capital area focussed particularly on the characteristics and timing of venture-backed initial public offerings (IPOs). In these works, many scholars use constructs from new institutional economics, for example asymmetric information and reputation in their theories and hypotheses. Megginson and Weiss (1991), for example, apply Booth and Smith's (1986) certification hypothesis for capital markets characterised by asymmetric information to the field of venture capital; comparing a sample of 320 offerings from venture-backed firms between 1983 and 1987 with an equal number of offerings without venture-backing they find

[123] Management buyouts and buy-ins are here classified as buyouts. It should be noted that these groups are heterogeneous; many management buyouts are very small and might be more appropriately grouped into the venture capital area (see Appendix E on the characteristic features of venture capital and buyout firms)

that those aided by venture capitalists were able to go public at a significantly younger age. Megginson and Weiss conclude that the presence of venture capitalists in the offering firm certifies the quality of the issue, thereby lowering information asymmetries and IPO costs.[124] Lerner (1994) finds in a sample of 350 privately held biotech firms financed by venture capitalists between 1978 and 1992 that older venture company firms are better able to time IPOs near market peaks than are younger ones and that venture capitalists choose to IPO their portfolio companies when equity valuations are high and rely on private financings when equity valuations are low. Gompers (1996) examines data from a sample of 433 venture-backed IPOs between 1978 and 1987 and from a sample of the first IPOs of 62 venture capital funds between 1983 and 1993. He finds that young venture capitalists take their portfolio companies public earlier than established venture capital firms in order to build a reputation and successfully raise capital for new funds (the grandstanding hypothesis).[125] He also finds that young venture capitalists time an IPO to precede or coincide with periods of fundraising for follow-on funds. Black and Gilson (1998) hypothesize that venture capital firm and entrepreneur enter into an implicit contract over (future) control, wherein the venture capital firm undertakes to effect an IPO exit of the portfolio company (entailing private benefits of control for the entrepreneur) if the venture is successful. They argue that venture capital firms would not refuse to IPO successful portfolio companies, even if suboptimal for the venture capital firm, because of possible detrimental effects to their reputation that would jeopardise their future access to high quality venture opportunities (Black & Gilson, 1998, pp. 262–263). Lin and Smith (1998) also emphasize the role of reputation: In a sample of 2,634 IPOs between 1979 and 1990 (thereof 497 with venture-backing) they find evidence suggesting that venture capital firms' decisions to sell shares in the IPO are affected by their reputation.

5.2.2 The decision on exit time

Much of the existing literature on the exit timing of private equity investments has analysed data samples of empirical private equity transactions and identified relationships between investment duration or exit time, on the one hand, and characteristics of the investment, the private equity firm, or the capital market environment, on the other hand (e.g. Cumming

[124] Bottazzi and Da Rin's (2002) results on certification in Europe are inconclusive: Measuring the impact of venture capital on the amount of funds raised (normalised by the company's value of assets) in a sample of 511 IPOs on *Euro.nm*, they find that venture-backed companies raise on average 60% more funds than non-venture-backed firms, thus supporting the hypothesis of certification. However, after controlling for R&D intensity at IPO (reducing the sample size by almost one half) they find that the effect of venture-backing becomes statistically insignificant

[125] Bottazzi and Da Rin (2002) do not find that European venture capital-backed firms go public earlier than other firms. However, for 80% of the sample the dependent variable *time-to-listing* was calculated using the difference between "the creation of the relevant 'new' market and the firm's IPO" rendering the results of the analysis effectively meaningless (see the discussion by van Ours at the end of the publication)

& Johan, 2010; Cumming & MacIntosh, 2001; Giot & Schwienbacher, 2007; Gompers, 1996; Jelic, 2011; Lerner, 1994; Ljungqvist & Richardson, 2003b; Megginson & Weiss, 1991; Wright, Robbie, Romanet et al., 1994). Other contributions to research in this area have interviewed private equity firms about factors that influence their exit timing or about their divestment objectives (e.g. Paffenholz, 2004; Povaly, 2007; Wall & Smith, 1997).

Only very few studies have looked into the decision rules that private equity firms employ for timing their portfolio company exits. Relander, Syrjänen, and Miettinen (1994), for example, questioned 24 venture capital firms located in 11 European countries on how they "decide when the price and time are right" for selling their (technology-based) portfolio investments and whether they "have a minimum price under which [they] would not sell the firm" (pp. 142–143). [126] The responses contain a number of simple strategic decision heuristics (e.g. sell when "[the] venture is in a transition stage" or when "the venture or the fund have matured") and financial decision rules (e.g. sell when "waiting would not raise the internal rate of return", "absolute and relative returns are compared to future expectations"); some venture capital firms appear to also require a minimum IRR or price, which can be "determined by a feeling" (Relander et al., 1994, p. 143). Wall and Smith (1997) conclude from 30 unstructured interviews with venture capital funds in 14 European countries that "most VCs [venture capitalists] view price, or their IRR, as the overriding factor determining their approach to exit" and that "where other factors were mentioned [by venture capitalists], it was often because of their impact on the IRR" (p. 7). Other studies underline the importance of returns: Survey data from Paffenholz (2004, pp. 157 and 219) suggest that many private equity firms view the maximisation of sale proceeds ("Maximierung der Verkaufserlöse") as the primary divestment objective; Loos (2006) concludes from an analysis of the average returns, deal sizes, and holding periods of just over 3,000 leveraged buyout transactions undertaken by 84 private equity firms that "buyout

[126] Relander, Syrjänen, and Miettinen (1994) do not specify sample sizes for individual questions, but make a general note that some venture capitalists did not respond to every question, or provided multiple responses (p. 139)

firms appear to be efficiently optimizing their exit strategy with respect to highest achievable average IRR" (p. 188).

A valuable contribution in this area was made by Cumming and MacIntosh (2001, 2003) who put forward a theoretical model of (efficient) venture capital investment duration. Based on the general assumption that the ability of the venture capital firm to add value to the portfolio company investment diminishes over the holding period, they postulate that, under idealised conditions (i.e. liquid exit markets, an infinite time-horizon etc.), "a VC [venture capitalist] will exit from an investment when the projected marginal value added, as a result of the VC's efforts [PMVA], at any given measurement interval, is less than the projected marginal cost [PMC] of those efforts" (Cumming & MacIntosh, 2001, p. 447).[127] Cumming and MacIntosh (2001) and Cumming and Johan (2010) use this theory and additional assumptions to develop hypotheses concerning the effects of various factors on venture capital investment duration. They present survey data from venture capital firms in the U.S and Canada, yielding statistically significant results for some of these factors (e.g. investment stage, industry sector, availability of capital, and the number of new investment opportunities). Povaly (2007) measures the importance that 50 buyout firms in Europe attribute to the cost of monitoring portfolio company investments. His results show that, among a choice of 9 factors possibly impacting the decision on exit time, factors *monitoring requirements* and *capacity of private equity managers* received the lowest mean importance rating from buyout firm respondents (p. 303); he concludes from this that the "'*value-add and monitoring cost*' concept" is not applicable to the European buyout industry (p. 306).

5.2.3 The decision on exit channel

Private equity firms can terminate their engagement in portfolio company investments in various ways, often referred to as *exit channels* or *exit routes*. Typical exit channels are an initial public offering (IPO), the sale of the portfolio company to a strategic acquirer (trade sale), the sale to another private equity firm (secondary sale), the sale of the portfolio company to its management (buy-back), and a write-off of the investment.[128] One branch of existing literature on private equity exits has conducted empirical studies of how the choice of exit channel is affected by characteristics of the portfolio company, the private equity firm, or the capital market environment. As in earlier research, many of these studies use theories and constructs from new institutional economics to predict or explain the choices of private equity firms.

[127] Cumming and MacIntosh (2003) define cost as "all the direct and overhead costs associated with creating value, as well as the opportunity cost associated with alternative deployments of capital" (pp. 109–110)

[128] Strictly speaking, a write-off only affects the company accounts and does not necessarily terminate a private equity firm's engagement in the portfolio company

Schwienbacher (2005), for example, uses an agency theory-based approach to predict (with mixed success) the effect of syndication and monitoring devices on the probabilities of various exit routes. Cumming and MacIntosh (2003) suppose that venture capital firms "generally choose the timing and form of exit that maximize the proceeds of exit" (p. 112). They use agency theory, asymmetric information, and Black and Gilson's (1998) implicit contract over control hypothesis to evaluate the influence of a wide range of factors on the exit channel preferences of venture capital firms (see Cumming & MacIntosh, 2003, Table 1, for a summary overview). From this they derive a general rank ordering of exit channels by venture capital preference and testable hypotheses regarding the effect of specific factors (the ratio of exit proceeds to investment cost, investment duration, and whether or not the portfolio company is a high-technology firm) on the rank ordering of exit channels; empirical tests of these hypotheses yielded varied results (see Cumming & MacIntosh, 2003, pp. 185–197). Other works in this area include Cumming and MacIntosh (2006), Nahata (2003), Sudarsanam (2005), and Povaly (2007, p. 312).

Another branch of existing research examines the decision problem by modelling the choice of exit channel, under consideration of varying aspects and assumptions. Aghion, Bolton and Tirole (2004), for example, model the optimal design of active monitors' exit options, considering their demand for liquidity and costs of monitoring. Bienz and Leite (2008) model the exit channel decision for venture capital firms in consideration of portfolio companies' profitability levels and their respective needs for oversight after the exit. Under the conditions of the model, venture capital firms maximise their returns by realising portfolio company investments in a defined pecking order of exit channels: Highly profitable companies with little need for oversight go public and less profitable companies with more need for oversight are sold in a trade sale. Bayar and Chemmanur (2011) model the choice for venture capital-backed portfolio companies between an IPO and a trade sale. They use their model to make predictions regarding the equilibrium choice between IPOs and trade sales, under consideration of a company's standing in product market competition, private benefits of control for the entrepreneur, potential synergies of the portfolio company with the acquiring firm, and a variance between IPOs and trade sales in the degree of information asymmetry and bargaining power between firm insiders and outside purchasers. Another related strand of research focuses on the role of convertible securities in the exit decision of venture capital firms (e.g. Arcot, 2005; Bascha & Walz, 2001; Berglöf, 1994; Hellmann, 2006).

5.3 Development of Research Focus and Hypotheses

5.3.1 Exit decision power

The exit is a crucial stage in the life cycle of a private equity investment. In practise, the decisions when and how to exit a portfolio company investment (i.e. the decisions on exit time and exit channel) can be led either by the private equity firm or by the portfolio company. Naturally, the two parties can disagree about the appropriate action (e.g. Bascha & Walz, 2001; Berglöf, 1994, pp. 247–248; Kaplan & Strömberg, 2004; Sahlman, 1990, p. 509).[129] For a better understanding of the exit decision it therefore appears useful to investigate the distribution of decision power between the private equity firm and portfolio company management. In general, private equity firms control portfolio companies (and their exits) through majority ownership positions (mostly buyout transactions), board representation and contractual arrangements (see, e.g. Sahlman, 1990, p. 509, or Fenn et al., 1997, p. 53, on board control; see, e.g. Lerner et al., 2005, pp. 288–295, on the securities used for venture investments and on covenant provisions). But there are a number of good arguments for private equity firms to share exit decision power with portfolio company managers: Firstly, company managers that are excluded from the exit decision could be less motivated or even uncooperative during the exit process — this could negatively affect the sale value of the company (see Povaly, 2007, pp. 276–278, on the importance of portfolio company management in the exit process). Secondly, private equity firms that ignore the exit preferences of their portfolio company managers might suffer reputational damage among entrepreneurs and managers of future investment opportunities — with possibly detrimental consequences to their access to deal-flow (Black & Gilson, 1998, p. 263).

One of the early contributions to private equity literature draws a connection between the distribution of exit decision power and the longevity of buyouts: Wright, Robbie, Thompson et

[129] This is apparent, for example, when considering the possible implications for company management of an IPO compared to those of a trade sale to a large competitor with sizeable business overlap

al. (1994) hypothesize that the distribution of decision power between portfolio company management, buyout institution, and the portfolio company influences the duration of buyouts (the decision power hypothesis). They contend that, for example, smaller buyouts should be associated with later exits because company managers of smaller buyouts should generally have larger equity holdings in the buyout and thus be in a better position "to continue to pursue an entrepreneurial career rather than exiting through a sale to a third party and becoming managerial employees again or retiring" (p. 218). Wright, Robbie, Thompson et al. derive support for their hypothesis from a sample of around two thousand UK management and employee buyouts that exited between 1981 and 1990. The data shows that, consistent with their expectations, in each year, buyouts with larger transaction values were significantly more likely to exit through IPO, trade sale, or secondary buyout than buyouts with smaller transaction values.[130] From the assumption of Wright, Robbie, Thompson et al. (1994) that managers of smaller buyouts should generally have larger equity holdings in the buyout and thus command more decision power in relation to the buyout firm, I develop the hypothesis that buyout firms with larger transaction sizes generally have more decision power in relation to their portfolio companies than buyout firms with smaller transaction sizes have (H4).

5.3.2 The decision on exit time

For the investment decision many private equity firms require that the expected rate of return of the proposed investment exceeds a defined minimum amount — modern portfolio theory and the capital asset pricing model do not appear to play a very important role (see Chapter 3 for more detail on minimum return requirements). Similarly, private equity firms also appear to employ simple rules of thumb for the exit decision. The empirical data points from previous studies (see the review of existing literature in Chapter 5.2.2) were used to formulate a set of

[130] Other scholars have put forward other explanations for this effect. Using a dataset obtained from "one of the largest institutional investors in private equity in the U.S.", Ljungqvist and Richardson (2003b) also find that larger investments are exited significantly faster than smaller ones. They argue that because "shorter holding periods imply higher IRRs, ceteris paribus, this suggests that PEF [private equity fund] managers focus their attention on those investments that have the largest impact on their fund returns" (p. 20)

(financial) decision rules for the survey questionnaire in this thesis; two additional decision rules for the survey questionnaire were prompted by the research of Cumming and MacIntosh (2001) and Tykvová (2003). Cumming and MacIntosh hypothesize that duration is shorter for earlier stage investments than it is for later stage investments because of early culling of poor investment projects ("the lemons ripen quickly, while the plums take time to mature"; Cumming & MacIntosh, 2001, p. 451); their data reveal statistically significant relationships between stage and duration for the sample of U.S. firms; their results for the Canadian sample are less supportive.[131] Tykvová (2003) develops a two-period model of the decision of venture capital firms on the timing and extent of IPOs; she finds that low-quality portfolio company investments are liquidated early (after the first period), whereas high-quality portfolio companies are taken public after the first or second period, depending on the consulting intensity of the project.[132] Based on these results, it is expected that private equity firms will more often choose to immediately begin the exit process for investments that are clearly underperforming than they will do for investments that are clearly performing (H5).

5.3.3 The decision on exit channel

Much of the existing research in this area has concentrated on how the choice of exit channel is affected by characteristics of the portfolio company, the private equity firm, or the capital market environment. This thesis takes a different approach in that it asks private equity firms directly what importance they attribute to criteria for deciding upon the exit channel of a portfolio company investment. Earlier studies have emphasized the importance of price for the exit channel decision (e.g. Cumming & MacIntosh, 2003; Relander et al., 1994, p. 141; Wall & Smith, 1997). Based on these results, it is expected that private equity firms view price as the most important criterion for deciding the exit channel of portfolio investments (H6).

5.4 Results and Discussion

5.4.1 The distribution of exit decision power between private equity firms and portfolio companies

Unlike most of the rating scales used in the survey questionnaire in this thesis, the rating scales that were used to record the distribution of decision power are bipolar, labelled, and unnumbered. The corresponding data analysis employs non-parametric statistical methods only, as these methods were deemed more appropriate for this data (see the introduction to this thesis for more detail on the statistical methods employed). An early screening revealed considerable

---

131 Cumming and MacIntosh (2001) attribute the weaker support from the Canadian data to institutional factors, such as legislation and the liquidity of secondary markets

132 A more recent empirical study by Schmidt, Steffen, and Szabó (2010) finds additional support for the supposed early culling of poor quality investments

differences in the response patterns of buyout firm respondents and venture capital firm respondents. Most of the analyses were therefore conducted separately for buyout firms and venture capital firms, and exclude eleven questionnaires from generalist or other type private equity firms (whose responses mostly lie between the mean ratings of buyout firms and venture capital firms).

Figure 11 shows that only few venture capital and buyout firms (correspondingly, less than 5% of all private equity firms in the survey sample; 95% CI [1.6%, 8.5%]) generally accept a junior position in relation to the portfolio company when deciding upon the appropriate time to begin an exit process.[133] This outcome is not surprising, considering the level of control rights that are typically held by private equity firms through ownership, board representation or contractual provisions. But the data also show that a sizeable percentage of venture capital and buyout firms (claim to) frequently share exit decision power with portfolio company management: Around one third of all private equity firms (95% CI [24.0%, 39.7%]) correspondingly state that they generally accept a joint lead position. The graph also shows a pronounced difference in the response patterns of venture capital and buyout firms: The distribution of responses from venture capital firms is skewed towards joint control, whereas the distribution of responses from buyout firms is skewed towards control by the private equity firm; Mann-Whitney U-tests are statistically significant ($U = 1{,}581$, $p < .0005$, two-tailed, $n_{VC} = 73$, $n_{BO} = 71$, mean $\text{rank}_{VC} = 86.3$, mean $\text{rank}_{BO} = 58.3$).

[133] Four respondents specified another party as general lead decision-maker under *other* in the questionnaire: Three of these respondents referred to a majority or lead investor and one buyout firm respondent specified the "Board of Directors"

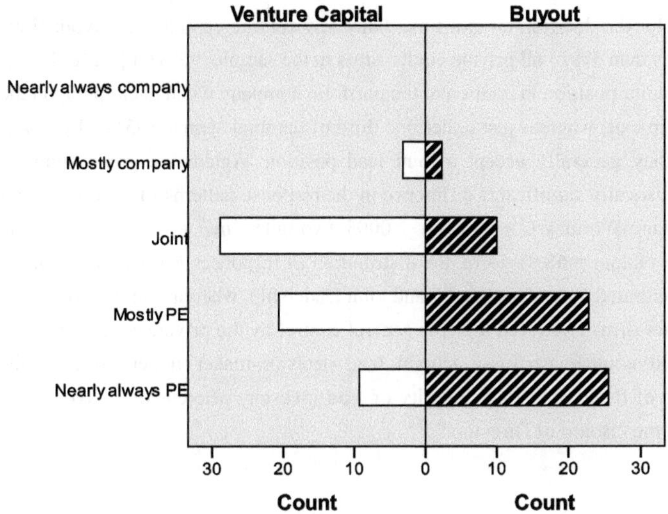

Figure 11. Distribution of decision power between the private equity firm (PE) and the portfolio company for the decision when to begin an exit process (n = 123). The categories on the y-axis represent the response items contained in the survey questionnaire; the double x-axis represents the number of survey responses by category for each firm type. *Venture capital* also includes eight firms of related firm types, such as "growth equity" and "business angel". *Buyout* also includes two firms of related firm types ("industry specific buyout" and "restructuring buyout"). All figures are based on country-weighted survey data. The weights reflect the ratio of a country's share of private equity firms in the frame population to its share of firms in the survey sample.

It was suggested earlier that there are sound reasons for private equity firms to involve portfolio company management in the exit decision: Their active involvement should help to ensure a smooth exit process and enhance a private equity firm's reputation among company managers and entrepreneurs — potential facilitators of future deal-flow. Accordingly, the observed differences between venture capital and buyout firms might be explained by differences in their respective gains from sharing exit decision power with the portfolio company. Buyout firms might, for example, be less concerned about the reputational effects of not involving company managers in the exit decision because they are not bound by implicit contracts over control as venture capital firms are supposed to be; in fact, Black and Gilson's discussion of implicit contracts over control expressly excludes buyout firms (Black & Gilson, 1998, p. 245). A venture capital firm that is known to disregard the exit preferences of its entrepreneurs might suffer reputational damage within the community of entrepreneurs and therefore have difficulties to attract high-quality investment opportunities (Black & Gilson, 1998, p. 263); this regulating effect of reputation can be assumed to be less functional in buyout markets, where target companies are larger and ownership is often separated from management.

Figure 12 relates to the exit channel decision and shows a pattern of responses that is very similar to the graph for the decision on exit time. Only few venture capital and buyout firms (correspondingly, less than 5% of all private equity firms in the sample; 95% CI [1.2%, 7.5%]) generally assume a junior position in relation to the portfolio company when deciding upon the appropriate channel to exit, whereas just under one third of the total sample (95% CI [21.4%, 36.6%]) state that they generally accept a joint lead position. Again, the graph shows a pronounced (and statistically significant) difference in the response patterns of venture capital and buyout firms (Mann-Whitney $U = 1{,}624$, $p < .0005$, two-tailed, $n_{VC} = 73$, $n_{BO} = 71$, mean $rank_{VC} = 85.8$, mean $rank_{BO} = 58.9$). Here, the distribution of responses from venture capital firms is largely concentrated around *mostly PE* and joint leadership, whereas the distribution of responses from buyout firms is skewed towards general control by the private equity firm. Six respondents specified another party as general lead decision-maker under *other* in the questionnaire: Three of these refer to a majority or lead investor, whereas one buyout firm respondent specified the "Board of Directors".[134]

[134] Other responses are "consortium" and "with advisers"

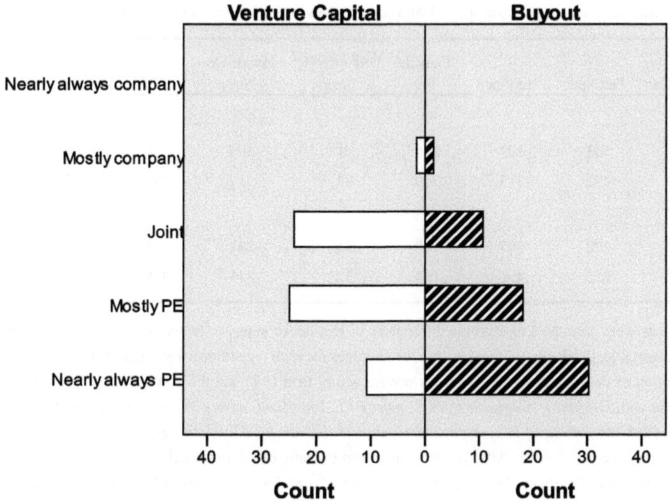

Figure 12. Distribution of decision power between the private equity firm (PE) and the portfolio company for the exit channel decision (n = 123). The categories on the y-axis represent the response items contained in the survey questionnaire; the double x-axis represents the number of survey responses by category for each firm type. *Venture capital* also includes eight firms of related firm types, such as "growth equity" and "business angel". *Buyout* also includes two firms of related firm types ("industry specific buyout" and "restructuring buyout"). All figures are based on country-weighted survey data. The weights reflect the ratio of a country's share of private equity firms in the frame population to its share of firms in the survey sample.

5.4.2 The influence of firm characteristics on the evaluation of exit decision power

The results of the Mann-Whitney *U*-tests presented in Table 32 show significant results for the industry specialisation variable (venture capital firms only) and for the management style variable (buyout firms only). The higher level of control exerted by buyout firms that employ a hands-on management style is coherently reflected in the significantly increased decision power of these buyout firms compared to buyout firms that employ a supportive management style. Implicit contracts over control could explain the absence of such an effect in the sample of venture capital firms.

Table 32

Connections between firm characteristics (dichotomous variables) and respondents' ratings of exit decision power

Decision	EU - US/Can	GeoSpec	IndSpec	Outside Inv	Well/Under - Loss[a]	Hands On - Supp	CEF
Venture Capital							
Exit time	353	503	322 *	386	91	506	360
Exit channel	377	492	315 **	390	82	517	349
Buyout							
Exit time	405	492	607	118	26	231 ***	406
Exit channel	385	452	495	164	32	313 ***	389

Note. Mann-Whitney *U*-tests were employed to examine differences in exit decision power between the two subsamples of each dichotomous column variable; the displayed numbers are the *U*-values for each type of decision and subsample of private equity firms. The distribution of decision power between the private equity firm (PE) and the portfolio company (PC) was recorded on a bipolar scale with five steps: *nearly always PE, mostly PE, joint lead, mostly PC, nearly always PC*; for the analysis these steps were coded into numbers 5 to 1, respectively (*exit decision power*). All figures, except those relating to EU - US/Can, are based on country-weighted survey data. The weights reflect the ratio of a country's share of private equity firms in the frame population to its share of firms in the survey sample. *Venture capital* also includes eight firms of related types, such as "growth equity" and "business angel". *Buyout* also includes two firms of related types ("industry specific buyout" and "restructuring buyout"). *Exit time* relates to the decision when to begin an exit process for an investment; *exit channel* relates to the decision how to exit an investment. EU - US/Can denotes headquarter location: EU = Europe; US/Can = United States of America or Canada. GeoSpec refers to firms, for which respondents specified whether or not they specialise in geographical areas. IndSpec refers to firms, for which respondents specified whether or not they specialise in industry sectors. Outside Inv refers to whether or not respondents specified that their firm sources the majority of its fund capital from outside investors. Well/Under - Loss refers to the preferred performance of target companies: Well/Under ="well-performing" or "underperforming"; Loss = "loss-making". Hands On - Supp denotes management style: Hands on = "hands-on"; Supp = "supportive". CEF refers to firms, for which respondents specified whether or not they mostly manage investments in (closed-end) funds with a fixed lifetime.

$^{*}p < .10$. $^{**}p < .05$. $^{***}p < .01$. All *p*s are two-tailed and calculated using the exact test; in each test, *n* exceeded 10 for each subsample unless otherwise noted.

[a]One of the subsamples contained less than 10 data points.

The results of the Spearman rank correlation tests presented in Table 33 show statistically significant associations almost exclusively for the sample of venture capital firm respondents. In this subsample, exit decision power is significantly positively associated with Age, Funds, and Capital. These results could signify the presence of a mechanism similar to Gompers's (1996) grandstanding hypothesis: Younger (and smaller) venture capital firms might share more exit decision power with portfolio company management than older venture capital firms in order to build a reputation among entrepreneurs.

Table 33

Spearman rank correlations between firm characteristics (ordinal scale and continuous variables) and respondents' ratings of exit decision power

Decision	Age (yrs)	Funds	Capital (€m)	Investments	Investment Size (€m)
Venture Capital					
Exit time	.29 **	.30 **	.17	-.12	.04
Exit channel	.35 ***	.53 ***	.38 ***	-.03	.16
Buyout					
Exit time	-.14	-.15	.24 *	-.12	.09
Exit channel	.00	-.06	.20	-.06	.06

Note. The distribution of decision power between the private equity firm (PE) and the portfolio company (PC) was recorded on a bipolar scale with five steps: *nearly always PE, mostly PE, joint lead, mostly PC, nearly always PC*; for the analysis these steps were coded into numbers 5 to 1, respectively (*exit decision power*). Correlations were tested pairwise, using country-weighted data. Weighted n ranges between 64 and 73. The weights reflect the ratio of a country's share of private equity firms in the frame population to its share of firms in the survey sample. A positive correlation coefficient signifies an increase in decision power of the PE in relation to the PC as the value of the firm characteristic variable increases. *Venture capital* also includes eight firms of related firm types, such as "growth equity" and "business angel". *Buyout* also includes two firms of related firm types ("industry specific buyout" and "restructuring buyout"). *Exit time* relates to the decision when to begin an exit process for an investment; *exit channel* relates to the decision how to exit an investment. Age is the number of years a respondent's firm has been in existence. Funds is the number of private equity funds a respondent's firm has raised. Capital is the rough total capital under management of a respondent's firm in € millions. Investments is the rough number of company investments managed by a respondent's firm. Investment Size is a respondent firm's rough typical investment size (equity stake) in € millions. Range specifications were replaced by their means, and amounts in other currencies were converted to € amounts using the averages of market exchange rates over the time of the survey.

$^{*}p < .10$. $^{**}p < .05$. $^{***}p < .01$. All ps are two-tailed.

It was hypothesized that buyout firms with larger transaction sizes generally have more decision power in relation to their portfolio companies than buyout firms with smaller transaction sizes have (H4). Consistent with this hypothesis, the Spearman rank correlations in Table 33 show that the decision power of private equity firms in the sample tended to increase with their investment size, albeit very slightly. But these effects are not statistically significant (alpha = .05, one-tailed). Additional Mann-Whitney U-tests also did not yield statistically significant differences in the decision power ratings of buyout firms with larger transaction sizes (i.e. buyout firms with typical investment sizes greater than the median typical investment size of the entire sample of buyout firms) and buyout firms with smaller transaction sizes (i.e. buyout firms with typical investment sizes smaller than, or equal to the median typical investment size of the entire sample of buyout firms) (exit time: $U = 495$, $p = .101$, one-tailed, $n_1 = 33$, $n_2 = 36$; exit channel: $U = 552$, $p = .101$, one-tailed, $n_1 = 33$, $n_2 = 36$). A post-hoc power analysis of the corresponding parametric test (independent samples t-test) in approximation of a power analysis for the Mann-Whitney U-test shows that, based on a minimum required statistical power of .80 and an alpha level of .05 (one-tailed), the corresponding parametric tests would have been sensitive enough to detect medium effect sizes ($d > 0.6$). Subject to the limitations of the analysis (moderate sensitivity of statistical tests, no multivariate statistical analysis), it is concluded that the results do not support the hypothesis developed from the assumptions of Wright, Robbie, Thompson et al. (1994) that buyout firms with larger transaction sizes generally have more decision power in relation to their portfolio companies than buyout firms with smaller transaction sizes have.

5.4.3 The usage of decision rules for initiating an exit process

Figure 13 shows the usage of decision rules for choosing when to begin the exit processes of performing investments and underperforming investments. All means lie within a comparatively tight range around the midpoint of the rating scale and all 95% confidence intervals are narrower than the smallest interval of the rating scale. Additional analysis revealed that 93.0% (76.1%) of all survey respondents attributed a frequency rating of 3 or higher (on a scale with five numbered steps ranging from 5 [*very often*] to 1 [*never*]) to at least two (three) decision rules for performing investments; correspondingly, 83.6% (65.3%) of all survey respondents attributed such a frequency rating to at least two (three) decision rules for underperforming investments.[135] These results suggest that all the decision rules specified in the questionnaire are — to varying degrees — employed by the underlying population of private equity firms for deciding upon the time to initiate the exit process for an investment. Although no single rule appears to dominate the choice, two structurally equivalent decision heuristics (no major increase of price or multiple expected; no major increase of IRR expected) generated higher mean frequency ratings than any other rule, both for performing investments as well as for underperforming investments. This is of particular interest, because these heuristics can under certain conditions deliver the same results as a policy of maximising net present value — for example, if the value increase of the investment is expected to decline over the holding period and the rate of the expected major increase in price (net of any additional cost) reflects the investment's opportunity cost of capital (see Appendix J for an analytical illustration of this). Under these assumptions, the decision heuristics are also largely comparable to Cumming and MacIntosh's (2001, p. 447) postulation that "a VC [venture capitalist] will exit from an investment when the projected marginal value added, as a result of the VC's efforts [PMVA], at any given measurement interval, is less than the projected marginal cost [PMC] of those efforts".

[135] For the purpose of this analysis, structurally equivalent rules, that is, rules that differentiate only in the metric used, were treated as a single rule

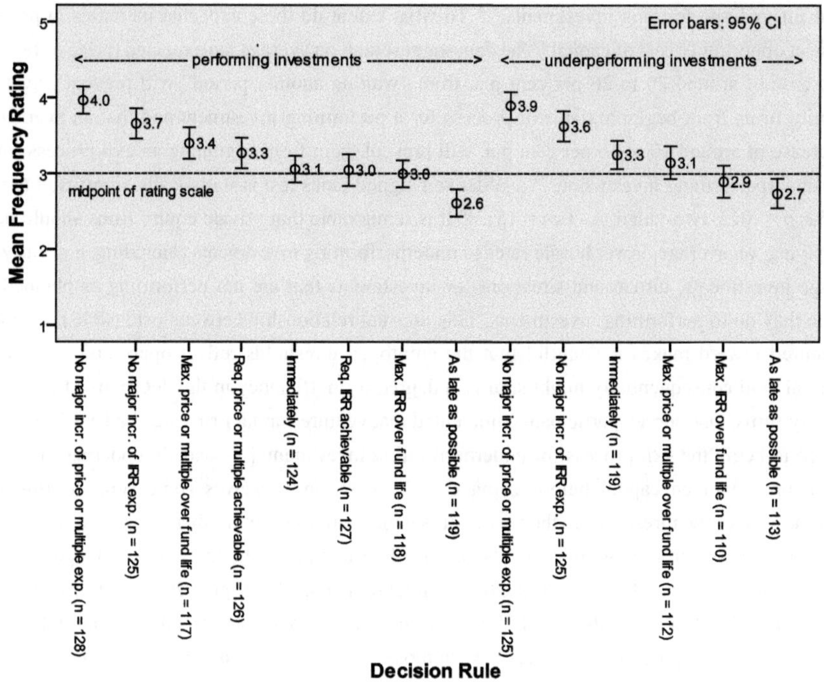

Figure 13. Usage of decision rules for initiating the exit processes of performing investments and underperforming investments. Frequencies of usage were measured on numbered 5-point rating scales, ranging from 5 (*very often*) to 1 (*never*). Two decision heuristics that refer to required levels of return were measured for performing investments only. CI = confidence interval. Req. = required. Incr. = increase. Exp. = expected. IRR = internal rate of return. Max. = maximum. All figures are based on country-weighted survey data. The weights reflect the ratio of a country's share of private equity firms in the frame population to its share of firms in the survey sample.

Table 34 shows a summary of respondents' reports concerning the expected *major increase* of price or IRR that causes them to delay beginning an exit process for performing investments and for underperforming investments.[136] To what extent do these expected increases in price reflect opportunity cost of capital? The data suggest that, on average, an expected (price or IRR) increase of around 20 to 26 per cent p.a. from "waiting another period" will prevent private equity firms from beginning an exit process for a performing investment and that an average increase of around 10 to 16 per cent p.a. will prevent them from beginning an exit process for an underperforming investment;[137] a Wilcoxon signed ranks test is statistically significant (z = 2.52, p = .012, two-tailed, n - ties = 15).[138] It is remarkable that private equity firms should be applying, on average, lower hurdle rates to underperforming investments (including, e.g. early-stage investments, turnaround situations, or investments that are not performing as planned) than they do to performing investments. This unusual relationship between ostensible risk and required reward makes it doubtful that the employed thresholds reflect opportunity cost of capital, and consequentially might signify a degree of inefficiency in the decisions of private equity firms. One survey participant commented that venture capital firms are "bad at [deciding when to begin the exit process for underperforming investments] — usually underperformers suck up too much capital before going down". This view receives some support from a comparison of the thresholds in the survey data with the rates of return that private equity firms typically require from new investments, as specified in existing literature (e.g. Elango et al., 1995; Manigart et al., 2002, pp. 300–302; Ruhnka & Young, 1991, pp. 120–127; Vater, 2003, pp. 124–125): While, the thresholds for performing investments are broadly in line with the reported return requirements (especially with those for later stage and buyout investments), the figures for underperforming investments are considerably lower than most of the reported return requirements for new investments.

---

136 A breakdown of responses within the two types of investment categories by firm type (venture capital and buyout) is not presented here as no substantial differences were apparent

137 Some caution is required here as the units of the underlying amounts (i.e. percentages or percentage-points) were not clearly specified

138 A corresponding parametric test was not significant at alpha = .05, two-tailed. This outcome does not stand in conflict with the result of the non-parametric test as the data do not meet the normality assumption of the parametric test and the valid sample size was smaller than 30

Table 34

Thresholds for delaying the begin of an exit process

Category	Metric	*n*	*Mdn*	*M*	95% CI of *M* LB	95% CI of *M* UB	*SD*
Performing investments	price	25	20	32.2	20.3	44.1	28.6
	IRR	10	20	18.5	11.3	25.6	10.2
	none	6	6	10.5	1.1	19.9	8.9
	All performing	41	20	25.6	17.9	33.3	24.4
Underperforming investments	price	15	15	16.1	9.3	23.0	12.5
	IRR	10	17	17.2	10.2	24.1	9.7
	none	6	10	11.4	3.7	19.1	7.3
	All underperforming	31	10	15.6	11.6	19.5	10.7

Note. The statistics summarise respondents' specifications regarding the expected *major increase* of price or IRR p.a. that causes them to delay beginning an exit process for performing investments and for underperforming investments. LB = lower boundary. UB = upper boundary. Two data points for underperforming investments (0 and -10) were excluded from the analysis. Some caution in the interpretation is required as the units of the underlying amounts (i.e. percentages or percentage-points) were not clearly specified. All figures are based on country-weighted survey data. The weights reflect the ratio of a country's share of private equity firms in the frame population to its share of firms in the survey sample.

It was hypothesized that private equity firms will more often choose to immediately begin the exit process for investments that are clearly underperforming than they will do for investments that are clearly performing (H5). The survey data are largely supportive of this hypothesis, but the size of effect is small. Figure 13 shows that, as predicted, the strategy to begin the exit process immediately generated a higher mean frequency rating for underperforming investments than for performing investments, and a paired samples test is statistically significant ($n = 118$, $t = -1.9$, $df = 117$, $p = .031$, one-tailed, $d = -0.21$).[139] Further analysis shows that the hypothesized effect is not statistically significant within the sample of buyout firm respondents alone ($n = 54$, $t = -1.1$, $df = 53$, $p = .148$, one-tailed, $d = -0.19$). But this does not contradict the support for Hypothesis 5: A two-way mixed analysis of variance with the frequency rating of the decision rule to begin an exit process immediately as dependent variable, the performance condition (performing or underperforming) as a within-subjects factor, and firm type (buyout or venture capital) as a between-subjects factor yields a statistically significant main effect of performance, $F(1, 125) = 5.75$, $p = .018$, partial $\eta^2 = .04$, whereas the interaction effect of performance and firm type is statistically non-significant, $F(1, 125) = 0.10$, $p = .751$, partial $\eta^2 < .005$.

[139] Non-parametric Wilcoxon Tests yielded results comparable to the presented parametric results

Additional exploratory analyses suggest that buyout firms tend towards an opposing, delaying strategy for their underperforming investments: Figure 13 shows that the decision rule to begin the exit process as late as possible yielded the lowest mean frequency ratings, overall (possibly induced by the unwelcome prospect of having to conduct "fire-sales" at the end of a fund's lifetime). But within the sample of buyout firm respondents (and not within the sample of venture capital firm respondents), the decision heuristic to begin the exit process as late as possible generated a significantly higher mean frequency rating for underperforming investments than for performing investments ($n = 51$, $t = -3.2$, $df = 50$, $p = .002$, two-tailed, $d = -0.46$); the size of effect is medium to large. This result remains unchanged when investigating the effects of firm type and the performance condition in combination: A two-way mixed analysis of variance with the frequency rating of the decision rule to begin as late as possible as dependent variable, the performance condition (performing or underperforming) as a within-subjects factor and firm type (buyout or venture capital) as a between-subjects factor yields a statistically non-significant main effect of investment performance, $F(1, 114) = 0.60$, $p = .441$, partial $\eta^2 = .01$, whereas the interaction effect of investment performance and firm type is statistically significant, $F(1, 114) = 13.35$, $p < .0005$, partial $\eta^2 = .11$. These results might be explained by the differing business models of buyout firms and venture capital firms: As buyout firms typically hold fewer, but larger investments, the termination of a single poor quality investment project has a greater relative impact on overall fund performance; buyout firms could therefore be more inclined to delay beginning the exit process for their underperforming investments in order to have more opportunity to actively enhance the value of these investments or benefit from an unexpected improvement of market conditions.

Last, a number of respondents made specifications under *other* in the survey questionnaire. Some of these responses suggest that the exit timing is also dependent on the availability of an exit opportunity (e.g. "[begin the exit process] when exit opportunities aris[e]" or "when there is competition for the asset"). Evidently, the ability of private equity firms to sell a company investment, at any given point in time, at its (supposed) fair market value cannot generally be taken for granted. This increases the complexity of making optimal exit decisions because private equity firms cannot rely on the future liquidity of exit markets in their calculations. Other responses suggest that judgement and intuition play an important role for deciding when to begin the exit process for underperforming investments (e.g. "[begin the exit process] when you feel you can generate acceptable value" or "if we do not believe we can improve"). This could imply that the decision problem for underperforming investments is viewed as too complex for the application of standard decision rules. This interpretation ties in with the observation that the mean frequency rating of the rather more ambitious decision strategy of attempting to realise the maximum price or multiple over the lifetime of the fund is significantly lower for underperforming investments than for performing investments ($n = 109$, $t = 2.5$, $df = 108$, $p = .013$, two-tailed, $d = -0.26$).

5.4.4 The influence of firm characteristics and exit decision power on the evaluation of decision rules for initiating an exit process

5.4.4.1 Decision rules for performing investments

As regards performing investments, Table 35 exhibits two effects that are particularly noteworthy: Firstly, respondents from private equity firms located in Europe attributed significantly higher frequency ratings to the decision rules involving a required price or return (i.e. begin the exit process as soon as a required price or multiple is expected to be achieved, or, as soon as a required IRR is expected to be achieved) than respondents from private equity firms located in the United States of America and Canada. This result possibly signifies more rigid internal regulations on return requirements in private equity firms in Europe compared to those in the United States of America and Canada, or in other words, private equity managers in Europe might have less freedom to decide upon the appropriate exit time than their counterparts in the United States of America and Canada. Secondly, respondents from private equity firms with an industry specialisation strategy attached significantly higher frequency ratings to the decision rules that aim to maximise price or return over the lifetime of the fund. This suggests that industry-specialised private equity firms are more confident in their ability to time exits optimally over their fund lifetimes — which is possibly justified by their specialised knowledge of the industry.

Table 35

Connections between firm characteristics (dichotomous variables) and respondents' usage of decision rules for initiating the exit processes of performing investments

Decision rule	EU - US/Can	BO - VC	GeoSpec	IndSpec	Outside Inv[a]	Well/Under - Loss[a]	Hands On - Supp	CEF[a]
Immediately	0.25	-0.32 $^{*+}$	0.06	-0.09	-0.37 $^{++}$	0.09	-0.10	0.38 *
As late as possible	-0.32 $^{*+}$	-0.33 $^{*+}$	-0.14	0.14	-0.40	-0.29	0.11	-0.44 $^{**b++}$
Req. price or multiple achievable	0.54 $^{***+++}$	0.29 $^{++}$	0.05	0.17	0.20	-0.32	0.55 $^{***+++}$	0.26 $^{+}$
Req. IRR achievable	0.41 $^{**b++}$	0.26	0.20	0.14	-0.09	0.62	0.29 $^{+}$	-0.22
No major incr. of price or multiple exp.	0.07	0.33 ^{*b}	-0.03	-0.04	-0.31	0.48	-0.07	0.10
No major incr. of IRR exp.	0.13	0.13	-0.01	-0.21	-0.24	1.31 $^{***++}$	-0.26	-0.22
Max. price or multiple over fund life	-0.07	0.01	-0.07	0.48 $^{**++}$	-0.15	0.10	0.29	0.03
Max. IRR over fund life	-0.03	-0.09	-0.06	0.62 $^{***+++}$	-0.29	0.61	0.39 $^{*+}$	-0.27 $^{+}$

Note. The figures denote effect sizes (Cohen's *d*), which are calculated by dividing the differences in mean frequency ratings of the two subsamples of a dichotomous column variable by the pooled standard deviation. Frequencies of usage were measured on numbered 5-point rating scales, ranging from 5 (*very often*) to 1 (*never*). All figures, except those relating to EU - US/Can, are based on country-weighted survey data. The weights reflect the ratio of a country's share of private equity firms in the frame population to its share of firms in the survey sample. EU - US/Can denotes headquarter location: EU = Europe; US/Can = United States of America or Canada. BO - VC denotes firm type: BO = buyout; VC = venture capital; VC includes eight firms of related types, such as "growth equity" and "business angel"; BO includes two firms of related types ("industry specific buyout" and "restructuring buyout"). GeoSpec refers to firms, for which respondents specified whether or not they specialise in geographical areas. IndSpec refers to firms, for which respondents specified whether or not they specialise in industry sectors. Outside Inv refers to whether or not respondents specified that their firm sources the majority of its fund capital from outside investors. Well/Under - Loss refers to the preferred performance of target companies: Well/Under ="well-performing" or "underperforming"; Loss = "loss-making". Hands On - Supp denotes management style: Hands on = "hands-on"; Supp = "supportive". CEF refers to firms, for which respondents specified whether or not they mostly manage investments in (closed-end) funds with a fixed lifetime. Req. = required. Incr. = increase. Exp. = expected. IRR = internal rate of return. Max. = maximum.

$^{*}p < .10$. $^{**}p < .05$. $^{***}p < .01$. All *p*s are two-tailed and relate to independent samples *t*-tests for equality of means; in each case *df* (pairwise) ranges between 93 and 126. ^{+}p, ^{++}p, and ^{+++}p denote respective significance levels for the Mann-Whitney *U*-test.

[a]One of the subsamples has a data count of less than 30.

[b]Equal variances not assumed.

The results of the Spearman rank correlation tests between ordinal scale or continuous firm characteristic variables and respondents' frequency ratings of exit strategies are presented in Table 36. The strongest significant effects ($p < .05$, two-tailed) are associated with the characteristics Capital and Investment Size.

Table 36

Spearman rank correlations between firm characteristics (ordinal scale and continuous variables) and respondents' usage of decision rules for initiating the exit processes of performing investments

Decision rule	Age (yrs)	Funds	Capital (€m)	Investments	Investment Size (€m)
Immediately	.03	.15 (*)	-.20 **	-.08	-.29 ***
As late as possible	-.07	-.17 *	-.18 *	-.05	-.10
Req. Price or multiple achievable	-.06	-.09	-.17 **	-.10	.04
Req. IRR achievable	-.06	-.01	-.16 *	-.11	.03
No major incr. of price or multiple exp.	.06	.03	.11	.12	.03
No major incr. of IRR exp.	-.03	.02	.05	.13	-.04
Max. price or multiple over fund life	-.07	-.10	-.08	.00	.04
Max. IRR over fund life	-.16 *	-.11	-.08	-.03	.01

Note. Frequencies of usage were measured on numbered 5-point rating scales, ranging from 5 (*very often*) to 1 (*never*). Correlations were tested pairwise, using country-weighted data. Weighted n ranges between 124 and 148. The weights reflect the ratio of a country's share of private equity firms in the frame population to its share of firms in the survey sample. Age is the number of years a respondent's firm has been in existence. Funds is the number of private equity funds a respondent's firm has raised. Capital is the rough total capital under management of a respondent's firm in € millions. Investments is the rough number of company investments managed by a respondent's firm. Investment Size is a respondent firm's rough typical investment size (equity stake) in € millions. Range specifications were replaced by their means, and amounts in other currencies were converted to € amounts using the averages of market exchange rates over the time of the survey. Req. = required. Incr. = increase. Exp. = expected. IRR = internal rate of return. Max. = maximum.

$^{*}p < .10$. $^{**}p < .05$. $^{***}p < .01$. All ps are two-tailed. Parentheses denote that the respective Spearman rank correlations within the buyout and venture capital subsamples were not significant at alpha = .10.

5.4.4.2 Decision rules for underperforming investments

As regards underperforming investments, the results shown in Table 37 corroborate the earlier observation of differences between buyout firms and venture capital firms in the early culling of poor quality investments as well as in the delaying of exit processes for such investments: Compared to respondents from venture capital firms, respondents from buyout firms attached significantly lower frequency ratings to the strategy to begin the exit process immediately, and significantly higher frequency ratings to the strategy to begin the exit process as late as possible; effect sizes are medium to large.[140]

[140] It should be noted that such differences also occurred between respondents from private equity firms that specialise in geographic areas and those that do not specialise in geographic areas — no plausible explanation was identified for these results

Table 37

Connections between firm characteristics (dichotomous variables) and respondents' usage of decision rules for initiating the exit processes of underperforming investments

Decision rule	EU - US/Can	BO - VC	GeoSpec	IndSpec	Outside Inv[a]	Well/Under - Loss[a]	Hands On - Supp	CEF[a]
Immediately	-0.31 *	-0.46 $^{**++}$	-0.38 $^{*++}$	0.24	-0.26	-0.21	-0.27 $^{+}$	0.23
As late as possible	0.27	0.46 $^{**+++}$	0.84 $^{***+++}$	-0.06	0.20	0.27	0.05	-0.38 $^{*++}$
No major incr. of price or multiple exp.	0.02	0.26	-0.33 $^{*+}$	-0.07	0.40 $^{++}$	1.03 **	-0.43 $^{**++}$	0.68 $^{***+++}$
No major incr. of IRR exp.	0.01	0.12	-0.11	-0.07	0.33 $^{++}$	1.08 $^{***++}$	-0.50 $^{**+++}$	0.29 $^{+}$
Max. price or multiple over fund life	0.09	0.42 $^{**++}$	-0.34 $^{*+}$	-0.08	0.38 $^{+}$	0.65 $^{+}$	0.13	0.45 $^{**++}$
Max. IRR over fund life	0.02	0.22	-0.11	0.18	0.28	0.62 $^{++}$	0.08	0.21

Note. The figures denote effect sizes (Cohen's *d*), which are calculated by dividing the differences in mean frequency ratings of the two subsamples of a dichotomous column variable by the pooled standard deviation. Frequencies of usage were measured on numbered 5-point rating scales, ranging from 5 (*very often*) to 1 (*never*). All figures, except those relating to EU - US/Can, are based on country-weighted survey data. The weights reflect the ratio of a country's share of private equity firms in the frame population to its share of firms in the survey sample. EU - US/Can denotes headquarter location: EU = Europe; US/Can = United States of America or Canada. BO - VC denotes firm type: BO = buyout; VC = venture capital; VC includes eight firms of related types, such as "growth equity" and "business angel"; BO includes two firms of related types ("industry specific buyout" and "restructuring buyout"). GeoSpec refers to firms, for which respondents specified whether or not they specialise in geographical areas. IndSpec refers to firms, for which respondents specified whether or not they specialise in industry sectors. Outside Inv refers to whether or not respondents specified that their firm sources the majority of its fund capital from outside investors. Well/Under - Loss refers to the preferred performance of target companies: Well/Under ="well-performing" or "underperforming"; Loss = "loss-making". Hands On - Supp denotes management style: Hands on = "hands-on"; Supp = "supportive". CEF refers to firms, for which respondents specified whether or not they mostly manage investments in (closed-end) funds with a fixed lifetime. Incr. = increase. Exp. = expected. IRR = internal rate of return. Max. = maximum.
$^{*}p < .10$. $^{**}p < .05$. $^{***}p < .01$. All *p*s are two-tailed and relate to independent samples *t*-tests for equality of means; in each case *df* (pairwise) ranges between 89 and 123. ^{+}p, ^{++}p, and ^{+++}p denote respective significance levels for the Mann-Whitney *U*-test.
[a]One of the subsamples has a data count of less than 30.

The results of the Spearman rank correlation tests between ordinal scale or continuous firm characteristic variables and respondents' frequency ratings of exit strategies are presented in Table 38. It seems that all correlation coefficients for the rather more ambitious decision rules that aim to maximise price or return over the lifetime of the fund are negative, whereas many correlation coefficients for more simple decision rules are positive; eight of these relationships are statistically significant (alpha = .05, two-tailed): It appears that, with increasing age, experience, and size, private equity firms more frequently employ the simple decision heuristics, and less frequently employ the more ambitious decision rules, for underperforming investments.

Table 38

Spearman rank correlations between firm characteristics (ordinal scale and continuous variables) and respondents' usage of decision rules for initiating the exit processes of underperforming investments

Decision rule	Age (yrs)	Funds	Capital (€m)	Investments	Investment Size (€m)
Immediately	.05	.14	-.02	.20 **	-.19 (**)
As late as possible	-.02	.04	.09	-.13	.26 ***
No major incr. of price or multiple exp.	.16 (*)	.18 (**)	.28 ***	.28 ***	.09
No major incr. of IRR exp.	.06	.17 (*)	.22 **	.24 ***	.06
Max. price or multiple over fund life	-.13	-.11	-.18 **	-.21 **	-.07
Max. IRR over fund life	-.11	-.01	-.06	-.08	-.01

Note. Frequencies of usage were measured on numbered 5-point rating scales, ranging from 5 (*very often*) to 1 (*never*). Correlations were tested pairwise, using country-weighted data. Weighted *n* ranges between 117 and 144. The weights reflect the ratio of a country's share of private equity firms in the frame population to its share of firms in the survey sample. Age is the number of years a respondent's firm has been in existence. Funds is the number of private equity funds a respondent's firm has raised. Capital is the rough total capital under management of a respondent's firm in € millions. Investments is the rough number of company investments managed by a respondent's firm. Investment Size is a respondent firm's rough typical investment size (equity stake) in € millions. Range specifications were replaced by their means, and amounts in other currencies were converted to € amounts using the averages of market exchange rates over the time of the survey. Incr. = increase. Exp. = expected. IRR = internal rate of return. Max. = maximum.

*$p < .10$. **$p < .05$. ***$p < .01$. All *p*s are two-tailed. Parentheses denote that the respective Spearman rank correlations within the buyout and venture capital subsamples were not significant at alpha = .10.

5.4.4.3 The influence of decision power on the evaluation of decision rules

The data presented in Table 39 show that the distribution of exit decision power between the private equity firm and the portfolio company has only a limited influence on private equity firms' evaluations of exit decision rules. The strongest effects ($p < .05$, two-tailed, $d > 0.30$) are associated with the decision rule to begin the exit process immediately. From the direction of effects it appears that the evaluation of this strategy by buyout firms that tend to hold less exit timing decision power than other buyout firms more closely resembles the evaluation of venture capital firms, and vice versa.

Table 39

Spearman rank correlations between the extent of decision power held by the private equity firm and its usage of exit decision rules

	Exit decision power of private equity firm			
	Performing investments		Underperforming investments	
Decision rule	BO	VC	BO	VC
Immediately	-.23 *	.35 ***	-.46 ***	.21
As late as possible	.03	-.05	.21 *	.18
Req. Price or multiple achievable	-.16	.15	.	.
Req. IRR achievable	-.25 **	.16	.	.
No major incr. of price or multiple exp.	.20 *	-.15	.22 *	-.07
No major incr. of IRR exp.	.17	.12	-.01	.06
Max. price or multiple over fund life	.28 **	-.05	.20	-.11
Max. IRR over fund life	.02	.14	-.07	-.08

Note. The distribution of decision power between the private equity firm (PE) and the portfolio company (PC) regarding the decision when to begin an exit process for an investment was recorded on a bipolar scale with five steps: *nearly always PE, mostly PE, joint lead, mostly PC, nearly always PC*; for the analysis these steps were coded into numbers 5 to 1, respectively (*exit decision power*). Frequencies of usage of exit decision rules were measured on numbered 5-point rating scales, ranging from 5 (*very often*) to 1 (*never*). Correlations were tested pairwise, using country-weighted data. Weighted *n* ranges between 57 and 70. The weights reflect the ratio of a country's share of private equity firms in the frame population to its share of firms in the survey sample. *Venture Capital* (VC) also includes eight firms of related firm types, such as "growth equity" and "business angel". *Buyout* (BO) also includes two firms of related firm types ("industry specific buyout" and "restructuring buyout"). Incr. = increase. Exp. = expected. IRR = internal rate of return. Max. = maximum.
$^{*}p < .10$. $^{**}p < .05$. $^{***}p < .01$. All *ps* are two-tailed.

5.4.5 The importance of criteria for the exit channel decision

The results presented in Figure 14 show that private equity firms generally attach importance to a broad range of criteria when deciding on the exit channel for a portfolio company investment: 8 of the 10 factors queried in the survey generated mean importance ratings with 95% confidence intervals above the midpoint of the rating scale; further analysis revealed that 71.7% of all survey respondents attributed an importance rating of 3 or higher (on a scale with five numbered steps ranging from 5 [*very important*] to 1 [*not important*]) to eight factors, or more.

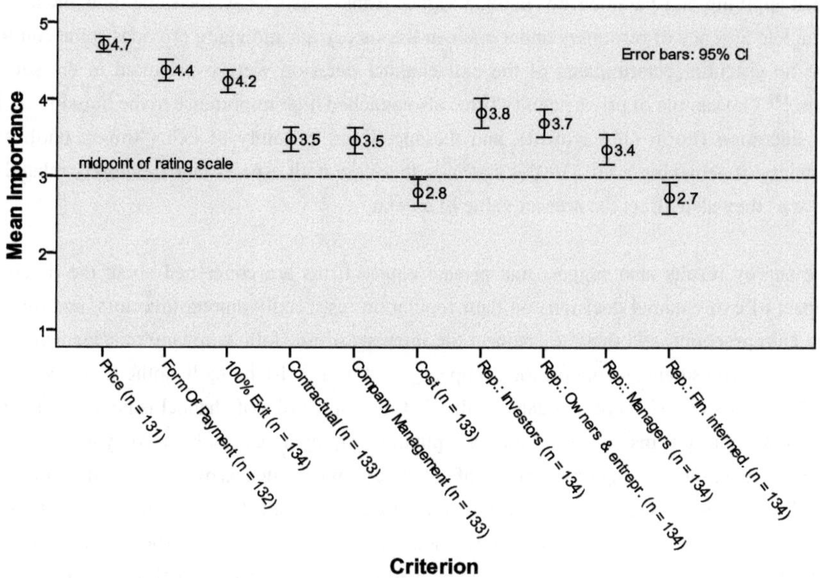

Figure 14. Importance of criteria for deciding which exit channel to choose for a company investment. Importance ratings were measured on numbered 5-point scales, ranging from 5 (*very important*) to 1 (*not important*). CI = confidence interval. Rep. = reputation. Entrepr. = entrepreneurs. Fin. intermed. = financial intermediaries. All figures are based on country-weighted survey data. The weights reflect the ratio of a country's share of private equity firms in the frame population to its share of firms in the survey sample.

It was hypothesized that private equity firms view price as the most important criterion for deciding the exit channel of portfolio investments (H6). Consistent with the prediction, Figure 14 shows that Price generated a higher mean importance rating than any other criterion did. Paired samples tests of the mean differences in importance ratings between Price and the other criteria in the survey questionnaire were statistically significant in every case ($p < .001$, one-tailed, $n > 128$), and effect sizes were large ($d > 0.5$) in all cases except for the paired sample of Price and Form Of Payment. The statistical significance of these results remains unchanged when testing responses from venture capital and buyout firms separately from each other, or when applying non-parametric Wilcoxon Signed Ranks Tests.[141] At the same time, the almost complete absence of responses under *other* in the survey questionnaire provides some comfort that no essential determinants of the exit channel decision were overlooked in the survey form.[142] The sample of private equity firms also attached high importance to the liquidity of the consideration (Form Of Payment), and the speed and certainty of exit ("timing until, and certainty of achieving a full [100%] exit") — these are both aspects that are closely related to Price as they also affect the present value of an exit.

The survey results also suggest that private equity firms are concerned about the potential impact of exit channel decisions on their reputation (especially among investors, and owners and entrepreneurs) and that they respect the interests of portfolio company management. The former provides general support for Gompers's (1996) grandstanding hypothesis; in extension of Gompers's (1996) work, the data signify that the choice of exit channel is not only affected by private equity firms' concern for their reputation among investors, but also by their concern for their reputation among other groups of contract partners, such as owners and entrepreneurs. Finally, the results suggest that private equity firms do not attribute very high importance to Cost as a criterion for the exit channel decision. This is consistent with earlier empirical results (Povaly, 2007, p. 312), and is possibly explained by a comparatively small marginal effect of costs on the net proceeds of different exit channels.

5.4.6 The influence of firm characteristics on the evaluation of criteria for the exit channel decision

The results of the independent samples *t*-tests presented in Table 40 exhibit a number of significant links between the importance that private equity firm managers attribute to exit channel decision criteria and various characteristics of their private equity firms. A number of these links involve firm type: The sample of buyout firm respondents rated the importance of almost every decision criterion higher than the sample of venture capital firm respondents did; these differences are statistically significant for one half of the queried decision criteria, including the four highest-rated thereof. It appears that buyout firms generally spend more consideration to the exit channel decision than do venture capital firms. Such an effect could be caused by implicit contracts over control in the venture capital industry: If venture capital firms and entrepreneurs have an "ex ante joint preference that the venture capital fund exit through an IPO" (Black & Gilson, 1998, p. 258) and venture capital firms are penalized for refusing an IPO exit to successful entrepreneurs, the choice of exit channel becomes more of

141 Detailed test results are available from the author upon request

142 One venture capital respondent specified that "exits are nearly always by M&A not IPO so there is not much choice in the matter", another venture capital respondent specified: "the highest financial reward"

an automatic consequence (of the entrepreneur's success) rather than an active decision. Another (non mutually exclusive) explanation for this effect could lie in the different business models of buyout and venture capital firms: Buyout firms usually manage a small number of medium to large company investments, whereas venture capital firms typically manage a greater number of small company investments. The average number of investments per partner is lower for buyout firms than it is for venture capital firms (Metrick & Yasuda, 2010, Table 1). Consequentially, buyout firms might therefore devote more management attention to individual investments than do venture capital firms. This resource-based interpretation could also explain the significant decrease in the importance that private equity firms attach to the (monitoring-intensive) assessment of contractual obligations and risks, as the private equity firms' numbers of investments rise (see Table 41).

Table 40

Connections between firm characteristics (dichotomous variables) and respondents' importance ratings of criteria for deciding which exit channel to choose for a company investment

Criterion	EU - US/Can	BO - VC	GeoSpec	IndSpec	Outside Inv[a]	Well/Under - Loss[a]	Hands On - Supp	CEF[a]
Price	-0.06	$0.37^{**\,b}$	-0.08	-0.19	$0.50^{*\,+++}$	0.74	-0.15	-0.07
Form Of Payment	0.09^{+}	$0.60^{***\,b\,+++}$	-0.03	-0.01	0.23	$1.00^{**\,++}$	0.22	0.34
100% Exit	$0.48^{***\,+++}$	$0.33^{*\,++}$	0.23^{+}	0.16	-0.16	0.40	0.01	0.27
Cost	0.04	0.05	0.31^{++}	0.14	-0.30	0.19	-0.02	$-0.39^{**\,b\,++}$
Contractual	0.13	0.20	0.15	0.22^{+}	0.32^{+}	0.17	0.29^{+}	0.16
Company Management	-0.29	0.28	0.05	0.05	0.18	0.68^{*}	-0.14	0.27
Rep.: Investors	-0.14	$0.44^{**\,+++}$	0.21	$-0.38^{(**)\,+++}$	0.45	0.62^{++}	-0.27	0.17
Rep.: Owners & entrepreneurs	-0.13	0.20	0.18	-0.15	0.33	$0.74^{*\,++}$	-0.18	0.04
Rep.: Managers	-0.01	$0.43^{**\,++}$	0.23	$-0.36^{(**)\,(++)}$	0.26	0.14	-0.28^{+}	0.26
Rep.: Financial intermediaries	0.04	0.02	0.10	-0.18	-0.10	0.06	-0.23	-0.30^{+}

Note. The figures denote effect sizes (Cohen's *d*), which are calculated by dividing the differences in mean importance ratings of the two subsamples of a dichotomous column variable by the pooled standard deviation. Importance ratings were measured on numbered 5-point scales, ranging from 5 (*very important*) to 1 (*not important*). All figures, except those relating to EU - US/Can, are based on country-weighted survey data. The weights reflect the ratio of a country's share of private equity firms in the frame population to its share of firms in the survey sample. EU - US/Can denotes headquarter location: EU = Europe; US/Can = United States of America or Canada. BO - VC denotes firm type: BO = buyout; VC = venture capital; VC includes eight firms of related types, such as "growth equity" and "business angel"; BO includes two firms of related types ("industry specific buyout" and "restructuring buyout"). GeoSpec refers to firms, for which respondents specified whether or not they specialise in geographical areas. IndSpec refers to firms, for which respondents specified whether or not they specialise in industry sectors. Outside Inv refers to whether or not respondents specified that their firm sources the majority of its fund capital from outside investors. Well/Under - Loss refers to the preferred performance of target companies: Well/Under ="well-performing" or "underperforming"; Loss = "loss-making". Hands On - Supp denotes management style: Hands on = "hands-on"; Supp = "supportive". CEF refers to firms, for which respondents specified whether or not they mostly manage investments in (closed-end) funds with a fixed lifetime. Rep. = reputation.

$^{*}p < .10$. $^{**}p < .05$. $^{***}p < .01$. All *p*s are two-tailed and relate to independent samples *t*-tests for equality of means; in each case *df* (pairwise) ranges between 103 and 132. ^{+}p, ^{++}p, and ^{+++}p denote respective significance levels for the Mann-Whitney *U*-test.

[a]One of the subsamples has a data count of less than 30.

[b]Equal variances not assumed.

Other significant effects in Table 40 involve the preferred performance of target companies: Respondents from private equity firms targeting well- or underperforming companies rated, on average, the importance of every decision criterion higher than respondents from firms targeting loss-making companies did. The effect is significant, and particularly strong, for the decision criteria Form Of Payment, Reputation Among Investors, and Reputation Among Owners And Entrepreneurs. These results could be caused by the special characteristics of private equity firms that target loss-making (e.g. *restructuring* or *turnaround*) opportunities. Restructuring firms might, for example, place less importance on the form of payment because the higher average returns of successful turnaround investments dwarf any possible effects from this criterion (see Kraft, 2001, pp. 312–323, for empirical evidence of the higher average returns of turnaround investors). Then, restructuring firms might attach less importance to their reputation among owners and entrepreneurs, because many of their new investment opportunities are likely to be sourced from debt-holders rather than equity-holders, and because the senior managers of their target companies are typically replaced after the transaction has been consummated (see Kraft, 2001, pp. 162–163, on the replacement of senior management by turnaround and restructuring firms). And finally, the lower importance that these private equity firms attach to their reputation among investors (as decision criterion for the exit channel) could be the result of lower information asymmetries between private equity firms and investors within the comparatively closely knit market for turnaround investments.

Asymmetric information could also explain the lower emphasis that industry-specialised private equity firms place on reputational criteria. The observed effects match the lower ratings that industry-specialised private equity firms place on the respective reputational objectives (see Table 11 in Chapter 3.4.2) and might similarly be ascribed to lower information asymmetries between such private equity firms and their contract partners. Another notable result is the higher importance that respondents from private equity firms located in the EU attached to the criterion 100% Exit. This effect could result from the increased risks and challenges in European jurisdictions of undertaking a squeeze-out of minority shareholders (see Ventoruzzo, 2010, on legal differences between the United States of America and Europe).

The results of the Spearman rank correlation tests between ordinal scale or continuous firm characteristic variables and private equity firm respondents' importance ratings of criteria are presented in Table 41. The strongest significant effects ($p < .05$, two-tailed) are associated with the characteristics Age and Investments. The implication of the statistically significant negative correlation between private equity firm age and the Cost criterion is ambiguous: It appears that either increasingly well-established private equity firms tend to become less mindful of cost or private equity firms that do not divert too much attention on the cost of exit channels tend to become more successful (and therefore reach a higher age).[143]

[143] It has to be noted that a possible bias in the data cannot be excluded as older, more successful private equity firms might feel less of a need to misrepresent their true attention to cost than younger private equity firms

Table 41

Spearman rank correlations between firm characteristics (ordinal scale and continuous variables) and respondents' importance ratings of criteria for deciding which exit channel to choose for a company investment

Criterion	Age (yrs)	Funds	Capital (€m)	Investments	Investment Size (€m)
Price	.09	.12	.00	.09	.06
Form Of Payment	-.05	-.01	.02	-.22 (***)	.12
100% Exit	-.10	.04	.00	-.11	.08
Cost	-.24 ***	-.03	-.12	-.14	-.08
Contractual	-.05	.04	-.15 *	-.22 ***	.03
Company Management	.04	.10	.01	.04	.01
Rep.: Investors	-.05	-.10	-.14	-.09	.05
Rep.: Owners & entrepreneurs	-.04	-.04	-.17 *	-.01	-.09
Rep.: Managers	.05	.02	-.05	.01	.11
Rep.: Financial intermediaries	.02	.03	.04	.09	.06

Note. Importance ratings were measured on numbered 5-point scales, ranging from 5 (*very important*) to 1 (*not important*). Correlations were tested pairwise, using country-weighted data. Weighted *n* ranges between 137 and 152. The weights reflect the ratio of a country's share of private equity firms in the frame population to its share of firms in the survey sample. Age is the number of years a respondent's firm has been in existence. Funds is the number of private equity funds a respondent's firm has raised. Capital is the rough total capital under management of a respondent's firm in € millions. Investments is the rough number of company investments managed by a respondent's firm. Investment Size is a respondent firm's rough typical investment size (equity stake) in € millions. Range specifications were replaced by their means, and amounts in other currencies were converted to € amounts using the averages of market exchange rates over the time of the survey. Rep. = reputation.
$^{*}p < .10$. $^{**}p < .05$. $^{***}p < .01$. All *p*s are two-tailed. Parentheses denote that the respective Spearman rank correlations within the buyout and venture capital subsamples were not significant at alpha = .10.

5.4.7 The influence of decision power on the evaluation of criteria for the exit channel decision

Table 42 shows only few statistically significant connections between the extent of decision power held by private equity firms and the importance attributed to criteria for deciding which exit channel to choose for a company investment. Generally, there seems to be a slight trend of respondents from buyout firms to attribute less importance to decision criteria, the more decision power they hold. This trend is significant for the Cost criterion only (alpha = .05, two-tailed). Overall, the distribution of exit decision power between the private equity firm and the portfolio company appears to have only a limited influence on how private equity firms evaluate decision criteria for the exit channel.

Table 42

Spearman rank correlations between the extent of decision power held by the private equity firm and the importance attributed to criteria for deciding which exit channel to choose for a company investment

	Exit decision power of private equity firm	
Criterion	BO	VC
Price	-.13	-.23 *
Form Of Payment	-.03	.04
100% Exit	-.06	-.09
Cost	-.27 **	.13
Contractual	-.08	.12
Company Management	-.12	.00
Rep.: Investors	-.20 *	-.12
Rep.: Owners & entrepreneurs	-.07	.07
Rep.: Managers	-.14	-.07
Rep.: Financial intermediaries	.09	.08

Note. The distribution of decision power between the private equity firm (PE) and the portfolio company (PC) regarding the exit channel decision for an investment was recorded on a bipolar scale with five steps: *nearly always PE, mostly PE, joint lead, mostly PC, nearly always PC*; for the analysis these steps were coded into numbers 5 to 1, respectively (*exit decision power*). Importance ratings of decision criteria were measured on numbered 5-point scales, ranging from 5 (*very important*) to 1 (*not important*). Correlations were tested pairwise, using country-weighted data. Weighted n ranges between 69 and 71. The weights reflect the ratio of a country's share of private equity firms in the frame population to its share of firms in the survey sample. *Venture Capital* (VC) also includes eight firms of related firm types, such as "growth equity" and "business angel". *Buyout* (BO) also includes two firms of related firm types ("industry specific buyout" and "restructuring buyout"). Rep. = reputation.

$^{*}p < .10$. $^{**}p < .05$. $^{***}p < .01$. All ps are two-tailed.

5.5 Conclusions

5.5.1 Distribution of exit decision power

Less than 5% of the private equity firms in the survey sample generally assume a junior position in relation to the portfolio company, when deciding upon the appropriate time to begin an exit process or when deciding upon the appropriate channel to exit, whereas around one third of the private equity firms in the survey sample generally accept a joint lead position for these decisions. The data also reveal a marked (and statistically significant) difference in the distributions of responses between buyout firms and venture capital firms: While the responses from buyout firms are skewed towards control by the private equity firm (both decision types), the responses from venture capital firms are skewed towards joint control for the decision on exit time and are more varied for the decision on exit channel. A bivariate exploratory analysis of connections between respondents' ratings of exit decision power and the characteristics of their private equity firms yielded a number of statistically significant relationships. Ratings from venture capital firms are associated, for example, with the industry specialisation (whether or not a private equity firm specialises in industry sectors), age and number of funds. Ratings from buyout firms are linked primarily to the firm's management style (hands-on or supportive). Last, the test results do not support the hypothesis developed from Wright, Robbie, Thompson et al. (1994) that buyout firms with larger transaction sizes generally have more decision power in relation to their portfolio companies than buyout firms with smaller transaction sizes have.

The following conclusions are drawn from these results: Firstly, the data show that — consistent with the typical level of control rights held through their ownership position, board representation or contractual provisions — private equity firms are mostly not prepared to let the decision on exit time or channel be dominated by portfolio company management or a third party. At the same time, the results also exhibit a sizeable proportion of private equity firms that are generally prepared to share exit decision power with portfolio company management.

Secondly, the data reveal that venture capital firms commonly share significantly more exit decision power with portfolio company management than do buyout firms. This and a number of other effects observed in the data can be explained by the existence of implicit contracts over control in the venture capital industry. In addition, the survey data appear to signify an effect that bears resemblance to Gompers's (1996) grandstanding hypothesis: Younger (and smaller) venture capital firms could be sharing more exit decision power with portfolio company management than older venture capital firms in order to build a reputation.

Thirdly, the lack of support for the hypothesis developed from the assumptions of Wright, Robbie, Thompson et al. (1994) puts into question their reasoning that smaller buyouts are associated with later exits because the company managers of smaller portfolio companies have increased exit decision power in relation to the buyout firm.

5.5.2 Decision rules for initiating an exit process

The private equity firms in the sample employ a number of decision heuristics for deciding when to begin the exit process of performing investments and of underperforming investments. The decision heuristics to begin the exit process when no major increase of price or multiple is expected from waiting another period or when no major increase of IRR is expected from waiting another period yielded the highest mean frequency ratings of all decision heuristics for both performing investments and underperforming investments. Many private equity firms also specified the amount that constitutes a *major increase* in price or IRR for their firm. These data suggest that, on average, an expected (price or IRR) increase of around 20 to 26 per cent p.a. from "waiting another period" will prevent private equity firms from beginning an exit process for a performing investment and that an average increase of around 10 to 16 per cent p.a. will prevent them from beginning an exit process for an underperforming investment.[144] The test results support the hypothesis that private equity firms will more often choose to begin the exit process immediately for investments that are clearly underperforming than they will do for investments that are clearly performing. A bivariate exploratory analysis of connections between respondents' frequency ratings of individual decision heuristics for performing investments and the characteristics of their private equity firms yielded a number of statistically significant relationships. The ratings that private equity firm respondents assigned to individual decision heuristics is, for example, associated with firm location (Europe or United States of America/Canada), firm type (buyout or venture capital), industry specialisation (whether or not the firm has an industry specialisation strategy), and with the amount of capital under management. An analysis of connections between respondents' frequency ratings of individual decision heuristics for underperforming investments and the characteristics of their private equity firms yielded statistically significant relationships, for example, with firm type (buyout or venture capital), strategic focus (geographical specialisation, specialisation by target performance), external funding, management style, fund type, the amount of capital under management, and the number of investments held. The distribution of exit decision power between the private equity firm and the portfolio company appears to have only a limited influence on private equity firms' evaluations of exit decision rules.

The following conclusions are drawn from these results: Firstly, private equity firms generally do not rely on one single rule for deciding upon when to begin an exit process for performing or underperforming investments, instead, they appear to choose the decision rule for a particular exit decision and investment from a selection of decision heuristics.

Secondly, the decision rules employed most frequently by the sample of private equity firms (no major increase of price or multiple expected; no major increase of IRR expected) are — under certain conditions — consistent with a policy to maximise net present value (and also resemble the exit behaviour predicted by Cumming & MacIntosh, 2001). However, the specifications of private equity firms regarding the thresholds for these decision rules make it doubtful that the respective conditions are met, possibly signifying a degree of inefficiency in the decisions of private equity firms.

Thirdly, the data support the hypothesized tendency towards an (increased) early culling of poor quality investments — albeit the observed size of effect is small. At the same time, the data

[144] Some caution is required here as the units of the underlying amounts (i.e. percentages or percentage-points) were not clearly specified

show a contrasting (and stronger) tendency of buyout firms to procrastinate the exits of poor quality investments more frequently than those of other investments.

Fourthly, additional specifications from respondents suggest that the availability of exit opportunities plays an important role for the exit timing decision. Evidently, exit markets are not always liquid — this is a concern for decision rules that pre-suppose fully liquid exit markets.

Fifthly, for underperforming investments the data show a tendency of larger, more experienced private equity firms to more frequently employ the simpler decision heuristics, and less frequently employ the more ambitious decision rules; some private equity firms appear to regard the decision on exit time as altogether too complex for the application of pre-defined decision heuristics.

5.5.3 Criteria for the exit channel decision

The survey data show that private equity firms attach importance to a wide range of criteria for deciding which exit channel to choose for a company investment. As expected, price generated a higher mean importance rating than any other criterion. The decision criteria Form Of Payment and timing until, and certainty of achieving a full (100%) exit also generated comparatively high mean importance ratings from the sample of survey respondents. A bivariate exploratory analysis of connections between respondents' importance ratings of individual criteria and the characteristics of their private equity firms yielded a number of statistically significant relationships. Respondents' ratings were particularly frequently linked to firm type (buyout or venture capital) and sometimes also to industry specialisation, preferred performance of target companies, firm age and a firm's number of investments. In addition, respondents from private equity firms located in Europe attributed significantly higher importance ratings to the decision criterion 100% Exit than respondents from private equity firms located in the United States of America and Canada. And respondents' ratings of the Cost criterion are significantly negatively correlated with Age. Respondents' ratings are generally not significantly associated with the exit decision power of the private equity firm or with size criteria.

The following conclusions are drawn from these results: Firstly, private equity firms view price as the most important criterion for deciding the exit channel of portfolio company investments, whereas the form of payment and the speed and certainty of a (full) exit also play an important role. The older a private equity firm, the less importance it attaches to the associated cost.

Secondly, the data show that a private equity firm's choice of exit channel is (also) affected by reputational concerns — these results support Gompers's (1996) grandstanding hypothesis; in extension of Gompers's (1996) work, the results show that the choice of exit channel is not only affected by private equity firms' concern for their reputation among investors, but also by their concern for their reputation among other groups of contract partners, such as owners and entrepreneurs. The results also suggest that the level of importance that private equity firms attach to such reputational concerns is affected by the degree of asymmetric information between the private equity firms and its contract partners.

Thirdly, buyout firms generally bestow more attention on the exit channel decision than do venture capital firms. This can be explained, in part by the existence of implicit agreements in the venture capital industry that govern the choice of exit channel (Black & Gilson, 1998), and in part by larger transaction sizes (in conjunction with fewer investments per fund) in the buyout industry.

Fourthly, legal differences between countries (concerning, for example, the squeeze-out of minority shareholders) can affect the exit decision.

6 Summary of Results

6.1 Summary of Chapters

The aim of this doctoral thesis was to improve our understanding of decision-making in private equity firms, whereas particular emphasis was placed on the objectives, minimum return requirements, success measures, decision metrics, exit decision power, and exit decision rules of private equity firms. The analysis and discussion of proprietary survey data from 136 private equity firms (mostly venture capital and buyout firms) located in the United States of America, Canada, and Europe yields a multitude of new facts and insights. As regards objectives, the results show that private equity firms attach particularly high importance to the objective of delivering high returns to investors and to reputational objectives, the latter of which strengthens a central assumption of popular private equity theories and also supports the idea that at-stake reputation is a genuine incentive for private equity firms to align their interests with those of their investors and contract partners. The analysis reveals several statistically significant connections between respondents' importance ratings of objectives and certain characteristics of their private equity firms. These suggest that a private equity firm's desire for reputation is linked to the degree of asymmetric information about the quality of the private equity firm between the private equity firm and its principal contract partners and that a private equity firm's appetite for risk is linked to its business focus. The data do not provide clear support for Lerner and Schoar's (2004) prediction of a (direct) link between the liquidity of investors' interests in the funds of a private equity firm and the intensity of asymmetric information about the quality of the private equity firm between inside investors and outside investors; instead, they appear to suggest that this relationship is moderated by reputation. If this holds true, Lerner and Schoar's theory on the causes of illiquidity should be extended to account for the effects of reputation.

The survey data on minimum return requirements provide empirical evidence of their (expected) important role for investment decisions in private equity firms. Survey respondents attach particularly high importance ratings to minimum level IRRs and minimum level money multiples; in comparison, the sample of private equity firms attaches little importance to minimum level discount rates in discounted cash flow models. The survey results also provide information on determinants of the minimum return that private equity firms require for a particular investment: Factors such as investment stage and quality of management generated particularly high importance ratings from the sample of private equity firms. A comparison of mean importance ratings across all factors appears to support the idea that idiosyncratic risk plays an important part for a private equity firm's assessment of investment opportunities. Bivariate statistical tests show a number of significant relationships between individual characteristics of private equity firms and the importance ratings that respondents assigned to various factors. I conclude from these results that a private equity firm's investment strategy and associated risk profile are important determinants of the levels of minimum return required from new investments and that the current degree of diversification plays a role for the importance that private equity firms attach to idiosyncratic risk when evaluating new investment opportunities. The results do not support the idea of Ruhnka and Young (1991, pp. 125–128) that a decline in the level of minimum return required from earlier to later stages of investment is caused by a decrease in internal risks.

The empirical analysis of the survey data on private equity firms' success measures and decision metrics is preceded in this thesis by a discussion of the quality of the multiple and IRR for performance measurement in private equity firms, in which I find defensible arguments for the popularity of these metrics. The results of the empirical analysis offer strong support for the expected prominent role that the money multiple and IRR play in private equity firms — both in terms of measuring investment success (ex post) and as criteria for key decisions regarding portfolio investments (ex ante). In comparison to these metrics, success measures that are based on modern portfolio theory and the capital asset pricing received, on average, far lower mean importance ratings. One deficiency of both the IRR and the multiple is their unreliability (in comparison to the net present value) for ranking and selecting investment projects that are mutually exclusive. As the data suggest that most private equity firms do have to decide between mutually exclusive investment opportunities, I conclude that at least some private equity firms forfeit better performance by inappropriately employing the IRR and multiple for the appraisal of mutually exclusive investment opportunities. In the survey, item non-response was particularly high for measures of risk or risk-return for individual investments. The available data suggest that private equity firms generally employ a range of methods for such purpose, whereas only few firms employ beta-based metrics. I attribute these results to the widespread use of risk-adjusted minimum return requirements and to market imperfections in private equity markets. Otherwise, the importance that private equity firms assigned to individual success measures is frequently associated with firm type, external funding, and fund horizon, and is generally not associated with the age, size, geographical location, and investment focus of private equity firms. I ascribe the former results to a tendency of private equity firms to select metrics that offer a high measurement quality for the average investment and to a streamlining influence of external funding on a firm's choice of metrics.

As concerns the exit decision, I find that private equity firms are mostly not prepared to let the decision on exit time or channel be dominated by portfolio company management or a third party — even though a considerable proportion of private equity firms are generally prepared to share exit decision power with portfolio company management. I also find that venture capital firms commonly share significantly more exit decision power with portfolio company management than buyout firms do and ascribe this effect to the existence of implicit contracts over control in the venture capital industry. The survey data do not support the assumption of Wright, Robbie, Thompson et al. (1994) that smaller buyout portfolio companies have more exit decision power than larger buyout portfolio companies. As regards rules for deciding when to begin the exit process for performing and for underperforming investments, the data show that the sample of private equity firms attach medium or high frequency ratings of usage to a wide range of rules and that most private equity firms attach high frequency ratings to at least two decision rules. I conjecture from this that private equity firms typically choose the decision rule for a particular exit decision and investment from a selection of heuristics, rather than relying on one universal decision rule for all exit decisions. Further analysis shows that the decision rules that are most popular with private equity firms are — under certain conditions — consistent with a policy to maximise net present value. But the survey data make it doubtful that the respective conditions are met. Otherwise, I find only weak empirical support for an early culling of poor quality investments — instead, I detect a contrasting tendency of buyout firms to procrastinate the exits of such investments. I also find that, for exiting underperforming investments, a private equity firm's usage of the simpler decision heuristics tends to increase with its age, experience, and size. Last, the survey data show that private equity firms attach importance to a wide range of criteria for the exit channel decision. Price stands out as the most important criterion, followed by the related criteria form of payment, and timing until, and certainty of achieving a full (100%) exit. Reputational concerns also play an important role, whereas the importance attached to these concerns appears to be linked to the degree of asymmetric information between the private equity firm and its contract partners. The data also suggest that, overall, buyout firms devote more attention to the choice of exit channel than do venture capital firms.

6.2 Additional Conclusions

A comprehensive review of the study results yields some additional observations and conclusions. Firstly, decision rules and metrics from modern portfolio theory and CAPM apparently do not play an important role in private equity. It would appear that market "imperfections" render the central models of established financial theory less useful for decision-making in a private equity environment. Instead, the survey results show that private equity firms typically use simple IRR- or multiples-based rules of thumb for their investment decisions. This from an academic viewpoint rather unsatisfactory situation is hardly the result of a lack of theoretical knowledge: Private equity firms are regarded as specialists in finance (often referred to as *financial investors*), and many of their executives are recruited from the leading universities and business schools. It appears more likely that modern portfolio theory and the capital asset pricing model are merely less useful to private equity firms, because the real-world characteristics of private equity markets, involving asymmetric (or absent) information, illiquidity, and exposure to idiosyncratic risk, only rarely satisfy the demanding requirements of conventional finance theory.

Alternative theoretical models could offer new solutions. Many empirical results in this thesis can be explained using theories and constructs which represent new institutional economics and include agency theory, asymmetric information, and Black and Gilson's (1998) implicit contract over control hypothesis. Future research could explore the suitability of alternative theories and ideas for decision-making in private equity firms. Some of the study results bring to mind Simon's (1979) theories of bounded rationality, which were developed in an endeavour to

> replace the classical model with one that would describe how decisions could be (and probably actually were) made when the alternatives of search had to be sought out, the consequences of choosing particular alternatives were only very imperfectly known both because of limited computational power and because of uncertainty in the external world, and the decision maker did not possess a general and consistent utility function for comparing heterogeneous alternatives (Simon, 1979, pp. 500–501).

Simon (1979) suggests various means of simplifying intractable decision problems, one of which is to "look for satisfactory choices instead of optimal ones" (p. 501). The employment by private equity firms of minimum return requirements for evaluating new investments and their use of return thresholds for the exit decision (as shown in this study) could indeed signify that private equity firms aspire to *satisfice* rather than to *maximise*. And the range of decision rules that private equity firms employ for choosing when to begin an exit process for a company investment is reminiscent of Gigerenzer and Selten's (2002a) *adaptive toolbox* of decision heuristics.[145] They argue that the employment of simple decision heuristics does not have to imply lower quality decisions than optimising decision algorithms:

> Optimization is often based on uncertain assumptions, which are themselves guesswork, and as a consequence, there may be about as many different outcomes of optimizing strategies as there are sets of assumptions. In these real-

145 An adaptive toolbox is characterised by Gigerenzer and Selten (2002b) largely as a set of "fast and frugal" decision-making heuristics that are "adapted to particular environments" (p. 8)

word cases, it is possible that simple and robust heuristics can match or even outperform a specific optimizing strategy (Gigerenzer & Selten, 2002b, p. 4)

Secondly, it is noteworthy that the responses of private equity firms are frequently connected to their firm type (buyout firm or venture capital firm) and investment strategy, but only rarely connected to their being located in Europe or the United States of America and Canada).[146] The former is consistent with other recent findings (e.g. Borell, 2011) and underlines the importance of making a distinction between private equity firms with different types and strategies; future research on decision-making in private equity firms should take these differences into account. The latter result suggests that the views of European private equity firms on the determinants and rules of decision-making usually do not differ materially from those of private equity firms in the United States of America and Canada. This is particularly noteworthy in light of earlier studies that have highlighted differences in private equity markets across the Atlantic Ocean (e.g. Black & Gilson, 1998; Manigart et al., 2002; Schwienbacher, 2005; Wright, Robbie, Romanet et al., 1994[147]). One possible explanation for these deviating results is that differences between the two geographical regions relate mainly to external factors, such as legality and the liquidity of stock and buyout markets, rather than to factors within private equity firms.

6.3 Implications for Practitioners

For practitioners, the study provides defensible arguments for the employment of the multiple and IRR to measure and manage the performance of company investments. It contends that under typical conditions of private equity investing these metrics can deliver reasonably valid and reliable results (as compared to NPV), provided that they are used in connection with hurdle rates that reflect the investment's opportunity cost of capital over the (expected) holding period. The study also illustrates how, under certain conditions (e.g. if the value increase of the investment is expected to decline over the holding period and the rate of the expected major increase in price, net of any additional cost, reflects the investment's opportunity cost of capital), the most popular exit decision rules can be consistent with NPV-maximising strategies.

At the same time, the discussion in this thesis points out a number of issues of concern: Firstly, private equity firm executives need to be well acquainted with the limitations and deficiencies of multiples and IRRs for measuring and managing the performance of portfolio company

[146] In two instances (i.e. the importance ratings of the metric Capital Gain and of the exit channel criterion 100% Exit), statistically significant associations with geographic location are attributed to legality. These findings are consistent with recent results of Cumming, Schmidt, and Walz (2010), showing an effect of legality on venture capital governance

[147] More precisely, Manigart et al. (2002) distinguish between the United States and the United Kingdom on the one hand, and Belgium, France and the Netherlands (denoted as *continental Europe*) on the other hand

investments: In particular, the two metrics can be misleading when used to rank (and select between) mutually exclusive investment opportunities, to compare performance across investments, to evaluate unsuccessful investments or investments with complex cash flow streams, or when used to evaluate investments with sizeable interim cash flows. The survey results suggest that at least some private equity firms are forfeiting better performance by inappropriate application of the multiple and IRR. In the above-mentioned situations private equity firms should exercise particular caution and possibly consider the use of alternative methodologies, such as profitability indices, public market equivalents, or modified IRRs. Secondly, the average importance that private equity firms attach to the multiple and IRR for various types of decisions in the life-cycle of a company investment appears to vary. It is unclear why, for example, the multiple should be more important for the original investment decision than for the subsequent decision to increase or reduce the investment in a portfolio company. Last, the survey results suggest that for the sell or hold decision, private equity firms apply lower hurdle rates to poor quality portfolio company investments than they do to high quality portfolio company investments — this policy is hardly in line with the standards that private equity firms apply to new investments.[148]

6.4 Contribution to Literature

This study makes three principal contributions to private equity literature. Firstly, the study makes available a unique set of novel empirical facts about the determinants and rules of decision-making in private equity firms. This dataset helps to improve our understanding of private equity firms and affords a basis for future theoretical work. Secondly, this thesis contributes to existing private equity theory by testing and discussing hypotheses that are developed from the available stock of theories and ideas, including, for example, Lerner and Schoar's (2004) hypotheses concerning the reasons for the illiquidity of private equity funds and Ruhnka and Young's (1991) assumptions regarding the determinants of minimum return requirements. It also sheds light on how private equity firms assess principal theoretical constructs such as return, risk and reputation and draws attention to previously unknown interrelations and connections, such as the streamlining effect of external funding on a private equity firm's choice of success measures, the tendency of buyout firms to procrastinate the exiting of poor quality investments, and the implied relationship between asymmetric information and reputation. Last, the review and discussion of success measures in this thesis also makes a contribution to the body of literature on performance measurement.

[148] From a theoretical viewpoint the higher reluctance to exit poor quality investments is somewhat reminiscent of Kahneman and Tversky's (1986, pp. S254–S257) finding that people choose risk-seeking strategies in order to avoid looming losses

6.5 Suggestions for Future Research

Much of the research in this thesis is of an exploratory and descriptive nature and should be regarded as a starting point for further study. Future research on decision-making in private equity firms could engage in the following areas. Firstly, the cross-sectional survey design in this thesis could be complemented by in-depth case study research;[149] such research could establish in more detail *how* private equity firms conduct their investment and disinvestment decisions and place more focus on reasons and motives of private equity firm behaviour. Secondly, theoretical models and additional cross-sectional data could be used to examine the impact of decision-making on firm success, and to identify successful decision strategies. Last, theoretical research could pursue two alternative courses: One branch of research could attempt to extend or amend models of conventional financial theory for the "imperfections" and peculiarities of private equity markets, while a competing branch of research could explore the suitability of models of bounded rationality for private equity decision problems.

[149] One example of existing case study research in this field is the paper by Wright, Robbie, Thompson et al. (1994) on the longevity and life-cycle of buyouts, which contains three case studies besides cross-sectional survey data

7 Zusammenfassung in deutscher Sprache

Gegenstand dieser Arbeit ist die Erkundung von Determinanten und Regeln der Entscheidungsfindung in Private Equity-Unternehmen. Dazu wurde eine empirische Untersuchung durchgeführt, in deren Mittelpunkt die folgenden Aspekte der Entscheidungsfindung stehen: die Ziele von Private Equity-Unternehmen und ihre Mindestrenditeforderungen bei Neuinvestitionen, die Kennzahlen, welche Private Equity-Unternehmen zur Erfolgsmessung verwenden (*Erfolgskennzahlen*) und welche sie als Entscheidungskriterien verwenden (*Entscheidungskennzahlen*), die Entscheidungsmacht von Private Equity-Unternehmen im Verhältnis zu ihren Portfoliounternehmen bei Desinvestitionen, die Entscheidungsregeln, welche von Private Equity-Unternehmen eingesetzt werden, um zu entscheiden, wann ein Desinvestitionsprozess beginnen soll, sowie die wichtigsten Determinanten der Entscheidung über den Exitkanal.[150] Das Phänomen *Private Equity* hat sich innerhalb der letzten Jahrzehnte von einer Randerscheinung zu einem globalen Wirtschaftszweig mit messbarem Einfluss auf nationale Ökonomien entwickelt. Neuere Forschungsbefunde belegen beispielsweise, dass Private Equity die Entwicklung neuer Produkte und Dienstleistungen stimuliert, die Produktivität von Unternehmen verbessert und das Branchenwachstum beschleunigt (vgl. Bernstein, Lerner, Sørensen & Strömberg, 2009; Boucly, Sraer & Thesmar, 2011; Davis, Haltiwanger, Jarmin, Lerner & Miranda, 2009; Lerner, Sørensen & Strömberg, 2008; Romain & van Pottelsberghe, 2004). Trotz des dramatischen Rückgangs der Private Equity-Aktivität seit dem Beginn der jüngsten Finanzkrise liegt das weltweit verwaltete Private Equity-Vermögen (investierte und für Investitionen verfügbare Mittel) laut aktuellen Schätzungen von Branchenorganisationen bei ca. USD 2,5 Billionen (vgl. Preqin, 2011, S. 15; TheCityUK, 2011, S. 3).[151] Über den Einsatz (und die Freisetzung) dieser enormen volkswirtschaftlichen Ressourcen entscheiden lediglich einige tausend Private Equity-Unternehmen; jedoch ist bisher nur wenig darüber bekannt, wie diese Organisationen ihre Entscheidungen treffen.

Bestehende Literatur zur Entscheidungsfindung in Private Equity-Unternehmen befasst sich vielfach mit den Entscheidungskriterien und kognitiven Prozessen bei der Auswahl und Beurteilung von Neuinvestitionen (vgl. z. B. Borell, 2011; Dimov, Shepherd & Sutcliffe, 2007;

---

150 Der Exitkanal bezeichnet hier, auf welche Weise ein Private Equity-Unternehmen sein Engagement in einer Portfoliogesellschaft beendet. Typische Exitkanäle sind der Börsengang (mit Anschlusstransaktionen), der Verkauf an einen strategischen Käufer (*Trade Sale*), der Verkauf an ein anderes Private Equity-Unternehmen (*Secondary Sale*), der Verkauf an das Management der Portfoliogesellschaft (*Buy-back*) oder die Abschreibung der Investition

151 Diese Angabe beinhaltet auch Immobilienfonds mit einem geschätzten Anteil von 16% (vgl. Preqin, 2011, S. 15)

Dixon, 1991; Elango, Fried, Hisrich & Polonchek, 1995; Kollmann & Kuckertz, 2010; Lockett, Murray & Wright, 2002; Manigart et al., 2002; Murray & Lott, 1995; Muzyka, Birley & Leleux, 1996; Petty & Gruber, 2011; Shepherd, Zacharakis & Baron, 2003; Ruhnka & Young, 1991; Tyebjee T. T. & Bruno, 1981; Vater, 2003) sowie mit Faktoren, die den Zeitpunkt oder Kanal der Desinvestition von Portfoliogesellschaften beeinflussen (vgl. z. B. Black & Gilson, 1998; Cumming & Johan, 2010; Cumming & MacIntosh, 2003; Gompers, 1996; Lerner, 1994; Lin & Smith, 1998; Megginson & Weiss, 1991; Povaly, 2007; Relander, Syrjänen & Miettinen, 1994; Schwienbacher, 2005; Wall & Smith, 1997; Wright, Robbie, Thompson & Starkey, 1994). Im Bereich Wagniskapital haben einige Arbeiten darüber hinaus Theorieansätze oder theoretische Modelle für die Bestimmung des Desinvestitionszeitpunkts (vgl. z. B. Cumming & MacIntosh, 2001; Tykvová, 2003) oder für die Wahl des Exitkanals hervorgebracht (vgl. z. B. Aghion, Bolton & Tirole, 2004; Arcot, 2005; Bascha & Walz, 2001; Bayar & Chemmanur, 2011; Berglöf, 1994; Bienz & Leite, 2008; Black & Gilson, 1998; Hellmann, 2006; Schwienbacher, 2005). Dennoch sind viele als grundlegend erscheinende Aspekte der Entscheidungsfindung bislang weitgehend unerforscht, so z. B. die Ziele von Private Equity-Unternehmen, ihre Erfolgs- und Entscheidungskennzahlen, die Bestimmungsfaktoren von Mindestrenditeforderungen bei Neuinvestitionen oder die Entscheidungsregeln, welche in der Praxis für Desinvestitionen eingesetzt werden.

Zielsetzung dieser Arbeit ist es, einen Beitrag zur Verbesserung des Erkenntnisstands über die Entscheidungsfindung in Private Equity-Unternehmen zu leisten; die Ergebnisse sollen die Entwicklung neuer Ansätze und Theorien auf diesem Gebiet fördern und die Qualität von Entscheidungen in der Praxis erhöhen. Der Forschungsansatz ist im Hinblick auf den begrenzten Umfang der einschlägigen Literatur überwiegend explorativ und deskriptiv; gleichwohl werden aus der bestehenden Literatur falsifizierbare Hypothesen hergeleitet, die anhand eigener empirischer Daten überprüft werden.[152] Zur Datengewinnung wurde die Befragungsmethode ausgewählt. Dazu wurde ein standardisierter Fragebogen entwickelt, der sich an erprobten Designs früherer Private Equity-Befragungen sowie an Empfehlungen der Literatur orientierte. Nach mehreren Expertengesprächen und einem abschließenden Online-Pilottest wurde der Fragebogen im März 2009 an mehr als 2.300 Private Equity-Unternehmen mit Sitz in den USA, Kanada und elf europäischen Ländern jeweils postalisch, als druckfähiger Download und als Internetfragebogen zugänglich gemacht. Die Feldphase der Befragung dauerte etwas über zwei Monate, in dessen Lauf 136 verwertbare Antwortbögen von teilnahmeberechtigten Private Equity-Unternehmen eingingen (die *Stichprobe*). Eine Regressionsanalyse der Rücklaufquoten und Befragtenzahlen aus 16 Private Equity-Studien

[152] Zum Zwecke der Klarheit sind hypothesengeleitete Teile der Arbeit stets im Text als solche kenntlich gemacht

deutet darauf hin, dass die eher niedrige Rücklaufquote dieser Untersuchung in Höhe von 5,8% größtenteils auf die ungewöhnlich hohe Befragtenzahl zurückzuführen ist. Weitergehende Analysen der Befragungsqualität ergaben keine Anzeichen dafür, dass nicht-teilnehmende Befragte in den Untersuchungsmerkmalen wesentlich von teilnehmenden Private Equity-Unternehmen abweichen. Zudem zeigen die Qualitätsanalysen eine gute Übereinstimmung der Befragungsdaten mit verfügbaren Vergleichsdaten einer externen Datenquelle. Ländergewichtungen werden bei der Auswertung eingesetzt, um Unterschiede zwischen den Rücklaufquoten verschiedener Länder zu kompensieren. Die Stichprobe von 136 Private Equity-Unternehmen enthält 64 Wagniskapitalgesellschaften und 61 Buyout-Gesellschaften. Im Jahr der Erhebung waren diese Private Equity-Unternehmen durchschnittlich 9 bis 11 Jahre alt und hatten durchschnittlich 2 bis 3 Private Equity-Fonds verwaltet. Der Mittelwert (Median) des verwalteten Anlagevermögens (*Capital under Management*) belief sich auf €426,0 Millionen (€150,0 Millionen). Die Angaben der Befragten hinsichtlich des „Rough Average Return“ ihres Private Equity-Unternehmens über alle Fonds ergeben ein durchschnittliches IRR in Höhe von 33,5% und ein durchschnittliches Money Multiple in Höhe von 2,6. Bei der Auswertung der Daten wurden zumeist einfache uni- oder bivariate statistische Verfahren (parametrisch und nichtparametrisch) sowie vereinzelt lineare oder logistische Regressionsanalysen eingesetzt.

Die Untersuchungsergebnisse hinsichtlich der Ziele von Private Equity-Unternehmen zeigen (wenig überraschend), dass dem Renditeziel „Deliver High Returns to Investors“ die höchste Bedeutung beigemessen wird. Bemerkenswert ist jedoch die hohe Bedeutung, die Reputationszielen zugesprochen wird. Dieses Ergebnis untermauert erstmalig eine grundlegende Prämisse gängiger Private Equity-Theorien wie z. B. die *Grandstanding*-Hypothese von Gompers (1996) und die *Implicit Contract over Control*-Hypothese von Black und Gilson (1998). Des Weiteren unterstützt dieses Ergebnis die Vermutung einiger Autoren, dass die auf dem Spiel stehende Reputation ein realer Anreiz für Private Equity-Unternehmen ist, ihre Interessen an die ihrer Investoren und Vertragspartner anzugleichen (vgl. Fenn, Liang & Prowse, 1997, S. 43 ff.; Megginson & Weiss, 1991, S. 881; Sahlman, 1990, S. 513). Weiterhin deutet die Auswertung darauf hin, dass die Bedeutung des Reputationsziels für ein Private Equity-Unternehmen mit dem Ausmaß der Informationsasymmetrien hinsichtlich der Qualität des Private Equity-Unternehmens zwischen diesem und dessen wichtigsten Vertragspartnern verknüpft ist und dass ein Zusammenhang zwischen der Geschäftsausrichtung eines Private Equity-Unternehmens und dessen Risikobereitschaft besteht. Schließlich legt die Analyse nahe, dass die Theorie von Lerner und Schoar (2004) über die Gründe der Illiquidität von Private Equity-Fondsanteilen möglicherweise erweitert werden sollte, um die Wirkung von Reputationseffekten einzuschließen.

Die Befragungsergebnisse hinsichtlich der Mindestrenditeanforderungen von Private Equity-Unternehmen belegen empirisch ihre erwartungsgemäß bedeutende Rolle für Investitionsentscheidungen. Die Private Equity-Unternehmen in der Stichprobe sahen dabei vor allem Mindest-IRRs und Mindest-Multiples als wichtig an; dagegen scheinen Mindest-Kalkulationszinssätze im Rahmen der Kapitalwertmethode für sie nur von geringem Belang zu sein. Weitere Auswertungsergebnisse legen nahe, dass Faktoren wie z. B. die Investitionsphase und die Qualität des Managements der Portfoliogesellschaft eine besonders hohe Bedeutung für die Festlegung der Höhe der Mindestrenditeforderung an ein Investitionsprojekt haben und bestärken die Vermutung, dass dem unsystematischen Risiko eine wichtige Rolle bei Investitionsentscheidungen von Private Equity-Unternehmen zukommt. Die Resultate unterstützen nicht die Mutmaßung von Ruhnka und Young (1991, S. 125 ff.), dass eine Abnahme der Mindestrenditeforderungen von frühen zu späten Investitionsphasen durch eine Verminderung von internen Risiken (*Internal Risks*) verursacht wird.

Im Hinblick auf die Erfolgs- und Entscheidungskennzahlen von Private Equity-Unternehmen bringt die Arbeit in einem theoretischen Diskurs vertretbare Gründe für die Popularität der Multiple- und IRR-Methoden zur Performancemessung in Private Equity-Unternehmen hervor: Diese haben praktische Vorteile und können valide und zuverlässige Ergebnisse liefern, wenn sie in geeigneter Weise eingesetzt werden. Die empirische Untersuchung bestätigt die bedeutende Rolle dieser Kennzahlen für Private Equity-Unternehmen – sowohl bei der Messung von Investitionserfolg (ex post) als auch als Kriterium bei wesentlichen Entscheidungen hinsichtlich der Portfolioinvestitionen (ex ante). Erfolgskennzahlen, welche der modernen Portfoliotheorie und dem CAPM zuzurechnen sind, wird hingegen weitaus geringere Bedeutung beigemessen. Allerdings haben die IRR- und die Multiple-Methode als Akzeptanzkriterien für Investitionen hinlänglich bekannte Nachteile, beispielsweise im Fall sich gegenseitig ausschließender Investitionsprojekte. Da die Ergebnisse dieser Arbeit u. a. darauf hindeuten, dass die meisten Private Equity-Unternehmen oftmals über sich gegenseitig ausschließende Investitionsprojekte entscheiden müssen, wird in Verbindung mit Befragungsergebnissen hinsichtlich der Desinvestitionsentscheidung gefolgert, dass zumindest manche Private Equity-Unternehmen Performanceverluste durch unsachgemäße oder inkonsistente Anwendung von Entscheidungsheuristiken und -kriterien erleiden. Darüber hinaus zeigen die Ergebnisse, dass die Bedeutung, die Private Equity-Unternehmen einzelnen Erfolgskennzahlen beimessen, vielfach mit dem Unternehmenstyp (z. B. Buyout- oder Wagniskapitalgesellschaft), der Inanspruchnahme externer Finanzgeber (*Outside Investors*) und dem Fondshorizont verknüpft ist. Diese Resultate werden zum einen auf eine Tendenz bei Private Equity-Unternehmen zurückgeführt, Erfolgskennzahlen auszuwählen, die eine hohe Messqualität hinsichtlich der für ihre Investitionsstrategie typischen Investitionsprojekte aufweisen. Zum anderen werden sie mit einem straffenden Einfluss externer Finanzierung auf die

Kennzahlenauswahl eines Private Equity-Unternehmens begründet. Schließlich war in der Befragung die Nichtbeantwortung der Frage nach den verwendeten Maßgrößen für das Investitionsrisiko oder das Rendite-Risiko-Verhältnis besonders hoch; dieses Resultat ist möglicherweise die Folge einer weit verbreiteten Verwendung von risikoadjustierten Mindestrenditeforderungen bei Private Equity-Unternehmen.

Die Befragungsergebnisse hinsichtlich der Desinvestitionsentscheidung lassen erkennen, dass Private Equity-Unternehmen in der Regel nicht bereit sind, die Entscheidung über den Exitzeitpunkt oder -kanal vom Management der Portfoliogesellschaft oder einer Drittpartei beherrschen zu lassen, obschon ein großer Anteil der Befragten grundsätzlich willens ist, diese Entscheidungen mit dem Management der Portfoliogesellschaft zu teilen. Wagniskapitalgesellschaften scheinen dabei ihren Management-Teams gewöhnlich mehr Entscheidungsmacht zuzubilligen als Buyout-Gesellschaften es tun; dies wird vom Verfasser mit der Existenz von *Implicit Contracts over Control* nach Black und Gilson (1998) im Markt für Wagniskapital begründet. Die Annahme von Wright, Robbie, Thompson et al. (1994), dass kleinere Buyout-Portfoliogesellschaften bei der Desinvestitionsentscheidung über mehr Macht verfügen als größere Buyout-Portfoliogesellschaften, wird von den Befragungsergebnissen nicht unterstützt. Hinsichtlich der Entscheidung über den Beginn von Desinvestitionsprozessen für erfolgreiche (*Performing*) oder hinter den Erwartungen zurückbleibende (*Underperforming*) Beteiligungsengagements sprach die Stichprobe einer Vielzahl an Entscheidungsheuristiken eine mittlere oder hohe Nutzungshäufigkeit zu, wobei die meisten Private Equity-Unternehmen jeweils mindestens zwei Entscheidungsregeln eine hohe Nutzungshäufigkeit beimaßen. Diese Ergebnisse könnten darauf hindeuten, dass Private Equity-Unternehmen die jeweilige Entscheidungsregel für eine Desinvestition aus einem Vorrat an Entscheidungsheuristiken auswählen und sich nicht auf eine, für alle Desinvestitionen allgemeingültige Entscheidungsregel verlassen. Weitergehende Analysen zeigen, dass die unter Private Equity-Unternehmen beliebtesten Entscheidungsregeln unter bestimmten Bedingungen dieselben Ergebnisse wie Entscheidungen nach Maßgabe der Kapitalwertmaximierung erzielen können; indes lassen es die Befragungsergebnisse zweifelhaft erscheinen, dass diese Bedingungen für die Anwendungspraxis zutreffen. Bei der Entscheidung über die Desinvestition von hinter den Erwartungen zurückbleibenden Investitionen wird festgestellt, dass die Verwendung einfacher Entscheidungsheuristiken tendenziell mit dem Alter, der Erfahrung und der Größe des Private Equity-Unternehmens zunimmt. Außerdem zeigen die Ergebnisse eine lediglich schwache empirische Unterstützung für die Hypothese einer frühzeitigen Liquidation von Investitionen niedriger Qualität (*Early Culling*, vgl. Cumming & MacIntosh, 2001, S. 451) – stattdessen weisen weitere Auswertungen auf eine entgegengesetzte Tendenz unter Buyout-Gesellschaften, die Desinvestition solcher Portfoliogesellschaften hinauszuschieben. Schließlich stellt sich bei der Wahl des Exitkanals der Preis als wichtigstes Kriterium heraus, gefolgt von der Form der

Kaufpreiszahlung (z. B. in bar oder in Aktien) und der Terminierung und Sicherheit einer vollständigen Desinvestition. Bei dieser Entscheidung wird abermals der eigenen Reputation eine hohe Bedeutung beigemessen.

Eine übergreifende Betrachtung der Untersuchungsergebnisse führt zu weiteren Erkenntnissen. Zum Ersten spielen Entscheidungsregeln und -kennzahlen der modernen Portfoliotheorie und des CAPM für Private Equity-Firmen offenbar nur eine untergeordnete Rolle. Es wird in dieser Arbeit argumentiert, dass „Marktunvollkommenheiten" der Private Equity-Märkte (die asymmetrische Informationsverteilung zwischen den Marktteilnehmern, fehlende Informationen, die Illiquidität der Beteiligungen und der Fondsanteile sowie der teilweise geringe Diversifikationsgrad von Private Equity-Unternehmen und ihrer Fonds) die Zweckdienlichkeit der zentralen Modelle etablierter Finanztheorie für die Entscheidungsfindung in einem Private Equity-Umfeld vermindern. Viele der empirischen Ergebnisse in dieser Arbeit können dagegen anhand von Theorien und Konstrukten erklärt werden, die im Wesentlichen der neo-institutionalistischen Finanzierungstheorie zugerechnet werden: die Agency-Theorie, die asymmetrische Informationsverteilung und die *Implicit Contract over Control*-Hypothese von Black und Gilson (1998). Möglicherweise bieten alternative theoretische Ansätze, z. B. aus dem Bereich der begrenzten Rationalität, weitere Anknüpfungspunkte für die Erklärung der Entscheidungen von Private Equity-Unternehmen. So erinnert der Einsatz einfacher Kennzahlen und grober Mindestrenditeforderungen bei Investitions- und Desinvestitionsentscheidungen durch Private Equity-Unternehmen an die *Satisfactory Choices* von Simon (1979, S. 501), welche optimierende Entscheidungen ersetzen sollen. Des Weiteren erinnert die Verwendung von Desinvestitionsheuristiken an die *Adaptive Toolbox* von Gigerenzer und Selten (2002a, S. 8), die sie weitestgehend als eine Anzahl von *Fast and Frugal* und an spezielle Umgebungsbedingungen angepasste Entscheidungsheuristiken beschreiben. Zum Zweiten lassen die Ergebnisse auf der einen Seite erkennen, dass sich Private Equity-Unternehmen mit unterschiedlicher Geschäftsausrichtung in vielen Befragungspunkten deutlich voneinander unterscheiden; dies sollte in zukünftigen Forschungsarbeiten zur Entscheidungsfindung in Private Equity-Unternehmen Berücksichtigung finden. Auf der anderen Seite zeigt die Auswertung nur wenige statistisch signifikante Verbindungen zwischen Befragungsdaten und dem geografischen Sitz des Unternehmens in Europa oder den USA und Kanada – offenbar unterscheiden sich die Ansichten europäischer Private Equity-Unternehmen über die Determinanten und Regeln der Entscheidungsfindung in der Regel nicht wesentlich von denen US-amerikanischer und kanadischer Private Equity-Unternehmen. Diese Erkenntnis steht auf den ersten Blick im Gegensatz zu früheren Untersuchungen, welche die Unterschiede zwischen Private Equity-Märkten in Europa und den USA herausstellen (vgl. z. B. Black & Gilson, 1998; Manigart et al., 2002; Schwienbacher, 2005; Wright, Robbie, Romanet et al., 1994). Eine mögliche Erklärung für diese abweichenden Ergebnisse ist, dass Unterschiede zwischen den geografischen Regionen vor allem auf externe Faktoren, wie beispielsweise das Rechtssystem oder die Liquidität der Aktien- und Buyout-Märkte, zurückzuführen sind und weniger auf Faktoren innerhalb der Private Equity-Unternehmen.

Die Untersuchungsergebnisse dieser Arbeit sollten sowohl für die Private Equity-Forschung als auch für die Private Equity-Praxis von Nutzen sein. Für Wissenschaftler bietet diese Arbeit neue Daten und neue Erkenntnisse über die Determinanten und Regeln der Entscheidungsfindung in Private Equity-Unternehmen; die Ergebnisse können zur Entwicklung neuer Ideen und Theorien auf diesem Forschungsgebiet beitragen. Für Praktiker bietet diese Arbeit ein Grundverständnis für mögliche Fallstricke bei der Entscheidungsfindung. Ein gesteigertes Bewusstsein für diese Gefahren sollte Private Equity-Unternehmen dabei unterstützen, die Qualität ihrer Entscheidungen zu verbessern. Diese Dissertation bietet mehrere Anknüpfungspunkte für zukünftige Forschungsarbeiten: Erstens könnte ergänzende Fallstudienforschung genauer untersuchen, *wie* Private Equity-Unternehmen ihre Investitions- und Desinvestitionsentscheidungen treffen und welche Gründe und Motive ihr Entscheidungsverhalten bestimmen. Zweitens könnte die Auswirkung verschiedener Entscheidungsheuristiken auf den Unternehmenserfolg anhand theoretischer Modelle oder zusätzlicher empirischer Daten untersucht werden; möglicherweise könnten so erfolgreiche Entscheidungsstrategien identifiziert werden. Drittens könnte die theoretische Forschung einerseits versuchen, die Modelle der etablierten Finanztheorien dahingehend zu erweitern oder modifizieren, dass sie die „Unvollkommenheiten" und Eigenheiten der Private Equity-Märkte berücksichtigen, andererseits könnte sie die Eignung von Modellen der begrenzten Rationalität für Private Equity-Entscheidungsprobleme erkunden.

Appendices

Appendix A Table of Hypotheses

Hypothesis	Basis	Result[a]	Comment[a]
H1: The more funds a private equity firm has raised, the more importance it tends to attribute to the Liquidity objective	Prediction by Lerner and Schoar (2004) that funds with a lower intensity of asymmetric information about the quality of the private equity firm between inside investors and outside investors should be associated with fewer transfer restrictions for investors	Not supported ($ps > .242$, multivar.)	The bivariate test result is statistically significant ($p < .05$), but the multivariate results are not; the multivariate analysis does not comprise all variables used by Lerner and Schoar and the sensitivities are not very high. The results reveal a strong link between the Liquidity objective and Age
H2a: The importance that buyout firms attribute to the MRR factor management quality is lower than the importance that venture capital firms attribute to the MRR factor management quality	Assumption by Ruhnka and Young (1991, pp.125-128) that a decline in the levels of minimum return requirement from earlier to later stages of investment, as the investment continues to develop, is caused by a decrease in *internal risks*, such as poor management quality, a high cash burn rate, or a lack of internal financial controls	Not supported ($p = .161$)	The directions of mean differences are consistent with the predictions, but very small and not statistically significant. The sensitivity of the statistical tests is moderate; no multivariate tests were conducted
H2b: The importance that buyout firms attribute to the MRR factor capital intensity is lower than the importance that venture capital firms attribute to the MRR factor capital intensity		Not supported ($p = .297$)	
H3: Private equity firms generally view money multiples and IRRs as more important than other metrics for measuring the success of portfolio company investments	Anecdotal evidence from existing literature	Supported ($ps < .0005$)	Strong effect sizes for all metrics tested
H4: Buyout firms with larger transaction sizes generally have more decision power in relation to their portfolio companies than buyout firms with smaller transaction sizes have	Assumption of Wright, Robbie, Thompson et al. (1994) that managers of smaller buyouts should generally have larger equity holdings in the buyout and thus command more decision power relative to the buyout firm	Not supported ($p = .101$)	The sensitivity of the statistical tests was moderate; no multivariate tests were conducted
H5: Private equity firms will more often choose to immediately begin the exit process for investments that are clearly underperforming than they will do for investments that are clearly performing	Empirical evidence on early culling of poor quality investments from Cumming and MacIntosh (2001) and implications from the model of Tykvová (2003)	Supported ($p = .018$)	The size of effect is small and the effect is not statistically significant for the sample of buyout firms only ($p = .148$). Instead, buyout firms show a contrary tendency to procrastinate the exits of such investments
H6: Private equity firms view price as the most important criterion for deciding the exit channel of portfolio investments	Anecdotal evidence from earlier empirical studies	Supported ($ps < .001$)	Strong effect sizes for all criteria tested, excepting the criterion Form Of Payment

[a]*ps* are one-tailed.

Appendix B Print Version of the Survey Form

Research Project
Performance Management and Exit Policies of Private Equity Firms

- We kindly ask for **about ten minutes** of your time to complete this questionnaire
- All participants returning completed questionnaires will receive a **summary report** of results
- The questionnaire is divided into three parts, as follows:

  Part A - **Performance measures** and **objectives** used to manage company investments

  Part B - **Decision power** and **decision criteria** for exiting company investments

  Part C - Some background information on **your private equity firm**

- In case you should not know the exact answer to a specific question please make an estimate. You may ignore questions that do not apply to your firm or where you are not willing to disclose information and return the partially completed questionnaire. A **glossary of terms** is provided on the back of this page
- All responses will be handled **strictly confidential** and will be used only for the purposes of this research project in compliance with Section 40 of the *German Federal Data Protection Act*. Any published material will contain **only aggregate data** and will not identify individual firms
- Please **contact** Mark Broere on +49 160 9028 4630 or at mark.broere@tu-cottbus.de for any **questions** related to this research project
- We would appreciate if you could **return the completed questionnaire** by fax, email or post to:

Mark Broere
Doctoral student
BTU Cottbus, Faculty 3
Chair of Business Administration and Corporate Finance
P.O. Box 10 13 44
03013 Cottbus, GERMANY

Fax (Europe): +49 6109 397 350
Fax (US): +1 402 272 7506

Prof. Dr. Klaus Serfling   Mark Broere

Thank you very much for participating in this survey and for returning the completed questionnaire

Glossary of Terms

Adjusted Present Value (APV)	The *net present value* of a project if financed solely by equity plus the *present value* of any financing benefits
Annualised Money Multiple	The multiple that when compounded over the years of the investment period equals the *money multiple*
Beta Coefficient	A measure of risk that describes how the expected return of a stock or portfolio is correlated to the return of the financial market as a whole
Capital Gain	The increase in sale price of an investment over its purchase price
Discounted Cash Flow (DCF)	see *net present value*
Excess IRR	The difference between deal or fund *IRR* and the compound annual growth rate of a public market index over a matched period of time
Exit	Any initial public offering (IPO), trade sale, secondary sale, buyback or write-off / liquidation of a company investment
Liquidity	The ease and speed with which an asset can be sold at fair market value in a timely fashion
Money Multiple (MM)	The sum of cash received from an investment (plus any residual value if not yet realised) divided by the sum of cash paid into the investment. Money multiples are often also called *investment multiples* or just *multiples.* Depending on whether residual value is included in the calculation, money multiples are also referred to as *total value to paid-in capital* (*TVPI*), or, *distributions to paid-in capital* (*DPI*)
Net Present Value (NPV)	The present value of cash inflows less the present value of cash outflows from a project
Present Value (PV)	The current worth of a future amount of money or stream of cash flows given a specified rate of return (*discount rate*)
IRR	*Internal rate of return* is the discount rate of cash flow that makes net present value equal zero
Public market equivalent (PME)	The *Public market equivalent* is calculated by comparing the value of a (private equity) investment to the value of the residual number of shares in a public market index after matching the investment's cash flow (both time and value) with hypothetical purchases and sales of shares in the public market index
Profitability Index (PI)	The present value of cash flow received from an investment divided by the present value of cash flow paid into the investment (effectively a *money multiple* based on present values)
Sharpe Ratio	Measures the (expected) excess return per unit of risk and is calculated as the (expected) premium return of an investment over the (expected) risk-free rate, divided by the standard deviation of (expected) returns
Time Weighted Return (TWR)	A measure of the compound rate of growth in a portfolio or project, that eliminates the distorting effects of additions and deductions to invested capital (also referred to as geometric mean returns)

Part A – Performance Measures and Objectives

1. Which financial ratios does your firm view as important for ***measuring*** the ***success*** of company investments?

	very important 5	4	3	2	not important 1
internal rate of return *(IRR)*	O	O	O	O	O
money multiple *(MM)*	O	O	O	O	O
annualised money multiple	O	O	O	O	O
capital gain	O	O	O	O	O
time weighted return *(TWR)*	O	O	O	O	O
net present value *(NPV)*, discounted cash flow *(DCF)* or adjusted present value *(APV)*	O	O	O	O	O
profitability index	O	O	O	O	O
public market equivalent *(PME)*	O	O	O	O	O
excess IRR	O	O	O	O	O
other:	O	O	O	O	O

2. In your firm, how important are estimates of ***IRR*** and ***money multiples*** *(MM)* when...

		very important 5	4	3	2	not important 1
... deciding to invest in a company	*IRR*	O	O	O	O	O
	MM	O	O	O	O	O
... deciding to increase the investment in a company	*IRR*	O	O	O	O	O
	MM	O	O	O	O	O
... deciding to reduce or exit a company investment	*IRR*	O	O	O	O	O
	MM	O	O	O	O	O
... considering major decisions at company level *(e.g. acquisitions, restructuring, expansion programmes)*	*IRR*	O	O	O	O	O
	MM	O	O	O	O	O

3. If so, what measures of ***investment risk*** or ***risk-return*** *(e.g. Sharpe ratio)* does your company typically calculate for individual company investments?

....

4. How important are the following ***objectives*** for your firm?

	very important 5	4	3	2	not important 1
deliver high returns to investors	O	O	O	O	O
achieve high certainty of returns to investors	O	O	O	O	O
generate high liquidity of investors' interests in your funds	O	O	O	O	O
generate high income for your firm	O	O	O	O	O
enhance your firm's reputation ...					
... among investors	O	O	O	O	O
... among company owners and entrepreneurs	O	O	O	O	O
... among company managers	O	O	O	O	O
... among financial intermediaries *(e.g. investment banks)*	O	O	O	O	O
other:	O	O	O	O	O

5. Which ***minimum return requirements*** *(sometimes called 'hurdle rates')* are important for investment decisions in your firm?

	very important 5	4	3	2	not important 1
minimum level IRR	O	O	O	O	O
minimum level money multiple *(MM)*	O	O	O	O	O
minimum level discount rate in discounted cash flow *(DCF)* model	O	O	O	O	O
other:	O	O	O	O	O

6. How often is your firm forced to **reject** investment **opportunities** that ***meet minimum return requirements***, because of limited capacities *(e.g. equity capital or staff)*

	very often 5	4	3	2	never 1
	O	O	O	O	O

7. In your firm, what ***factors*** influence the ***level*** of minimum return that you require from a particular investment?

	very important 5	4	3	2	not important 1
stage of investment *(seed, expansion, buyout etc.)*	O	O	O	O	O
industry sector of investment *(technology, consumer goods etc..)*	O	O	O	O	O
capital intensity of business	O	O	O	O	O
beta coefficient of business	O	O	O	O	O
financial leverage *(debt to equity-levels)*	O	O	O	O	O
quality of management team	O	O	O	O	O
expected number of investment years	O	O	O	O	O
capital market environment *(interest rates, stock market levels etc.)*	O	O	O	O	O
inflation rates	O	O	O	O	O
fundraising environment	O	O	O	O	O
profile of other investments already undertaken by the same fund	O	O	O	O	O
other:	O	O	O	O	O
None – same level for all investments O					

Part B – Exit Decisions

8. Who generally takes the lead on deciding ***when*** to begin an ***exit*** process?

	nearly always	mostly	joint lead	mostly	nearly always	
your private equity firm	O	O	O	O	O	company management

O other *(e.g. lead investor of the consortium)*: ....

9. Who generally takes the lead on deciding ***how*** *(IPO, trade sale etc.)* to ***exit***?

	nearly always	mostly	joint lead	mostly	nearly always	
your private equity firm	O	O	O	O	O	company management

O other *(e.g. lead investor of the consortium)*: ....

Research project on performance management and exit policies of private equity firms
Brandenburg University of Technology, Germany

Page 2 of 4

10. ***When*** do you ***begin*** the ***exit*** process for an investment that is clearly ***performing***?

	very often 5	4	3	2	never 1
immediately	O	O	O	O	O
as late as possible	O	O	O	O	O
as soon as a required ...					
*price or MM** is expected to be achieved	O	O	O	O	O
IRR is expected to be achieved	O	O	O	O	O
when no *major* increase of ...					
*... price or MM** is expected from waiting another period	O	O	O	O	O
... IRR is expected from waiting another period	O	O	O	O	O
whereas a *major* (price) / (IRR) increase is roughly ...... (%) / (%-points) p.a.					
Wait until the period in which you expect the maximum ...					
*... price or MM** over the lifetime of the fund	O	O	O	O	O
... IRR over the lifetime of the fund	O	O	O	O	O
other:	O	O	O	O	O

11. ***When*** do you ***begin*** the ***exit*** process for an investment that is clearly ***underperforming***?

	very often 5	4	3	2	never 1
immediately	O	O	O	O	O
as late as possible *(since conditions might improve)*	O	O	O	O	O
when no *major* increase of ...					
*... price or MM** is expected from waiting another period	O	O	O	O	O
... IRR is expected from waiting another period	O	O	O	O	O
... whereas a *major* (price) / (IRR) increase is roughly ...... (%) / (%-points) p.a.					
wait until the period in which you expect the maximum ...					
*... price or MM** over the lifetime of the fund	O	O	O	O	O
... IRR over the lifetime of the fund	O	O	O	O	O
other:	O	O	O	O	O

12. ***How important*** are the following criteria for deciding which ***exit route*** *(e.g. IPO, trade sale, secondary sale)* you choose for a company investment?

	very important 5	4	3	2	not important 1
price	O	O	O	O	O
form of payment *(cash, securities etc.)*	O	O	O	O	O
timing until, and certainty of achieving a full *(100%)* exit	O	O	O	O	O
cost	O	O	O	O	O
contractual obligations and risks *(representations, warranties etc.)*	O	O	O	O	O
interests of the investee company's management	O	O	O	O	O
impact on your firm's reputation ...					
... among investors	O	O	O	O	O
... among company owners and entrepreneurs	O	O	O	O	O
... among company managers	O	O	O	O	O
... among financial intermediaries *(e.g. investment banks)*	O	O	O	O	O
other:	O	O	O	O	O

** price and money multiple refer to the capital invested by your firm*

Research project on performance management and exit policies of private equity firms
Brandenburg University of Technology, Germany

Page 3 of 4

Part C – Your Private Equity Firm

13. ***Type*** of firm

- O business angel
- O venture capital firm
- O buyout firm
- O generalist
- O other: ....

14. Who provides the majority of your ***fund capital***?

- O parent company
- O outside investors
- O capital markets *(publicly-traded vehicles)*
- O private family
- O government, state or public institution
- O other: ....

15. ***General*** characteristics

does your firm mostly manage its investments in *(closed-end)* funds with a fixed lifetime? *(yes/no)*	....
If not, does your firm mostly undertake company investments with a limited or unlimited time horizon?	....
how many years has your private equity firm existed?	........yrs
how many private equity funds has your firm raised so far?	..........#
what is *(roughly)* your firm's total capital under management?	..................m€
how many company investments are *(roughly)* currently managed by your firm?	..........#

16. Investment ***focus***

does your firm specialise in industry sectors? *(yes/no)*	....
does your firm specialise in geographic areas? *(yes/no)*	....
does your firm mostly target majority or minority ownership stakes?	....
what is *(roughly)* your typical investment size (equity stake)?	......................m€
are your target firms preferably well-performing, underperforming or loss-making?	....

17. ***Performance*** characteristics

What average return has your firm *(roughly)* achieved across all funds

- IRR ....%
- MM ....

18. Management ***style***

- O hands-off
- O supportive
- O hands-on
- O other: ....

19. Any additional ***comment***

....

END

REPLY SHEET

Mark Broere
Doctoral student
BTU Cottbus, Faculty 3
Chair of Business Administration and Corporate Finance
P.O. Box 10 13 44
03013 Cottbus
GERMANY

Fax (Europe): +49 6109 397 350
Fax (US): +1 402 272 7506

Please send the (free) copy of summary results to:

Name: ....

Position: ....

Company: ....

Fax: ....

Email: ....

Appendix C Examples of Written Communications

Brandenburgische Technische Universität Cottbus

Brandenburg University of Technology
Faculty 3 – Mechanical, Electrical and Industrial Engineering
Chair of Business Administration and Corporate Finance

Mark Broere
Doctoral student

phone: +49 6109 397 349
fax: +49 6109 397 350
mobile: +49 160 9028 4630
e-mail: mark.broere@tu-cottbus.de

9 March 2009

Mr.

USA

By Fax:

Dear Mr.

Research Project on Performance Management and Exit Policies of Private Equity Firms

In the next several days, you will receive an invitation by mail to participate in a multi-national research project that is designed to understand how private equity firms manage their company investments.

This project is a major undertaking – one of the largest and most significant studies yet commenced in this area, involving around 2,500 private equity firms in North America and Europe.

We hope that you will agree to participate in the study by filling out the questionnaire you will receive in a few days. As in any study the reliability of the findings depends heavily on the cooperation of each person in the sample. Your name and the identity of your firm will not be divulged – any published material will contain only aggregate data and will not identify individual contributions.

We will greatly appreciate your cooperation.

Sincerely,

Mark Broere

Mark Broere, BTU Cottbus, Faculty 3, Chair of Business Administration and Corporate Finance, P.O. Box 10 13 44, 03013 Cottbus, Germany

Brandenburgische Technische Universität Cottbus

Brandenburg University of Technology
Faculty 3 – Mechanical, Electrical and Industrial Engineering
Chair of Business Administration and Corporate Finance

Mark Broere
Doctoral student

phone: +49 6109 397 349
fax: +49 6109 397 350
mobile: +49 160 9028 4630
e-mail: mark.broere@tu-cottbus.de

11 March 2009

Mr.

New York, NY 10001
USA

Dear Mr. ,

Research Project on Performance Management and Exit Policies of Private Equity Firms

I am inviting you and your private equity firm to participate in a research project to establish the objectives and performance measures that buyout firms and venture capitalists employ for managing investments, and to understand how exit decisions are taken.

The project is one of the most significant studies yet undertaken in this area and involves a survey of around 2,500 private equity firms in North America and Europe. It is part of my doctoral thesis under the mentorship of Prof. Dr. Klaus Serfling at the Chair of Business Administration and Corporate Finance at the Brandenburg University of Technology, Germany. With this research, I hope to contribute to an area of private equity that has yet received little attention, and thus help to promote a better understanding of private equity firms and the general private equity industry.

In return for completing the questionnaire, each survey respondent will receive a (free) summary report of results. Additionally, I will share the results of my study in a scientific publication. All responses will be handled strictly confidential and will be used only for the purposes of this research project in compliance with Section 40 of the *German Federal Data Protection Act*. Any published material will contain only aggregate data and will not identify individual firms.

The US National Venture Capital Association (NVCA), the European Private Equity & Venture Capital Association (EVCA), and Canada's Venture Capital & Private Equity Association (CVCA) are informed of this project and have received draft copies of the questionnaire for review.

Your responses will make a most important contribution to the project. A pre-test has shown that the form is typically completed in about ten minutes. To participate you can either

A. Complete the questionnaire online at www.privateequityexits.com (code: [illegible]), or,

B. Complete the enclosed questionnaire and return it by fax until **Friday, 27 March**.

If you have any questions including concerns about the confidentiality of your information in this study, please contact me under the above contact details.

Sincerely,

Mark Broere

Mark Broere, BTU Cottbus, Faculty 3, Chair of Business Administration and Corporate Finance, P.O. Box 10 13 44, 03013 Cottbus, Germany

Appendix D Table of Final Disposition Codes for the Sample Frame of Private Equity Firms

Category	Count
1. Returned questionnaires	
1.1 Complete	134 [a]
1.2 Partial or break-off with sufficient information	2 [a]
2. Eligible, "Non-Interview"	
2.1 Refusal, break-off or partial completion with insufficient information	
2.11 Explicit refusal	
2.111 Other person refusal	18
2.112 Known respondent-level refusal	18
2.12 Break-off, questionnaire too incomplete to process	3 [a]
2.121 Logged on to survey, did not complete any items	2
2.122 Logged on to survey, break-off before viewing first page of questionnaire	5
2.123 Insufficient quality of fax transmission	1 [a]
3. Unknown eligibility, "Non-Interview"	
3.1 Nothing known about respondent or address	
3.19 Nothing ever returned	2,076 [b]
3.3 Unknown whereabouts, mailing returned undelivered	40 [c]
3.9 Other	1
4. Not eligible	
4.1 Selected respondent screened out of sample	
4.11 Firm ceased to exist or otherwise not eligible (explicit)	35 [d]
4.12 Firm ceased to exist or otherwise not eligible (implicit)	30 [e]
4.7 No eligible respondent	4 [f]
4.9 Duplicate listing	4
Total	2,373

Note. The disposition codes are drawn from the 2009 Standard Definitions of the American Association for Public Opinion Research (AAPOR) for final dispositions of case codes for mail surveys and for internet surveys of specifically named persons.
[a]Questionnaires were allocated to these categories according to the following AAPOR guideline: "Less than 50% of all applicable questions answered (with other than a refusal or no answer) equals break-off, 50%-80% equals partial, and more that [*sic*] 80% equals complete" (AAPOR 2009 Standard Definitions, p. 12). The percentage completion of each questionnaire was calculated according to a pre-defined point system (available from the author upon request).
[b]Includes firms where no fax or email details were available for follow-up letters. No mailings were returned as undeliverable (the sender details were not supplied on the envelopes).
[c]Follow-up letters by fax and/or email generated error messages.
[d]Statement on company website, email response or press article specifying that firm has ceased to exist, is inactive or otherwise not eligible.
[e]Follow-up by fax and/or email generated error messages *and* company website either for sale or otherwise not available.
[f]These (completed) questionnaires were eliminated from the sample because of serious doubts about the profit-seeking nature of the private equity firm. The respective respondents attributed importance ratings of 1 or 2, on a numbered 5-point scale, ranging from 5 (*very important*) to 1 (*not important*), to the objective of delivering high returns to investors. Additional research revealed that all of these firms were directly or indirectly funded by a government, state or a public institution.

Appendix E Analysis of Determinants of Firm Performance

This analysis investigates the determinants of firm performance in the sample of private equity firms. Venture capital and buyout firms are reviewed separately from each other due to their disparate business models (despite having many features in common).[153] Most private equity firms are typically structured as limited partnerships; they conduct cyclical fundraisings, undertake investments for limited periods of time, assume an active role of sponsorship, and receive performance-related compensation. Buyout firms typically acquire majority ownership stakes in established medium-to-large companies; they frequently finance their purchases with substantial amounts of debt and manage only a small number of investments simultaneously. In contrast, venture capital firms typically acquire minority stakes of young, growing companies. Financing is mostly equity and frequently made available in steps (see Footnote 54 on staged financing). Venture capital firms often hold a sizeable number of company investments at one point in time. It is therefore perhaps no coincidence that the results in the descriptive section of this thesis exhibit a statistically significant difference between the performance of venture capital firms and that of buyout firms (see Table 8 in Chapter 2.3).

Linear regression analyses were conducted with *ln IRR* as dependent variable.[154] In order to increase the statistical power of the analysis, the predictor variables comprised only firm characteristic variables that were significantly associated with the IRR in bivariate tests. A screening of Spearman rank correlations between the IRR and other firm characteristic variables yielded three significant associations (alpha = .05, two-tailed): In the sample of venture capital firms the IRR is significantly positively correlated with Funds ($r_s = .34$, $p = .041$, two-tailed, $n = 37$) and in the sample of buyout firms the IRR is significantly negatively correlated with GeoSpec ($r_s = .\text{-}39$, $p = .004$, two-tailed, $n = 53$) and Investments ($r_s = .\text{-}28$, $p = .044$, two-tailed, $n = 53$). Table E1 presents summary results of the regression analyses that were performed with these variables.[155] The results suggest that the IRR of venture capital firms in the sample is positively related to firm experience (as measured by the number of funds raised) and that the IRR of buyout firms in the sample is negatively associated with geographical specialisation and, to a lesser extent, with the number of investments.

---

[153] Generalist and other type private equity firms are disregarded in this analysis

[154] IRRs were chosen rather than multiples because they offered a larger dataset

[155] Prior to the regression analyses, the data were screened for linearity, outliers, normality, multicollinearity, and homoscedasticity of residuals. None of these analyses gave rise to serious concern

Table E1

Summary results of linear regression analyses for venture capital and buyout firms with ln IRR as dependent variable

Variable	*B*	*SE B*	t	*p*	exp (*B*)	95% CI for exp (*B*) Lower	Upper
Venture capital sample (n = 30)							
Constant***	2.17	.29	7.5 ***	< .0005	8.74	4.83	15.83
Funds**	0.20	.09	2.2 **	.036	1.22	1.01	1.48
Buyout sample (n = 45)							
Constant***	3.90	.12	33.2 ***	< .0005	49.26	38.87	62.42
GeoSpec***	-0.39	.11	-3.5 ***	.001	0.67	0.54	0.85
Investments*	-0.01	.01	-1.8 *	.082	0.99	0.97	1.00

Note. Venture capital sample: $R^2 = .15$, $F(1, 28) = 4.86$, $p = .036$. Adjusted $R^2 = .12$. Buyout sample: $R^2 = .28$, $F(2, 42) = 8.08$, $p = .001$. Adjusted $R^2 = .24$. All figures are based on country-weighted survey data. The weights reflect the ratio of a country's share of private equity firms in the frame population to its share of firms in the survey sample. Ln IRR is the natural logarithm of the rough average IRR (in %) that a respondent's firm has achieved across all funds. Some amounts were expressly specified as *gross*. One amount was specified as *net*; this value was divided by 0.8 to arrive at a rough approximation of gross return. Response data also include one forecast value and three minimum return specifications (implied by ">" as prefix or "+" as suffix). *Venture capital* also includes eight firms of related firm types, such as "growth equity" and "business angel". *Buyout* also includes two firms of related firm types ("industry specific buyout" and "restructuring buyout"). Funds is the number of private equity funds a respondent's firm has raised. In one case a specified range was replaced by its mean value. One outlier with 23 funds was excluded from the regression analysis. GeoSpec refers to firms, for which respondents specified whether or not they specialise in geographical areas. Investments is the rough number of company investments managed by a respondent's firm. One outlier with 140 investments was excluded from the regression analysis.

Back-transformation of the regression model for venture capital firms yields the following relationship:

$$IRR = 8.74\, e^{.20\, Funds}\,.$$

Consequentially, the ratio between the predicted IRR of a venture capital firm that has raised n+1 funds and the predicted IRR of a venture capital firm that has raised n funds is calculated as follows:

$$\frac{IRR(n+1)}{IRR(n)} = \frac{8.74\, e^{.20(n+1)}}{8.74\, e^{.20(n)}} = e^{.20} = 1.22\,.$$

Thus, the model predicts an average increase in IRR by 22 per cent (95% CI [1.4, 47.6]) for every additional fund the venture capital firm has raised. A back-transformation of the regression model for buyout firms yields the following relationship:

$$IRR = 49.26\, e^{-39\, GeoSpec}\, e^{-.1\, Investments}\,,$$

with the following partial solutions:

$$IRR_{GeoSpec=0} = 49.26\, e^{-.1\, Investments}\,,$$

and

$$IRR_{GeoSpec=1} = 33.25\ e^{-.1\ Investments}\ .$$

Thus, controlling for the number of investments, the model predicts the IRR of buyout firms with a geographical specialisation to be almost one third less than that of buyout firms without a geographical specialisation. Applying the boundaries of the 95% confidence interval to the formula yields a (compounded) range for the decrease between 15 and 85 per cent. The decrease in predicted IRR for an increase in the number of investments is comparatively small. The factor of decrease in predicted IRR for every additional investment ranges between 0.97 and 1.00. For example, an additional 5 investments implies a change in predicted IRR between -14.2 and +1.0 per cent.

Appendix F Table of Pearson Correlations for Variables Used in the Logistic Regression Analysis for Predicting Survey Participation Status

Variable	1	2	3	4	5	6	7	8	9
1 Age (yrs)	1.00	-.19	-.10	-.01	-.07	-.04	.00	.02	.04
2 Funds Raised ($m)		1.00	-.06	-.11	.03	.02	-.03	.11	-.14
3 US & Canada			1.00	.58	.47	.52	.57	-.08	-.05
4 UK				1.00	.40	.45	.49	-.02	-.01
5 France					1.00	.37	.40	-.01	-.04
6 Germany						1.00	.45	.03	.06
7 Nordic							1.00	-.09	.01
8 Venture Capital								1.00	.46
9 Buyout									1.00

Note. n = 1.111. The data for sample frame characteristics were obtained from the Preqin database *Fund Manager Profiles* in February 2009. Funds Raised denotes the value of funds raised over the last ten years in $ millions. Private equity firm headquarter location was coded in five dummy variables, whereas *Nordic* stands for Denmark, Finland, Norway, and Sweden. The reference dummy (not included in the table) comprises Italy, the Netherlands, Spain, and Switzerland. The type of private equity firm was coded in two dummy variables, whereas the reference dummy (not included in the table) is *generalist*.

Appendix G Table of Independent Variable Definitions

Variable	Definition
	Ordinal scale and continuous variables
Age	Number of years a respondent's firm had been in existence (at the time of the survey)
Funds	Number of private equity funds a respondent's firm had raised until the time of the survey. In one case a specified range was replaced by its mean value
Capital	Rough total capital under management of a respondent's firm in € millions. In one case a specified range was replaced by its mean value. Amounts in other currencies were converted to € amounts using the average of the market exchange rate over the time of the survey
Investments	Rough number of company investments managed by a respondent's firm at the time of the survey
Investment Size	Respondent firm's (rough) typical investment size (equity stake) in € millions. Range specifications were replaced by their mean values. Amounts in other currencies were converted to € amounts using the averages of market exchange rates over the time of the survey
IRR	Rough average IRR (in %) that a respondent's firm had achieved across all funds (at the time of the survey). Some amounts were expressly specified as "gross". One amount was specified as "net"; this value was divided by .8 to arrive at a rough approximation of gross return. Response data also include one "forecast" and three minimum return specifications (implied by ">" as prefix or "+" as suffix)
Multiple	Rough average multiple that a respondent's firm had achieved across all funds (at the time of the survey). Some figures were expressly specified as "gross". Response data also include one "forecast" and two minimum return specifications (implied by ">" as prefix or "+" as suffix). Two extreme values ("50" and "1300") were excluded from the analysis
	Dichotomous variables
EU - US/Can	Private equity firm headquarter location: EU = Europe; US/Can = United States or Canada
BO - VC	Private equity firm type: BO = buyout; VC = venture capital; VC includes eight firms of related types, such as "growth equity" and "business angel"; BO includes two firms of related types ("industry specific buyout" and "restructuring buyout")
GeoSpec	Private equity firms, for which respondents specified whether or not they specialise in geographic areas
IndSpec	Private equity firms, for which respondents specified whether or not they specialise in industry sectors
Outside Inv	Refers to whether or not respondents specified that their firm sources the majority of its fund capital from outside investors
Majority - Minority	Ownership stake targeted by private equity firm: Majority = mostly majority; Minority = mostly
Well/Under - Loss	Preferred performance of target companies: Well/Under ="well-performing" or "underperforming"; Loss = "loss-making"
Hands On - Supp	Private equity firm management style: Hands on = "hands-on"; Supp = "supportive"
CEF	Private equity firms, for which respondents specified whether or not they mostly manage investments in (closed-end) funds with a fixed lifetime

Note. Categorical firm characteristic variables with more than two categories were re-coded into dichotomous variables by collapsing or disregarding categories in such a way that the new variables yielded a high contrast and satisfactory subsample sizes.

Appendix H Table of Spearman Rank Correlations for Independent Variables

Variable	1	2	3	4	5	6	7	8	9	10	11	12	13	14
1 Age (yrs)	1.00	.78***	.41***	.41***	.16*	-.08	.08	-.12	-.08	.00	.05	.04	-.27***	.21***
2 Funds		1.00	.52***	.46***	.22***	.07	-.01	-.01	.08	.04	-.03	.05	-.32***	.17**
3 Capital (€m)			1.00	.33***	.78***	-.02	.23***	.05	-.09	.16*	.35***	-.01	-.13	.16*
4 Investments				1.00	-.12	.06	-.46***	.06	-.04	-.02	-.43***	-.24***	-.35***	.22***
5 Investment Size (€m)					1.00	.01	.61***	.05	-.06	.24***	.63***	.09	-.01	.03
6 EU - US/Can						1.00	.03	.20**	-.15*	-.19**	-.10	.06	.03	.14*
7 BO - VC							1.00	.01	-.29***	.16*	.80***	.16*	.06	-.04
8 GeoSpec								1.00	.06	-.04	-.02	-.16*	.01	-.04
9 IndSpec									1.00	.09	-.17*	-.04	.18**	-.03
10 Outside Inv										1.00	.21**	.01	.15*	.34***
11 Majority - Minority											1.00	.23**	.14	-.02
12 Well/Under - Loss												1.00	-.09	-.03
13 Hands On - Supp													1.00	-.01
14 CEF														1.00

Note. Correlations were tested pairwise, using country-weighted data. Weighted n ranges between 95 and 156. The weights reflect the ratio of a country's share of private equity firms in the frame population to its share of firms in the survey sample. Age is the number of years a respondent's firm has been in existence. Funds is the number of private equity funds a respondent's firm has raised. Capital is the rough total capital under management of a respondent's firm in € millions. Investments is the rough number of company investments managed by a respondent's firm. Investment Size is a respondent firm's rough typical investment size (equity stake) in € millions. Range specifications were replaced by their means, and amounts in other currencies were converted to € amounts using the averages of market exchange rates over the time of the survey. EU - US/Can denotes headquarter location: EU = Europe; US/Can = United States of America or Canada. BO - VC denotes firm type: BO = buyout; VC = venture capital; VC includes eight firms of related types, such as "growth equity" and "business angel"; BO includes two firms of related types ("industry specific buyout" and "restructuring buyout"). GeoSpec refers to firms, for which respondents specified whether or not they specialise in geographical areas. IndSpec refers to firms, for which respondents specified whether or not they specialise in industry sectors. Outside Inv refers to whether or not respondents specified that their firm sources the majority of its fund capital from outside investors. Majority - Minority refers to targeted ownership stake: Majority = mostly majority; Minority = mostly minority. Well/Under - Loss refers to the preferred performance of target companies: Well/Under ="well-performing" or "underperforming"; Loss = "loss-making". Hands On - Supp denotes management style: Hands on = "hands-on"; Supp = "supportive". CEF refers to firms, for which respondents specified whether or not they mostly manage investments in (closed-end) funds with a fixed lifetime.

$^{*}p < .10$. $^{**}p < .05$. $^{***}p < .01$. All ps are two-tailed.

Appendix I Table of Pearson Correlations for Variables Used in the Linear Regression Analyses for the Importance of the Liquidity Objective

Variable	1	2	3	4	5
1 EU - US/Can	1.00	.04	.03	-.02	-.06
2 BO - VC		1.00	.29 ***	-.12	.19 **
3 Ln Capital			1.00	.36 ***	.44 ***
4 Funds				1.00	.53 ***
5 Ln Age					1.00

Note. n = 106. All figures are based on country-weighted data. The weights reflect the ratio of a country's share of private equity firms in the frame population to its share of firms in the survey sample. EU - US/Can denotes headquarter location: EU = Europe; US/Can = United States of America or Canada (reference). BO - VC denotes firm type: BO = buyout; VC = venture capital (reference); VC includes eight firms of related types, such as "growth equity" and "business angel"; BO includes two firms of related types ("indust ry specific buyout" and "restructuring buyout"). Ln Capital is the natural logarithm of the rough total capital under management of a respondent's firm in € millions. Funds is the number of private equity funds a respondent's firm has raised. Ln Age is the natural logarithm of the number of years a respondent's firm has been in existence. Range specifications were replaced by their means, and amounts in other currencies were converted to € amounts using the averages of market exchange rates over the time of the survey.

$^{*}p < .10$. $^{**}p < .05$. $^{***}p < .01$. All *p*s are two-tailed.

Appendix J Analytical Equivalence of the Policy to Maximise Net Present Value and thc Decision Rule to Begin an Exit Process When No Major Price Increase is Expected From Waiting Another Period

Consider a portfolio investment that begins in period 0 with a payment of a_0 and is realised after n periods for an amount s_n greater than zero. Throughout the holding period there are no cash flows other than a constant monitoring cost c for each holding period. Assuming a constant (non-negative) discount rate i, the NPV of the portfolio investment is calculated as follows:

$$NPV = -a_0 + \sum_{t=1}^{n} \frac{-c}{(1+i)^t} + \frac{s_n}{(1+i)^n}.$$

If the holding period is extended by one period, the incremental NPV amounts to

$$-a_0 + \sum_{t=1}^{n+1} \frac{-c}{(1+i)^t} + \frac{s_{n+1}}{(1+i)^{n+1}} - \left[-a_0 + \sum_{t=1}^{n} \frac{-c}{(1+i)^t} + \frac{s_n}{(1+i)^n}\right] = \frac{s_{n+1} - s_n(1+i) - c}{(1+i)^{n+1}}.$$

The denominator of this term is positive. Therefore, the incremental NPV is positive if the numerator is positive, too. This leads to the condition:

$$s_{n+1} - s_n > s_n i + c.$$

Thus, extending the holding period by one period will lead to an increase in NPV *only* if the price appreciation for the period is greater than the opportunity cost of the earlier sale plus the monitoring cost for the additional period. If the price increase of the portfolio investment decreases monotonically over time, the policy to maximise NPV can be achieved by extending the holding period as long as the above inequality holds true (assuming liquid markets and an infinite time horizon). Under uncertainty, the NPV-maximising decision is to continue the investment as long as the *expected* price increase from waiting an additional period exceeds the *expected* opportunity cost of the earlier sale plus the *expected* monitoring cost for the additional period. Similarly, the decision heuristic to begin an exit process when no major price increase is expected from waiting another period can conversely be formulated as: Continue the investment as long as the expected price increase from waiting another period exceeds a certain amount (i.e. the "major price increase"). It follows from this that, under these assumptions, the two rules are equivalent if the amount that defines the major price increase in the decision heuristic is the expected opportunity cost of the earlier sale plus the expected monitoring cost for the additional period.[156]

[156] Should the amount that a private equity firm demands for a continued investment exceed this amount there is a risk that the private equity firm will discontinue an investment, although the expected price increase still meets the NPV condition

References

> It was said that [the library] went on forever. It was said that you could wander for days among the distant shelves, that there were lost tribes of research students somewhere in there, that strange things lurked in forgotten alcoves and were preyed on by other things that were even stranger (Pratchett, 2001, pp. 2–3)

3i Group (2006, June 2). *3i makes 4.9x its money on Azzurri* [Press release]. Retrieved from http://www.3i.com/media/press-releases/azzurri_020606.html.

AGHION, P., BOLTON, P., & TIROLE, J. (2004). Exit options in corporate finance: Liquidity versus incentives. *Review of Finance*, *8*(3), 327–353. doi:10.1007/s10679-004-2542-0.

AKERLOF, G. A. (1970). The market for "lemons": Quality uncertainty and the market mechanism. *The Quarterly Journal of Economics*, *84*(3), 488–500.

American Psychological Association (2010). *Publication manual of the American Psychological Association* (6th ed.). Washington, DC: Author.

AMIHUD, Y., & MENDELSON, H. (2012). Liquidity, the value of the firm, and corporate finance. *Journal of Applied Corporate Finance, 24*(1), 17–32. doi:10.1111/j.1745-6622.2012.00362.x.

ARCOT, S. R. (2005). *Participating convertible preferred stock in venture capital exits.* LSE Ricafe Working Paper No. 20. Retrieved from http://ssrn.com/abstract=819843.

BADER, H. (1996). *Private Equity als Anlagekategorie: Theorie, Praxis und Portfoliomanagement für institutionelle Investoren* (Doctoral dissertation, University of St.Gallen, Switzerland). Bern, Switzerland: Paul Haupt.

BASCHA, A., & WALZ, U. (2001). Convertible securities and optimal exit decisions in venture capital finance. *Journal of Corporate Finance*, *7*(3), 285–306. doi:10.1016/S0929-1199(01)00023-2.

BAYAR, O., & CHEMMANUR, T. J. (2011). IPOs versus acquisitions and the valuation premium puzzle: A theory of exit choice by entrepreneurs and venture capitalists. *Journal of Financial and Quantitative Analysis* *46*(6), 1755–1793. doi:10.1017/S0022109011000408.

BERG, A. (2005). What is strategy for buyout associations? Berlin, Germany: VWF.

BERGLÖF, E. (1994). A control theory of venture capital finance. *The Journal of Law, Economics, and Organization*, *10*(2), 247–267.

BERNSTEIN, S., LERNER, J., SØRENSEN, M., & STRÖMBERG, P. (2009). Private equity, industry performance and cyclicality. In World Economic Forum (Ed.), *The global economic impact of private equity report 2010* (Globalization of Alternative Investments Working Papers No. 3, pp. 1–22). Geneva, Switzerland. Retrieved from http://www3.weforum.org/docs/WEF_IV_PrivateEquity_Report_2010.pdf.

BIENZ, C. & LEITE, T. (2008). *A pecking-order of venture capital exits*. Retrieved from http://ssrn.com/abstract=916742.

BLACK, B. S., & GILSON, R. J. (1998). Venture capital and the structure of capital markets: Banks versus stock markets. *Journal of Financial Economics, 47*(3), 243–277.

BODIE, Z., KANE, A., & MARCUS, A. J. (2008). *Investments* (7th, international ed.). Boston, MA: McGraw-Hill/Irwin.

BORELL, M. (2011). *Private equity in Europe: investment selection, resource allocation and financial distress*. (Doctoral dissertation, Johann Wolfgang Goethe-University, Frankfurt am Main).

BORTZ, J., & DÖRING, N. (2006). *Forschungsmethoden und Evaluation für Human- und Sozialwissenschaftler* (4th ed.). Heidelberg, Germany: Springer Medizin.

BOTTAZZI, L., & DA RIN, M. (2002). Venture capital in Europe and the financing of innovative companies. *Economic Policy, 17*(34), 231–269.

BOUCLY, Q., SRAER, D., & THESMAR, D. (2011). Growth LBOs. *Journal of Financial Economics, 102*(2), 432–453. doi:10.1016/j.jfineco.2011.05.014.

BREALEY, R. A., & MYERS, S. C. (1991). *Principles of corporate finance* (4th, international ed.). New York, NY: McGraw-Hill.

BREALEY, R. A., MYERS, S. C., & ALLEN, F. (2011). *Principles of corporate finance* (10th, global ed.). New York, NY: McGraw-Hill/Irwin.

BRYMAN, A. (2008). *Social research methods* (3rd ed.). Oxford, UK: Oxford University Press.

BUSHROD, L. (2004). Is it possible to benchmark private equity performance? *European Venture Capital Journal, 113*(September), 50–53.

BUSSE VON COLBE, W., & LAßMANN, G. (1990). *Betriebswirtschaftstheorie, Band 3: Investitionstheorie* (3rd ed.). Berlin, Germany: Springer.

CFA Institute (2010). Global investment performance standards: As adopted by the GIPS executive committee on 29 January 2010. Retrieved November 16, 2011, from http://www.cfapubs.org/doi/pdf/10.2469/ccb.v2010.n5.1.

CFA Institute, Investment Performance Council (2003). *Interpretive guidance for private equity*. Retrieved November 16, 2011, from http://www.gipsstandards.org/standards/guidance/archive/pdf/PrivateEquityGuidance.pdf.

CHALMERS, A. F. (1999). *What is this thing called science?* (3rd ed.). Indianapolis, IN: Hackett.

CHIAMPOU, G. F., & KALLETT, J. J. (1989). Risk/return profile of venture capital. *Journal of Business Venturing*, *4*(1), 1–10.

COCHRANE, J. H. (2005). The risk and return of venture capital. *Journal of Financial Economics*, *75*(1), 3–52.

Craigs Investment Partners (n.d.). *A guide to private equity – 08/09*. Retrieved September 27, 2011, from http://www.craigsip.com/userfiles/file/GuidePrivateEquity_280109.pdf.

CUMMING, D. J., & JOHAN, S. (2010). Venture capital investment duration. *Journal of Small Business Management*, *48*(2), 228–257. doi:10.1111/j.1540-627X.2010.00293.x.

CUMMING, D. J., & MACINTOSH, J. G. (2001). Venture capital investment duration in Canada and the United States. *Journal of Multinational Financial Management*, *11*(4-5), 445–463.

CUMMING, D. J., & MACINTOSH, J. G. (2003). Venture capital exits in Canada and the United States. *University of Toronto Law Journal*, *53*, 101–200. Retrieved from http://ssrn.com/abstract=321641.

CUMMING, D. J., & MACINTOSH, J. G. (2006). Firm, market and strategic factors in venture capital exits. In M. Bagella, L. Bechetti, & I. Hasan (Eds.), *Transparency, governance and markets* (pp. 67–93). Amsterdam, The Netherlands: Elsevier.

CUMMING, D. J., SCHMIDT, D., & WALZ, U. (2010). Legality and venture capital governance around the world. *Journal of Business Venturing*, *25*(1), 54–72. doi:10.1016/j.jbusvent.2008.07.001.

CUMMING, D. J., & WALZ, U. (2010). Private equity returns and disclosure around the world. *Journal of International Business Studies*, *41*(4), 727–754. doi:10.1057/jibs.2009.62.

DAMODARAN, A. (2005). *Marketability and value: Measuring the illiquidity discount*. Retrieved from http://ssrn.com/abstract=841484.

DAVIS, S. J., HALTIWANGER, J., JARMIN, R., LERNER, J., & MIRANDA, J. (2009). Private equity, jobs and productivity. In World Economic Forum (Ed.), *The global economic impact of private equity report 2009* (Globalization of Alternative Investments Working Papers No. 2, pp. 25–43). Geneva, Switzerland. Retrieved from http://www3.weforum.org/docs/WEF_IV_PrivateEquity_Report_2009.pdf.

DIMOV, D., SHEPHERD, D. A., & SUTCLIFFE, K. M. (2007). Requisite expertise, firm reputation, and status in venture capital investment allocation decisions. *Journal of Business Venturing, 22*(4), 481–502. doi:10.1016/j.jbusvent.2006.05.001.

DITTMANN, I., MAUG, E., & KEMPER, J. (2004). How fundamental are fundamental values? Valuation methods and their Impact on the performance of German venture capitalists. *European Financial Management, 10*(4), 609–638.

DIXON, R. (1991). Venture capitalists and the appraisal of investments. *Omega, 19*(5), 333–344.

EAGLE, D., GRINDER, B., & KIEFER, D. B. (2008). MIRR vs. IRR: Exploring the logic of the incremental reinvestment assumption. *Journal of International Finance & Economics, 8*(4), 69–75.

ELANGO, B., FRIED, V. H., HISRICH, R. D., & POLONCHEK, A. (1995). How venture capital firms differ. *Journal of Business Venturing, 10*(2), 157–179.

ELLIS, C., PATTNI, S., & TAILOR, D. (2012). *Measuring private equity returns and benchmarking against public markets*. BVCA Research Report. Retrieved from http://ssrn.com/abstract=1986783.

EMORY, C. W. (1985). *Business research methods* (3rd ed.). Homewood, IL: Irwin.

European Private Equity & Venture Capital Association (2006). *EVCA reporting guidelines: June 2006 (reprint January 2009)*. Retrieved November 16, 2011, from http://www.evca.eu/uploadedFiles/Home/Toolbox/Industry_Standards/evca_reporting_guidelines_2009.pdf.

FENN, G. W., LIANG, N., & PROWSE, S. D. (1997). The private equity market: An overview. *Financial Markets, Institutions & Instruments, 6*(4), 1–106.

FRANKE, G., & HAX, H. (2004). *Finanzwirtschaft des Unternehmens und Kapitalmarkt* (5th ed.). Berlin, Germany: Springer.

FRANZONI, F. A., NOWAK, E., & PHALIPPOU, L. (2011). *Private equity performance and liquidity risk.* Swiss Finance Institute Research Paper No. 09-43. Retrieved from http://ssrn.com/abstract=1517044.

GARSON, G. D. (2011, June). *Ordinal regression*. From: Statnotes: Topics in multivariate analysis. Retrieved September 29, 2011, from http://faculty.chass.ncsu.edu/garson/PA765/ordinalreg.htm.

Gigerenzer, G., & Selten, R. (Eds.) (2002a). *Bounded rationality: The adaptive toolbox*. Cambridge, MA: MIT Press.

GIGERENZER, G., & SELTEN, R. (2002b). Rethinking rationality. In G. Gigerenzer & R. Selten (Eds.), *Bounded rationality: The adaptive toolbox* (pp. 1–12). Cambridge, MA: MIT Press.

GIOT, P., & SCHWIENBACHER, A. (2007). IPOs, trade sales and liquidations: Modelling venture capital exits using survival analysis. *Journal of Banking & Finance, 31*(3), 679–702. doi:10.1016/j.jbankfin.2006.06.010.

GOMPERS, P. A. (1996). Grandstanding in the venture capital industry. *Journal of Financial Economics, 42*(1), 133–156.

GOMPERS, P. A., & LERNER, J. (1999). An analysis of compensation in the U.S. venture capital partnership. *Journal of Financial Economics, 51*(1), 3–44.

GOMPERS, P. A., & LERNER, J. (2001). The venture capital revolution. *Journal of Economic Perspectives, 15*(2), 145–168.

GOMPERS, P. A., & LERNER, J. (2004). *The venture capital cycle* (2nd ed.). Cambridge, MA: MIT Press.

GRABENWARTER, U. (2007). *The changing face of private equity*. Paper for the Private Equity World Germany 2007 conference. Retrieved September 30, 2011, from http://www.altassets.com/private-equity-knowledge-bank/article/nz12344.html.

GRABENWARTER, U., & WEIDIG, T. (2005). Exposed to the J-curve: Understanding and managing private equity fund investments. London, UK: Euromoney Books.

GROH, A. P., & GOTTSCHALG, O. (2006). *The risk-adjusted performance of US buyouts*. Paris, France: Groupe HEC; Chambre de Commerce et d'Industrie de Paris.

GROH, A. P., BAULE, R., & GOTTSCHALG, O. (2008). Measuring idiosyncratic risks in leveraged buyout transactions. *Quarterly Journal of Finance and Accounting, 47*(4), 5–23.

GROH, A. P., & LIECHTENSTEIN, H. VON (2011). The first step of the capital flow from institutions to entrepreneurs: The criteria for sorting venture capital funds. *European Financial Management, 17*(3), 532–559. doi:10.1111/j.1468-036X.2010.00583.x.

Groves, R. M., Fowler, F. J., Jr., Couper, M. P., Lepkowski, J. M., Singer, E., & Tourangeau, R. (2004). *Survey methodology*. Hoboken, NJ: Wiley.

Haarmann Hemmelrath (Ed.) (2002). Exit-Management in Beteiligungsgesellschaften: Ergebnisse einer Studie der Haarmann Hemmelrath Management Consultants GmbH in Zusammenarbeit mit der der Technischen Universität zu Braunschweig. Düsseldorf, Germany: Author.

HANNULA, M. (1999). *Expedient total productivity measurement* (Doctoral dissertation, Tampere University of Technology, Finland). Espoo, Finland: Finnish Academy of Technology.

HARRIS, R. S., JENKINSON, T., & KAPLAN, S. N. (2012). *Private equity performance: what do we know?* Fama-Miller Working Paper; Chicago Booth Research Paper No. 11-44; Darden Business School Working Paper No. 1932316. Retrieved from http://ssrn.com/abstract=1932316.

HELLMANN, T. (2006). IPOs, acquisitions, and the use of convertible securities in venture capital. *Journal of Financial Economics*, *81*(3), 649–679. doi:10.1016/j.jfineco.2005.06.007.

HOMMEL, U., RITTER, M., & WRIGHT, M. (2003). Verhalten der Beteiligungsfinanzierer nach dem "Downturn": Ergebnisse einer empirischen Untersuchung. *Finanz Betrieb*, *5*(5), 323–333.

HOMMEL, U., & SCHNEIDER, H. (2006). Die Kreditentscheidung im Rahmen von Leveraged-Buy-Out-Transaktionen. *Finanz Betrieb*, *7*(9), 521–525.

ISRAEL, G. D. (1992). *Determining sample size.* University of Florida. Retrieved September 30, 2011, from http://edis.ifas.ufl.edu/pdffiles/PD/PD00600.pdf.

JELIC, R. (2011). Staying power of UK buy-outs. *Journal of Business Finance & Accounting, 38*(7) & (8), 945–986. doi:10.1111/j.1468-5957.2011.02256.x.

JENSEN, M. C. (1989). Active investors, LBOs, and the privatization of bankruptcy. *Journal of Applied Corporate Finance*, *2*(1), 35–44.

JENSEN, M. C., & MECKLING, W. H. (1976). Theory of the firm: Managerial behavior, agency costs and ownership structure. *Journal of Financial Economics*, *3*(4), 305–360.

JOHNSON, T. P. & OWENS, L. (2003). *Survey response rate reporting in the professional literature*. Paper presented at the annual conference of the American Association for Public Opinion Research, Nashville, TN. Retrieved November 16, 2011, from http://www.amstat.org/sections/srms/proceedings/y2003/Files/JSM2003-000638.pdf.

JONES, C. M. & RHODES-KROPF, M. (2003). *The price of diversifiable risk in venture capital and private equity*. AFA 2003 Washington, DC Meetings. Retrieved from http://ssrn.com/abstract=342841.

KAPLAN, S. N. (1991). The staying power of leveraged buyouts. *Journal of Financial Economics*, *29*(2), 287–313. doi:10.1016/0304-405X(91)90004-4.

KAPLAN, S. N. & SCHOAR, A. (2003). *Private equity performance: Returns, persistence and capital flows.* MIT Sloan Working Paper No. 4446-03. Retrieved from http://ssrn.com/abstract=473341.

KAPLAN, S. N., & SCHOAR, A. (2005). Private equity performance: Returns, persistence, and capital flows. *The Journal of Finance*, *60*(4), 1791–1823. doi:10.1111/j.1540-6261.2005.00780.x.

KAPLAN, S. N., & STRÖMBERG, P. (2004). Characteristics, contracts, and actions: Evidence from venture capitalist analyses. *The Journal of Finance*, *59*(5), 2177–2210.

KASERER, C., & DILLER, C. (2004a). Cash-flows und Performance von europäischen Private Equity-Fonds. *Finanz Betrieb*, *6*(5), 400–407.

KASERER, C., & DILLER, C. (2004b). *European private equity funds - a cash flow based performance analysis.* CEFS Working Paper No. 2004-01, Technische Universität München, Germany. Retrieved from http://ssrn.com/abstract=547142.

KEMMERER, A. & WEIDIG, T. (2005). *Reporting value to the private equity fund investor.* Retrieved from http://ssrn.com/abstract=762305.

KIERULFF, H. (2008). MIRR: A better measure. *Business Horizons*, *51*(4), 321–329. doi:10.1016/j.bushor.2008.02.005.

KOLLMANN, T., & KUCKERTZ, A. (2010). Evaluation uncertainty of venture capitalists' investment criteria. *Journal of Business Research*, *63*(7), 741–747. doi:10.1016/ j.jbusres.2009.06.004.

KRAFT, V. (2001). *Private Equity-Investitionen in Turnarounds und Restrukturierungen* (Doctoral dissertation, University of St.Gallen, Switzerland). Frankfurt am Main, Germany: Campus.

LAKATOS, I. (1989). *The methodology of scientific research programmes* (Reprinted). *Philosophical papers: Vol. 1.* Cambridge, UK: Cambridge University Press.

LEBAS, M., & EUSKE, K. (2007). A conceptual and operational delineation of performance. In A. Neely (Ed.), *Business performance measurement: Theory and practice* (2nd ed., pp. 125–139). Cambridge, UK: Cambridge University Press.

LERNER, J. (1994). Venture capitalists and the decision to go public. *Journal of Financial Economics*, *35*(3), 293–316.

LERNER, J., HARDYMON, F., & LEAMON, A. (2005). *Venture capital and private equity: A casebook* (3rd ed.). New York, NY: Wiley.

LERNER, J., & SCHOAR, A. (2004). The illiquidity puzzle: Theory and evidence from private equity. *Journal of Financial Economics*, *72*(1), 3–40. doi:10.1016/S0304-405X(03)00203-4.

LERNER, J., SØRENSEN, M., & STRÖMBERG, P. (2008). Private equity and long-run investment: The case of innovation. In World Economic Forum (Ed.), *The global economic impact of private equity report 2008* (Globalization of Alternative Investments Working Papers No. 1, pp. 27–42). Geneva, Switzerland. Retrieved from http://www3.weforum.org/docs/WEF_IV_PrivateEquity_Report_2008.pdf.

LIN, I.-F., & SCHAEFFER, N. C. (1995). Using survey participants to estimate the impact of nonparticipation. *Public Opinion Quarterly*, *59*(2), 236–258. doi:10.1086/269471.

LIN, T. H., & SMITH, R. L. (1998). Insider reputation and selling decisions: The unwinding of venture capital investments during equity IPOs. *Journal of Corporate Finance*, *4*(3), 241–263. doi:10.1016/S0929-1199(98)00005-4.

LITVAK, K. (2004). *Venture capital limited partnership agreements: Understanding compensation arrangements*. University of Texas Law and Economics Research Paper No. 29; Columbia Law and Economics Research Paper No. 254. Retrieved from http://ssrn.com/abstract=555626.

LJUNGQVIST, A. & RICHARDSON, M. (2003a). *The cash flow, return and risk characteristics of private equity*. NBER working paper No. 9454. Cambridge, MA: National Bureau of Economic Research.

LJUNGQVIST, A. & RICHARDSON, M. (2003b). *The investment behavior of private equity fund managers*. Retrieved from http://ssrn.com/abstract=478061.

LOCKETT, A., MURRAY, G., & WRIGHT, M. (2002). Do UK venture capitalists *still* have a bias against investment in new technology firms. *Research Policy*, *31*(6), 1009–1030.

LONG, A. M., III (2008). *The common mathematical foundation of ACG's ICM and AICM and the K&S PME*. Retrieved November 16, 2011, from http://www.alignmentcapital.com/pdfs/research/acg_icm_vs_pme_2008.pdf.

LONG, A. M., III & NICKELS, C. J. (1996). *A private investment benchmark*. Retrieved November 16, 2011, from http://www.alignmentcapital.com/pdfs/research/icm_aimr_benchmark_1996.pdf.

LÖNNQVIST, A., & HANNULA, M. (2000). *Validating performance measures with the nomological network*. Tampere University of Technology, Tampere, Finland. Retrieved November 16, 2011, from http://www.tut.fi/units/tuta/teta/mittaritiimi/julkaisut/bryssel.pdf.

LOOS, N. (2006). *Value creation in leveraged buyouts: Analysis of factors driving private equity investment performance* (Doctoral dissertation, University of St.Gallen, Switzerland). Wiesbaden, Germany: Deutscher Universitäts-Verlag.

LÜCHINGER, B. & SCHNYDER, P. (2009). *Factors of success for secondary investing in the current market environment.* Retrieved November 16, 2011, from http://www.altassets.com/pdfs/partnersgroup_successinsecondaries.pdf.

MANCHOT, P. (2010). *Secondary Buyouts: Eine empirische Untersuchung von Werttreibern* (Doctoral dissertation, European Business School, Oestrich-Winkel, Germany, 2009). Wiesbaden, Germany: Gabler.

MANIGART, S., DE WAELE, K., WRIGHT, M., ROBBIE, K., DESBRIÈRES, P., SAPIENZA, H. J., & BEEKMAN, A. (2002). Determinants of required return in venture capital investments: a five-country study. *Journal of Business Venturing, 17*(4), 291–312.

MATZ, C. (2002). *Wettbewerbsentwicklung im deutschen Private-Equity-Markt: Strategieoptionen für Beteiligungskapital-Gesellschaften* (Doctoral dissertation, WHU – Otto Beisheim School of Management, Koblenz, Germany, 2001). Wiesbaden, Germany: Deutscher Universitäts-Verlag.

MAYER, H. O. (2008). Interview und schriftliche Befragung: Entwicklung, Durchführung und Auswertung (4th ed.). München, Germany: Oldenbourg.

MEGGINSON, W. L., & WEISS, K. A. (1991). Venture capitalist certification in initial public offerings. *The Journal of Finance, 46*(3), 879–903.

MEIER, D. (2006). *Post-investment value addition to buyouts: Analysis of European private equity firms* (Doctoral dissertation, RWTH Aachen, Germany, 2005). Wiesbaden, Germany: Deutscher Universitäts-Verlag.

METRICK, A., & YASUDA, A. (2010). The economics of private equity funds. *The Review of Financial Studies, 23*(6), 2303–2341. doi:10.1093/rfs/hhq020.

MÜLLER, E. (2011). Returns to private equity: Idiosyncratic risk does matter! *Review of Finance, 15*(3), 545–574. doi:10.1093/rof/rfq003.

MURRAY, G. C., & LOTT, J. (1995). Have UK venture capitalists a bias against investment in new technology-based firms? *Research Policy, 24*(2), 283–299. doi:10.1016/0048-7333(93)00767-N.

MUZYKA, D., BIRLEY, S., & LELEUX, B. (1996). Trade-offs in the investment decisions of European venture capitalists. *Journal of Business Venturing, 11*(4), 273–287.

MYERS, S. C., & MAJLUF, N. S. (1984). Corporate financing and investment decisions when firms have information that investors do not have. *Journal of Financial Economics*, *13*(2), 187–221. doi:10.1016/0304-405X(84)90023-0.

NAHATA, R. (2003). The determinants of venture capital exits. An empirical analysis of VC-backed portfolio companies. Working paper, Vanderbilt University, Nashville, TN.

NAHATA, R. (2009). Reputation in financial intermediation: Evidence from venture capital. In D. J. Cumming (Ed.), *Companion to venture capital [forthcoming]*. New York, NY: Wiley. Retrieved from http://ssrn.com/abstract=1431651.

NEUS, W., & WALZ, U. (2005). Exit timing of venture capitalists in the course of an initial public offering. *Journal of Financial Intermediation*, *14*(2), 253–277. doi:10.1016/j.jfi.2004.02.003.

NORSTRØM, C. J. (1972). A sufficient condition for a unique nonnegative internal rate of return. *Journal of Financial and Quantitative Analysis*, *7*(3), 1835–1839.

PAFFENHOLZ, G. (2004). *Exitmanagement: Desinvestitionen von Beteiligungsgesellschaften* (Doctoral dissertation, University of Cologne, Germany, 2004). Lohmar, Germany: Eul.

PAIER, D. (2010). Quantitative Sozialforschung: Eine Einführung. Wien, Austria: Facultas.

PETERSON, S., KASARDA, R., & GRIER, J. T. (in press). Public market equivalent measures for private equity returns. *Financial Analysts Journal*. Retrieved November 16, 2011, from http://www.scribd.com/doc/53831395/pme-paper.

PETTY, J. S., & GRUBER, M. (2011). "In pursuit of the real deal": A longitudinal study of VC decision making. *Journal of Business Venturing*, *26*(2), 172–188. doi:10.1016/j.jbusvent.2009.07.002.

PHALIPPOU, L. (2009). The hazards of using IRR to measure performance: The case of private equity. Retrieved from http://ssrn.com/abstract=1111796.

PHALIPPOU, L., & GOTTSCHALG, O. (2009). The performance of private equity funds. *The Review of Financial Studies*, *22*(4), 1747–1776. doi:10.1093/rfs/hhn014.

POSER, H. (2001). Wissenschaftstheorie: Eine philosophische Einführung. Stuttgart, Germany: Reclam.

POVALY, S. (2007). Private equity exits: Divestment process management for leveraged buyouts. Berlin, Germany: Springer.

PRATCHETT, T. (2001). *Guards! Guards!* New York, NY: HarperTorch.

Preqin (2009). *Fund manager profiles*. Retrieved February 23, 2009, from Preqin.

Preqin (2011). 2011 Preqin global private equity report. London, UK.

Private Equity Industry Guidelines Group (2004). *PEIGG reporting and performance measurement survey results*. Retrieved November 16, 2011, from http://www.peigg.org/images/PEIGG_Survey_Results.pdf.

Private Equity Industry Guidelines Group (2005). *Reporting and performance measurement guidelines*. Retrieved November 16, 2011, from http://www.peigg.org/images/PEIGG_Guidelines_3-1-05_FINAL1.pdf.

RAPPAPORT, A. (1990). The staying power of the public corporation. *Harvard Business Review*, *68*(1), 96–104.

REA, R. H. (1989). Factors affecting success and failure of seed capital/start-up negotiations. *Journal of Business Venturing*, *4*(2), 149–158.

RELANDER, K.-E., SYRJÄNEN, A.-P., & MIETTINEN, A. (1994). Analysis of the trade sale as a venture capital exit route. In W. D. Bygrave, M. Hay, & J. B. Peeters (Eds.), *Realizing investment value* (pp. 132–162). London, UK: Pitman.

REYES, J. E. (1990). Industry struggling to forge tools measuring risk: Traditional yardsticks falling short of the mark. *Venture Capital Journal*, *30*(September), 23–27.

REYES, J. E. (2003). Dare to compare: Is it fair to compare private equity returns with those from the public markets? A look at the problem and the potential solutions. *Venture Capital Journal*, *43*(8), 32–33.

ROMAIN, A., & VAN POTTELSBERGHE, B. (2004). *The economic impact of venture capital.* Discussion paper No. 18/2004, Series 1: Studies of the Economic Research Centre, Deutsche Bundesbank, Frankfurt am Main, Germany. Retrieved November 16, 2011, from http://www.bundesbank.de/download/volkswirtschaft/dkp/2004/200418dkp.pdf.

ROUSE, P., & PUTTERILL, M. (2003). An integral framework for performance measurement. *Management Decision*, *41*(8), 791–805. doi:10.1108/00251740310496305.

ROUVINEZ, C. (2003). Private equity benchmarking with PME+. *Venture Capital Journal*, *43*(8), 34–38.

RUHNKA, J., & YOUNG, J. E. (1991). Some hypotheses about risk in venture capital investing. *Journal of Business Venturing*, *6*(2), 115–133.

SAHLMAN, W. A. (1990). The structure and governance of venture-capital organizations. *Journal of Financial Economics*, *27*(2), 473–521.

SCHEFCZYK, M. (1998). Erfolgsstrategien deutscher Venture Capital-Gesellschaften: Eine Analyse der Investitionsaktivitäten und des Beteiligungsmanagements von Venture Capital-Gesellschaften. Stuttgart, Germany: Schäffer-Poeschel.

SCHEFCZYK, M. (2006). Finanzieren mit Venture Capital und Private Equity: Grundlagen für Investoren, Finanzintermediäre, Unternehmer und Wissenschaftler (2nd ed.). Stuttgart, Germany: Schäffer-Poeschel.

SCHMIDT, D. M., STEFFEN, S., & SZABÓ, F. (2010). Exit strategies of buyout investments: An empirical analysis. *The Journal of Alternative Investments*, *12*(4), 58–84. doi:10.3905/JAI.2010.12.4.058.

SCHWIENBACHER, A. (2005). *An empirical analysis of venture capital exits in Europe and in the United States*. EFA 2002 Berlin Meetings Discussion Paper. Retrieved from http://ssrn.com/abstract=302001.

SENDER, H. (2007, July 12). How Blackstone will divvy up its IPO riches: Schwarzman to hold $7.5 billion in stock; Peterson's big payday. *The Wall Street Journal*, p. C1. Retrieved November 16, 2011, from http://www.equilar.com/NewsArticles/061207_wsj.pdf.

SHAKESPEARE, W. (1997). The Tragedy of Hamlet, Prince of Denmark. In S. Greenblatt, W. Cohen, J. E. Howard, & K. Eisaman Maus (Eds.), *The Norton Shakespeare. Based on the Oxford Edition* (pp. 1659–1759). New York, NY: W. W. Norton.

SHEPHERD, D. A., ZACHARAKIS, A., & BARON, R. A. (2003). VCs' decision processes: Evidence suggesting more experience may not always be better. *Journal of Business Venturing*, *18*(3), 381–401. doi:10.1016/S0883-9026(02)00099-X.

SIMON, H. A. (1979). Rational decision making in business organizations. *American Economic Review*, *69*(4), 493–513.

SINK, D. S. (1985). Productivity management: Planning, measurement and evaluation, control and improvement. New York, NY: Wiley.

SOULIGNAC, C. (2002). *Why primary and secondary funds of funds are still of key interest*. Retrieved November 16, 2011, from http://www.altassets.com/private-equity-knowledge-bank/private-equity-sector-focus/fund-of-funds-/article/nz3101.html.

SUDARSANAM, P. S. & NWAGHODOH, U. (2005). *Exit strategy for UK leveraged buyouts: Empirical evidence on determinants*. Retrieved from http://ssrn.com/abstract=676849.

The American Association for Public Opinion Research (n.d.). *Do response rates matter?* Retrieved November 16, 2011, from http://www.aapor.org/Do_Response_Rates_Matter_1.htm.

The American Association for Public Opinion Research (2009). *Standard Definitions: Final dispositions of case codes and outcome rates for surveys* 6th edition. Retrieved November 16, 2011, from http://www.aapor.org/AM/Template.cfm?Section=Standard_Definitions1&Template=/CM/ContentDisplay.cfm&ContentID=1814.

TheCityUK (2011). *Private equity 2011.* Retrieved October 3, 2011, from http://www.thecityuk.com/assets/Uploads/PrivateEquity2011.pdf.

TVERSKY, A., & KAHNEMAN, D. (1986). Rational choice and the framing of decisions. *The Journal of Business*, *59*(4, Pt. 2), S251–S278.

TYEBJEE T. T. & BRUNO, A. V. (1981). *Venture capital decision making: Preliminary results from three empirical studies* (Frontiers of Entrepreneurship Research). Wellesley, MA: Babson College, pp. 281–320.

TYKVOVÁ, T. (2003). *The decision of venture capitalists on timing and extent of IPOs.* ZEW Discussion paper No. 03-12, Centre for European Economic Research (ZEW), Mannheim, Germany. Retrieved November 16, 2011, from ftp://ftp.zew.de/pub/zew-docs/dp/dp0312.pdf.

University of Massachusetts Amherst (2009). *Guidelines for creating an informed consent cover letter for no-risk surveys.* Retrieved May 25, 2010, from http://www.umass.edu/research/comply/surveystemplate.doc.

VATER, D. (2003). *Die Qualität deutscher Private-Equity-Unternehmen: Optimierungsmöglichkeiten bei der Vergabe von Beteiligungskapital* (Doctoral dissertation, Chemnitz University of Technology, Germany, 2002). Wiesbaden, Germany: Deutscher Universitäts-Verlag.

VENTORUZZO, M. (2010). Freeze-outs: Transcontinental analysis and reform proposals. *Virginia Journal of International Law*, *50*(4), 841–917.

WALL, J., & SMITH, J. (1997). Better exits. *The Journal of Private Equity*, *1*(2), 31–43. doi:10.3905/jpe.1997.409667.

WEGNER, C. (2007). *Buyout-Wertsteigerungstypen: Eine empirische Untersuchung der Growth-Buyouts in Deutschland* (Doctoral dissertation, Witten/Herdecke University Germany, 2003). München, Germany: Meidenbauer.

WEIDIG, T. & MATHONET, P.-Y. (2004). The risk profiles of private equity: Private equity is a risky asset, but private equity investments are not necessarily so. Retrieved from http://ssrn.com/abstract=495482.

WILKINSON, L., & Task Force on Statistical Inference (1999). Statistical methods in psychology journals: Guidelines and explanations. *American Psychologist, 54*(8), 594–604. Retrieved from http://www.apa.org/pubs/journals/releases/amp-54-8-594.pdf.

WOODWARD, S. E. (2009). *Measuring risk for venture capital and private equity portfolios*. Retrieved from http://ssrn.com/abstract=1458050.

WRIGHT, M., ROBBIE, K., ROMANET, Y., THOMPSON, S., JOACHIMSSON, R., BRUINING, J., & HERST, A. (1994). Harvesting, longevity and the life cycle of management buy-outs and buy-ins: A four-country study. In W. D. Bygrave, M. Hay, & J. B. Peeters (Eds.), *Realizing investment value* (pp. 82–109). London, UK: Pitman.

WRIGHT, M., ROBBIE, K., & THOMPSON, S. (1991). Corporate restructuring, buy-outs, and managerial equity: The European dimension. *Journal of Applied Corporate Finance, 3*(4), 47–58.

WRIGHT, M., ROBBIE, K., THOMPSON, S., & STARKEY, K. (1994). Longevity and the life-cycle of management buy-outs. *Strategic Management Journal, 15*(3), 215–227.

YIN, R. K. (2008). *Case study research: Design and methods* (4th ed.). Thousand Oaks, CA: Sage.

ZAR, J. H. (1972). Significance testing of the Spearman rank correlation coefficient. *Journal of the American Statistical Association, 67*(339), 578–580.

MIX
Papier aus verantwortungsvollen Quellen
Paper from responsible sources
FSC® C105338

If you have any concerns about our products, you can contact us on
ProductSafety@springernature.com

In case Publisher is established outside the EU, the EU authorized representative is:
Springer Nature Customer Service Center GmbH
Europaplatz 3, 69115 Heidelberg, Germany

Printed by Libri Plureos GmbH
in Hamburg, Germany